FRANCE AND THE INTERNATIONAL ECONOMY

A work of first-class scholarship which represents an important extension to our knowledge of post-war France in particular, and of Europe in general. [Lynch] shows a masterly grasp of the often complex and intricate data, and weaves it into a coherent and credible analysis of the forces of change and rigidity in France at that time. She is also careful to place her analysis in the wider economic and political context of the times.

Clifford Gulvin, *University of Portsmouth*

Essential reading for those teaching or researching French post-war economic policy, or the question of the internationalisation of the Western economies in the post-war period more generally.

Jan Windebank, *University of Sheffield*

Based on archival sources in France, Britain and the United States, *France and the International Economy* offers an innovative explanation of France's post-war economic resurgence which challenges many conventional accounts.

Frances Lynch argues that French plans, including those of Vichy, were primarily concerned with the role of France and its empire in the international economic system. The decision to sign the Treaty of Rome was not motivated primarily by the foreign policy imperative of containing the Federal Republic of Germany. More important was the economic necessity of creating a permanent institutional structure in western Europe which would meet the needs of the French economy better than the international system favoured by the United States and the United Kingdom.

France and the International Economy is a controversial and comprehensive account of a formative period in French economic history. It will be of interest to economic historians of France and Europe.

Frances M. B. Lynch is Reader in French Studies at the University of Westminster. Her publications include the co-authored *The Frontier of National Sovereignty* (1993).

ROUTLEDGE EXPLORATIONS IN ECONOMIC HISTORY

FRANCE AND THE INTERNATIONAL ECONOMY

From Vichy to the Treaty of Rome

Frances M. B. Lynch

London and New York

First published 1997
by Routledge
11 New Fetter Lane, London EC4P 4EE

Simultaneously published in the USA and Canada
by Routledge
29 West 35th Street, New York, NY 10001

©1997 Frances M. B. Lynch

Typeset in Times by Pure Tech India Limited, Pondicherry
Printed and bound in Great Britain by
T. J. International Ltd, Padstow, Cornwall

British Library Cataloguing in Publication Data
A catalogue record for this book is available from the British Library

Library of Congress Cataloging in Publication Data
Lynch, Frances M. B., 1955–
France and the international economy: from Vichy to the Treaty of
Rome/Frances M.B. Lynch.
p.   cm. – (Routledge explorations is economic history, ISSN 1359–7892)
Includes bibliographical references and index.
1. France–Economic policy–1945–   2. France–Foreign economic relations.
3. France–Economic conditions–1945–   I. Title. II. Series.
HC276.2.L9   1997
337.44′009′04–dc20   96–17106
ISBN 0–415–14219–9

CONTENTS

v

TABLES

PREFACE

When I began my research on the economic history of postwar France I was surprised that almost all the literature in English was written by Americans. Many years later this remains the case. Not only is this an intellectual curiosity but it has implications for Britain's understanding of France, of the role which France plays in the European Union and indeed of Britain's own history. The French government's decision to sign the Treaty of Rome in 1957 was to have profound effects on Britain and on its role in the world, yet it was and remains only partially understood. The realization that France had carved out a leadership role in Europe from which it could marginalize Britain produced a brief flurry of interest in the reasons for France's postwar transformation. It is my hope that this book might rekindle such interest and stimulate further research into the history of postwar France.

This book has taken a long time to complete. Over the years I have accumulated many debts and it is a great pleasure finally to be in a position to acknowledge at least some of them. Most of the research was carried out in Paris, where I experienced at first hand the beginnings of the belated modernization of a corner of the French state – the public archives. I owe a particular debt to the late Jean Bouvier for all his encouragement and advice. I also benefited greatly from the help of archivists in the Archives Nationales and particularly in the *section contemporaine*, in the Ministère de l'Economie, des Finances et du Budget, in the Ministère de l'Industrie and in the Quai d'Orsay and the Quai Branly. Among the historians and friends whom I was fortunate to meet in the course of carrying out my research in Paris I would like to mention Gérard Bossuat, Patrick Fridenson, Pierre Gerbet, Michel Margairaz, Cécile Méadel, Philippe Mioche and Philippe Mustar. Their own commitment and generosity was a constant source of inspiration to me.

Research for this book was not confined to Paris but took me to Washington, DC, Independence, Missouri, Lausanne, Brussels and London. I would like to thank the Nuffield Foundation for their financial assistance which made much of this possible. I was also fortunate to participate in a research group at the European University Institute, Florence, and to benefit from some of the vitality and driving force of the late Vibeke Sørensen.

My former colleagues in the Economic History Department of the University of Manchester helped me to discipline my thoughts and provided me with a stimulating intellectual environment. I would like to thank both them and the Arts Faculty of the University of Manchester for granting me leave to complete the final draft. Outside the Arts Faculty I benefited from lively and extensive discussions with David Edgerton and Kirsty Hughes. I also owe a particular debt to Isabel Warner, who over the years kept me abreast of recent literature including that in German. I was particularly fortunate that Patricia Cooke agreed to type and retype my book with an accuracy which was undiminished by the demands of new motherhood.

I owe a special debt to Alan Milward. Not only did he inspire the book but he contained his impatience to give me encouragement throughout. I am only sorry that this book is not a better tribute to his own scholarship.

What finally brought the book to completion was the birth of my daughter, Laura. I would like to think that my own mother Patricia has experienced comparable pleasure from her children.

ABBREVIATIONS

BIS	Bank for International Settlements
CAREC	Caisse autonome de la Reconstruction
CEEC	Committee for European Economic Cooperation
CFLN	Comité Français de Libération Nationale
CGA	Confédération Générale de l'Agriculture
CGE	Comité Général d'Etudes
CGP	Commissariat Général au Plan
CGT	Confédération Générale du Travail
CNC	Conseil National du Crédit
CNE	Conseil National Economique
CSF	Comptoir Sidérurgique de France
DGEN	Délégation Générale à l'Equipement National
DIME	Direction des industries mécaniques et électriques
ECA	Economic Cooperation Agency
ECSC	European Coal, Iron and Steel Community
EDC	European Defence Community
EDF	Electricité de France
EEC	European Economic Community
EPU	European Payments Union
ERP	European Recovery Programme
FDES	Fonds d'investissement pour le développement économique et social des territoires d'outre-mer
FEA	Foreign Economic Administration
FEE	Fonds d'expansion économique
FME	Fonds de modernisation et d'équipement
FRUS	Foreign Relations of the United States
GATT	General Agreement on Tariffs and Trade
GDP	Gross Domestic Product
GNP	Gross National Product
IBRD	International Bank for Reconstruction and Development
IMF	International Monetary Fund
INSEE	Institut national de la statistique et des études économiques

ABBREVIATIONS

IWA	International Wheat Agreement
MRP	Mouvement Républicain Populaire
NAC	National Advisory Council on International Monetary and Financial Problems
OCRPI	Office Central de Répartition des Produits Industriels
OEEC	Organization for European Economic Cooperation
ONIC	Office National Interprofessionnel des Céréales
PCF	Parti Communiste Français
RFC	Reconstruction Finance Corporation
RPF	Rassemblement du Peuple Français
SFIO	Section Française de l'Internationale Ouvrière
SHAEF	Supreme Headquarters of the Allied Expeditionary Forces
SOLLAC	Société Lorraine de Laminage Continu

Throughout the book the word 'ton' refers to metric tonnes.

ARCHIVAL REFERENCES

A.N.   Archives Nationales, Paris.
B.D.F.   Archives of the Banque de France.
B.O.E. OV   Archives of the Bank of England, Overseas Division.
F.J.M.   Fondation Jean Monnet pour l'Europe (Lausanne).
F.R.C.   Federal Records Center. Papers of Foreign Economic
            Administration (Suitland, Maryland).
M.A.E.   Ministère des Affaires Etrangères.
Min. Fin.   Ministère des Finances.
Min. Ind.   Ministère de l'Industrie.
N.A.C.   Papers of the National Advisory Council on International
            Monetary and Financial Problems (Washington, DC).
N.A.U.S.   National Archives of the United States (Washington, DC).
PRO   Public Records Office (London).
BOT   Board of Trade
CAB   Cabinet
FO   Foreign Office
T   Treasury
T.L.   Truman Memorial Library (Independence, Missouri).
U.S.T.   Archives of the United States Treasury Department.

INTRODUCTION

At its liberation in 1944 France was a country on the verge of civil war. Dismissed by Roosevelt as being irrelevant in his plans for a postwar international order, it had a culture which was considered to be incompatible with the characteristics of a modern industrialized economy.[1] The beginning of the Cold War, which was to enhance the importance of France in strategic terms, did little to alter perceptions of its economic strength or potential for change. Before the mid-1950s it was France which was thought of as the problem economy in Europe. This image changed with dramatic rapidity and by the late 1950s France began to impress the western world with the dynamism of its economy. Nowhere was this felt more keenly than in Britain. In the space of about ten years the relative economic and political strengths of France and Britain were reversed. National income per capita which, by 1963, had reached that of Britain was soon to surpass it, and France was able to reduce Britain to the position of begging for admission to the Common Market and then refusing its request. Nothing has changed fundamentally since then in spite of the ending of the Cold War.

Given the importance of these developments and the striking impact which they had on the United Kingdom's perceptions of France and of its own role, it is surprising how little is known about how France managed to overcome the legacies of its past to become a rich economy and to secure its future within a set of apparently permanent institutional arrangements in Europe.

The scale and nature of this transformation aroused great interest after 1955 among professional economists, politicians and ordinary visitors to France. For economists and historians until the late 1950s the challenge was to explain why France had not conformed to the pattern of economic development observed in the rest of western Europe in the nineteenth and twentieth centuries. The debate, which was started by American scholars, assumed an overtly political nature in France with left-wing historians blaming the apparently slow growth of the French economy on the failings of entrepreneurs, and of the middle class in general,

1

while right-wing historians attributed it to the legacy of the French Revolution of 1789.[2]

After the late 1950s the question suddenly became how to explain the success of the French economy in terms both of its own history and in comparison with other west European economies. This became more pressing when in the 1960s the French economy had the highest recorded growth rates in Europe next to Spain.

It was in the late 1940s that American interest in France increased significantly, stimulated in part by the importance which France had assumed in American foreign policy in the Cold War. It was at this time that the American historian David Landes developed a convincing theory about the reasons for France's apparent economic backwardness.[3] Essentially Landes argued that it was the system of values or culture in France which made people follow seemingly irrational policy choices. Thus the preference for status and control explained why family units in both industry and agriculture preferred to invest from their own resources, thereby sacrificing profits and expansion in order to retain control. That they were able to survive was because the state, which shared these values, had long protected them from outside competition through tariffs and later quantitative restrictions on trade.

Although the growing evidence of the decline of the family firm and the exodus from agriculture in the 1950s seemed to challenge Landes' thesis, the changes were explained in terms of changes in the behaviour of the state primarily. It was now argued that it was the state, through the process of indicative planning, which reduced the risks inherent in the decisions to invest and expand, and which was responsible for the growth of the economy.[4] Planning, therefore, as practised in postwar France, was considered until the mid-1950s as the logical continuation of the state intervention which, it was thought, was both symbol and cause of French 'backwardness'. Yet in the 1960s things changed abruptly. The French government's decision to expose French industry to increasing competition within the European Common Market did not have the disastrous consequences for the economy which many people had predicted.

The British Conservative government under Harold Macmillan, who in the late 1950s had told the British people that they had 'never had it so good', now became increasingly worried by developments across the Channel. Harold Macmillan's decision to try to copy elements of the French system of indicative planning, by setting up the National Economic Development Council in 1962, was partly motivated by panic. The experiment was ill-thought through and lacked any understanding of the reasons for the adoption of indicative planning in France or indeed of its economic effectiveness. Nonetheless, influenced by public discussion of the higher rate of economic growth in France, the Labour government under Harold Wilson continued the experiment, appointing George Brown as head of a new

INTRODUCTION

Department of Economic Affairs in 1964. The following year Andrew Shonfield published a book which, perhaps more than any other, provided a clear and apparently convincing justification for copying the French model of state economic intervention.[5]

However, the adoption of planning in Britain did not lead to any improvement in Britain's economic performance. The failure was, of course, partly attributable to ignorance of the real role of indicative planning in the French economy. It was to have profound implications for economic policy-making in Britain and for the long-term development of the British economy. Disillusionment with the ability of the state to control the economy then led to the adoption of the free-market policies of Margaret Thatcher in the 1980s.

Support for economic planning in France suffered a similar decline, although a number of different and often contradictory reasons are given for its demise.[6] For some it started as early as 1965 with the failure of the government's incomes policy which precipitated the resignation of Pierre Massé, the dynamic head of the Commissariat Général au Plan (CGP). For others it was that the plan was either a victim of its own success, or that the state was disengaging from the economy, or that the plan had been relegated to the status of a study group. Perhaps the most convincing explanation was the failure of the plan to prevent or reverse the economic crisis of the mid-1970s. The attempt of the incoming Socialist government in 1981 to revive the planning process failed.

This gradual demise of indicative planning was reinforced by the conclusion of major studies of the French economy completed in the 1970s. For Carré, Dubois and Malinvaud,[7] as well as for François Caron,[8] the origins of the postwar growth of the French economy lay in the years before the First World War. Contrary to the traditional view exemplified by Landes, French economic performance in the late nineteenth century and in the 1920s was now seen to have been more successful than had been admitted and more successful too than that of the United Kingdom. The fashion grew to explain growth in very long-run terms and France was seen as a country with richer resources than the United Kingdom and following a different pattern of development.[9]

Indeed when the period from the end of the nineteenth century to the 1970s was viewed as a whole it was the dismal performance of the economy in the 1930s which was seen as an aberration in a long period of growth. What had to be explained therefore were the reasons for the policy mistakes made in the 1930s, such as the failure to devalue the franc before 1936[10] or the costly social policies implemented by the Popular Front government.[11]

Once again the wheel of interpretation rotated full circle in the space of a decade. While in the 1960s British and French writers attributed France's success to technocratically sophisticated interventionism, by the late 1970s it was attributed to quite opposite causes including a 'natural' rate of growth which had been temporarily retarded by foolish state policies in the 1930s, and perhaps even in the 1950s.

Then in the 1980s Lévy-Leboyer, France's leading expert on the nineteenth century, challenged this optimistic view of the performance of the French economy in that century, on the basis of revised figures for the growth of the National Product.[12] What French historians, influenced by the late Jean Bouvier, now argue is that French economic performance should be analysed in terms of the resources available at any given period together with the constraints imposed upon the exploitation of those resources at a regional, national and international level. For them economic growth is the result of the successful management of these contradictions, its management an art rather than a science.[13]

At no time was this art practised more successfully than in the thirty years after 1945 – a period commonly referred to as the 'thirty glorious years'.[14] Even though growth rates in this period were lower than in the 1920s it was the fact that they were sustained over such a long stretch of time which made the period unique in French history.

Recent explanations, outside France, of France's success have, however, moved away from the uniqueness of the French experience and concentrated on the similarity between the growth of the French economy and that of other west European economies in the postwar period. In general there are two main lines of argument which take this view. One is that the high rates of economic growth recorded after 1945 were mainly the result of western European countries catching up with the levels of productivity of the technological leader, the United States. Put another way, the argument is that the higher rates of economic growth in western Europe compared with the United States or the United Kingdom were clear evidence of 'convergence'.[15] The second argument is that it was the Americans, through the institutional framework of cooperation set up within the European Recovery Programme (ERP), who changed the way in which the capitalist system operated in western Europe.[16] France is seen as typical of both of these processes.

While in many ways this is a persuasive argument, on its own it fails to explain how some of the factors which had impeded the more rapid industrialization of France since the nineteenth century were overcome in the post-1945 era. Even if these obstacles were not cultural, as David Landes was later to acknowledge,[17] and even if French behaviour had been entirely rational given the objective circumstances in which industry and agriculture had operated, what has to be explained is how these objective conditions were altered. How, for example, were the relatively high costs of capital and of coal and steel, which had inhibited investment and expansion in the past, brought into line with those in other countries after 1945?

For William James Adams[18] the answer lies in a combination of domestic policies and in changes in the external macroeconomic environment after

1958 such as the creation of the European Common Market and decolonization, both of which exposed French industry to an ever increasing and permanent degree of competition. Indicative planning worked, he claims, only in a very limited number of activities and could not in itself explain postwar growth. Nor does he give the French government any credit for creating an external environment conducive to the growth of the French economy. Its decision to sign the Treaty of Rome was, Adams asserts, taken for political rather than economic reasons. That the French economy benefited from participation in the Common Market was entirely fortuitous. Equally, since the British government's attitude to the Common Market negotiations in 1955–57 was based on economic rather than political considerations, it was understandable that Britain did not sign the Treaty of Rome.

These latest interpretations of the success of the postwar French economy are unsatisfactory in a number of respects. Placing so much emphasis on the beneficial effects of competition, when these effects were not felt until the 1960s in France, cannot explain the successful performance of the French economy in the 1950s, when it was the most protected economy in OEEC–Europe. Nor does this view properly fit into the story of the postwar development of the French economy, in the context of the relationship between France and western Europe established by the creation of the European Coal and Steel Community from 1950 onwards. To argue that the Treaty of Rome was a fortuitous political event with no integral connection to the development of the economy and that the French government took so important a decision for the future of the economy entirely on foreign policy grounds is to misunderstand the nature of the debate in France in the 1940s and 1950s. Only a detailed examination of French policy based on official records, in France and in a number of other countries, in the critical years between the end of the Second World War and the creation of the European Common Market, can explain the motivation and effectiveness of that policy. This is what this book sets out to provide.

The book takes as its starting point the moment of liberation when de Gaulle's provisional government stepped into the vacuum created by the collapse of the Vichy state. The government faced a number of problems, some stemming from the war and occupation, and others dating back to the beginning of the twentieth century or even earlier. Chapter 1 examines these problems as well as how they were perceived by planners in both Vichy and the Resistance. Chapter 2 then analyses the specific background to the Monnet Plan in the context of Franco-American relations, and in terms of its proposed solutions to the economic problems facing France. The importance of American aid to French economic and political reconstruction is examined in Chapters 3, 4 and 5. The remaining chapters of the book then analyse how the French state managed to create an external economic environment in which the growth process, started under the Monnet Plan, could be sustained rather than end in disaster as in 1929.

INTRODUCTION

NOTES

1 David S. Landes, 'French Entrepreneurship and Industrial Growth in the Nineteenth Century', *Journal of Economic History*, IX(1), May 1949.
2 See Introduction by François Crouzet (ed.), *The Economic Development of France since 1870* (Aldershot, 1993).
3 D. Landes, op. cit., 'French Entrepreneurship'.
4 P. Bauchet, *L'expérience française de planification* (Paris, 1958); J. Hackett and A. M. Hackett, *Economic Planning in France* (London, 1963); P. Massé, *Le Plan ou l'anti-hasard* (Paris, 1965); C. Gruson, *Origines et espoirs de la planification française* (Paris, 1968).
5 A. Shonfield, *Modern Capitalism: The Changing Balance of Public and Private Power* (London, 1965).
6 H. Rousso and P. Bauchet, *La Planification en crises (1965–1985)* (Paris, 1987).
7 J.-J. Carré, P. Dubois, and E. Malinvaud, *French Economic Growth* (Stanford and London, 1976). The French original was published in 1972.
8 F. Caron, *An Economic History of Modern France* (London, 1979).
9 P. K. O'Brien and C. Keyder, *Economic Growth in Britain and France 1780–1914. Two Paths to the Twentieth Century* (London, 1978); Richard Roehl, 'French Industrialization: A Reconsideration', *Explorations in Economic History*, 13(3), July 1976.
10 Alfred Sauvy, *Histoire économique de la France entre les deux guerres* (Paris, 1965); Tom Kemp, *The French Economy 1913–1939* (London, 1972); Julian Jackson, *The Politics of Depression in France, 1932–1936* (Cambridge, 1985).
11 Carré, Dubois and Malinvaud, op. cit.
12 M. Lévy-Leboyer and F. Bourguignon, *The French Economy in the Nineteenth Century. An Essay in Econometric Analysis* (Cambridge, 1990). The French original was published in 1985.
13 P. Fridenson and A. Straus (eds), *Le Capitalisme français. 19ᵉ–20ᵉ siècle. Blocages et dynamismes d'une croissance* (Paris, 1987).
14 Jean Fourastié, *Les Trente Glorieuses ou la Révolution Invisible de 1946 à 1975* (Paris, 1979).
15 M. Abramovitz, 'Catching Up, Forging Ahead and Falling Behind', *Journal of Economic History*, vol. 46, 1986, pp. 385–406; C. Feinstein, 'Benefits of Backwardness and Costs of Continuity', in A. Graham with A. Seldon (eds), *Government and Economies in the Postwar World* (London, 1990), pp. 284–93.
16 M. J. Hogan, *The Marshall Plan. America, Britain and the Reconstruction of Western Europe, 1947–52* (Cambridge, 1987); C. S. Maier, *In Search of Stability: Explorations in Historical Political Economy* (Cambridge, 1987).
17 D. Landes, 'Religion and Enterprise: The Case of the French Textile Industry', in E. Carter, R. Foster and J. Moody (eds), *Enterprise and Entrepreneurs in Nineteenth and Twentieth Century France* (Baltimore, 1976).
18 W. J. Adams, *Restructuring the French Economy. Government and the Rise of Market Competition since World War II* (Washington DC, 1989).

1

OUT OF THE ABYSS

At the moment of liberation France was without a legitimate government. The Vichy state to which the majority of the National Assembly had voted full powers in June 1940 had collapsed in the wake of the Allied victory. De Gaulle's claim to legitimacy in forming his provisional government in June 1944 rested on him being the sole leader of the French Resistance – a movement to which he argued the majority of the French people subscribed. The composition of his government was without precedent in French history. It included communists for the first time ever as well as socialists, radicals, independents and representatives from a new centre-left Catholic party, the Mouvement Républicain Populaire (MRP).

The economic situation facing de Gaulle's provisional government was grim. Although much of France's industrial capacity had remained intact during the first phase of hostilities in 1939/40, integration into the German war economy had led to a major reorientation of French trade and structure of production. The general level of production in both industry and agriculture had declined under the occupation due to shortages of supplies and of labour, although not all branches of activity were affected in the same way. Thus, for example, the textile industry, which had been deprived of its normal raw material imports, suffered a severe contraction, whereas the production of aluminium and of oils and sugar actually increased to meet the demand from Germany.[1]

The economic situation deteriorated still further in 1944 when, in the face of Allied bombing and the collapse of the German occupation, industrial production fell to about 40 per cent of the 1938 level.

THE LEGACY OF THE PAST

Exactly how much damage was caused by the entire war and occupation will no doubt always remain in dispute, but on any interpretation the account was grim. Budget deficits increased 3.5 times between 1939 and 1945. Public debt increased over fourfold. The money in circulation increased from 101,000 million francs in 1938 to 625,000 million francs in

FRANCE AND THE INTERNATIONAL ECONOMY

Table 1.1 Index of industrial production in France, 1941–44 (1938 = 100)

	General index	Extractive industries	Metals	Metal-working	Construction materials	Chemicals	Textiles	Gas	Electricity
1941	65	97	65	67	73	44	44	97	112
1942	59	99	55	62	69	38	35	100	108
1943	54	99	60	58	64	31	28	100	110
1944	41	61	32	39	34	17	–	66	84

Source: INSEE, *Annuaire Statistique. Résumé Rétrospectif* (Paris, 1951)

September 1944. Foreign indebtedness totalled 1282.7 million dollars in December 1945 compared with 261.8 million dollars at the end of 1939, whereas reserves of gold and foreign currencies fell from 3185.1 million dollars to 1817.8 million dollars over the same period, although most of the loss was in 1944 and 1945.

This damage to the country's financial position was mirrored by the physical damage. The number of buildings destroyed, 1,997,000, represented 20 per cent of the building stock and was over twice as many as in the First World War. The number of railway lines in working order in 1945 was just over 40 per cent of the prewar total. Two-thirds of the merchant fleet was lost. Agriculture suffered from the absence of 1 million men and the slaughter of 26 per cent of the livestock. As a result of a shortage of fertilizer and a reduction of imports average food rations in France at the end of the war were well below those in Britain – 35 per cent for meat, 65 per cent for fats and 62 per cent for sugar. The situation in industry was even worse. It was calculated that 12,500 million hours of work had been lost between 1940 and 1945 as a result of 765,952 workers being deported to Germany and 85,000 working for the German war economy in France.

This of course was a highly subjective calculation. Other aspects of the damage to French industry were easier to measure. The reduction in the stocks of raw materials ranged from 80 per cent of petroleum and 74 per cent of iron ore to 53 per cent of cotton and 29 per cent of coal. The loss of finished products was over half the output of steel, 100 per cent of the output of precision engineering industries and of heavy metal-working, and 77 per cent of the production of automobiles. Although only 7 per cent of machine tools were taken because they represented the newest and most sophisticated, the French were left with those whose average age was 29 in 1945.[2]

To such a catalogue of damage caused by war and occupation had to be added the damage caused to the economy in the interwar period. One measure of France's economic decline in that period was that by 1938 the level of industrial production was no higher than it had been in 1913. In other words the gains made in reconstructing the economy after the First World War had been completely reversed by the prolonged depression of the 1930s. Another measure was that there had been no net investment in

8

the French economy during the 1930s. Thus, recovery in 1945 was not only from war and occupation but from fifteen years of economic decline.

THE FRENCH ECONOMY BETWEEN THE WARS

Reconstruction after the First World had been rapid with GDP regaining its 1913 level by 1923 and rising to 34 per cent above it by 1929. While, in the absence of reparations from Germany on the scale intended, this had been financed through domestic inflation, the consequent fall in the external value of the franc was mild in comparison with the currency collapses elsewhere in Europe. When the French franc was finally stabilized *de jure*, by Prime Minister Poincaré in 1928, it had lost 80 per cent of its prewar value. Since the stabilized franc was judged to be relatively undervalued it gave French exports a competitive edge in international markets. Although the importance of these exports to the growth of the economy in the period 1926–30 has recently been challenged in favour of an explanation based on domestic fiscal policy,[3] what is not disputed is that when France's competitors moved rapidly into depression in 1929 the French economy was enjoying boom conditions. It continued to do so for another year before the contraction of exports made its impact on levels of production, prices and investment in France.

For many years the official explanation of the international depression, which was held by the political Right in France and elsewhere, attributed its severity to an over-expansion of credit in the 1920s encouraged under the rules of the Gold Exchange Standard. Since the result was that supply outstripped demand the remedy proposed by the Right was to allow production to fall and to restore the Gold Standard as the mechanism for determining the correct value of exchange rates.[4] In France where budget deficits after 1930–31 were seen to be raising the level of demand artificially, and hence interfering with the necessary decline in prices, the primary objective of government policy became that of balancing the budget through deflation.

But it was a policy which governments in Britain, the United States and Germany could not follow with impunity. Unemployment rates, which at their worst reached one-third of the labour force in Germany, forced these governments to adopt policies based on credit expansion in order to promote economic recovery. This necessitated the devaluation of the currency as in Britain and the United States or the imposition of draconian controls as in Nazi Germany.

In France widespread underemployment, particularly in the agricultural sector, shielded French governments initially from the worst effects of the depression. However, following the devaluations of sterling and the dollar, the government, both for balance of payments reasons and in response to pressure from sectional interests, stepped up the levels of protection in the

FRANCE AND THE INTERNATIONAL ECONOMY

Table 1.2 Movement in GDP, 1913–44 (1913=100.0)

	France	Germany	UK	USA
1918	63.9	82.0	113.2	114.8
1929	134.4	121.1	111.9	163.0
1932	114.7	102.0	106.2	117.1
1938	129.7	169.1	132.5	152.9
1944	65.2	207.5	161.6	318.7

Source: A. Maddison, *Dynamic Forces in Capitalist Development* (Oxford, 1991) pp. 212–15

economy. As well as increasing tariffs the government introduced quantitative restrictions on imports in 1931, thereby setting an example for other governments to follow. But protection and other forms of price support blocked the downward pressure on prices, making a nonsense of the government's deflationary policy.

The interpretation of the causes of the depression held by parties on the Left was that it was essentially a crisis of underconsumption of the sort which was endemic to the capitalist system. Where the communists differed from the socialists and radicals was over whether it was possible, or indeed desirable, for a government of the Left to promote recovery within the capitalist system. The failure of the Popular Front government's experiment in 1936–37, which was based on increasing the level of demand through a public works programme, a reduction in indirect taxation and the introduction of a 40–hour week without loss of pay, seemed to vindicate the communist party's rejection of reformist policies. Instead of promoting recovery the 'Blum experiment', as it was known, led to inflation, a foreign exchange crisis which precipitated the devaluation of the franc, and the downfall of the government after little more than one year in office.

The consequence of the failure of both right-and left-wing policies to produce a lasting recovery in the 1930s was that on the eve of the Second World War France, unlike any other developed country except the United States, had an economy which was weaker than that of 1929. The experience of the war years only widened the gap between France and the other industrialized powers, making the problem of France's economic decline a relative as well as an absolute one. No other major economy had fallen so far behind in such a relatively short period of time and it is this which makes the postwar transformation of the French economy a story of such exceptional and universal interest.

Paradoxically though this economic decline was not matched by a financial one. Indeed by 1939 the stock of gold accumulated in the official reserves was greater than in 1928, as Table 1.3 indicates. Even though France had run a deficit on current account throughout the 1930s, the strict monetary policies pursued in defence of the Poincaré franc until 1935 had attracted foreign capital fleeing from the effects of less orthodox policies elsewhere.

Table 1.3 Evolution of gold reserves of the Bank of France, 1928–39
(in tons of fine gold)

1928	1876.9
1929	2453.6
1930	3157.6
1931	4037.0
1932	4900.4
1933	4536.8
1934	4841.2
1935	3908.3
1936	2661.8
1937	2280.7
1938	2159.8
1939	2407.4

Source: Ministère des Finances, du Budget et des Affaires Economiques,
Inventaire de la situation financière (Paris, 1951)

But in 1935 not even Laval's stringent deflationary policies could stem the growing conviction that the Poincaré franc would have to be devalued. The persistence of the deficit on current account together with the election of a left-wing coalition government in 1936 caused confidence in the franc to evaporate. It did not return even after Blum's reluctant devaluation of the franc in September 1936.

One of the apparent benefits from accepting defeat in 1940 was that France conserved its gold reserves intact until 1944, having judiciously shipped them to more remote parts of the empire before signing the armistice. The gold which Germany seized in Paris in fact belonged to the Belgian government. But in view of the scale of the economic problems facing France these reserves were soon to be depleted.

PLANNING FOR THE POSTWAR

How France's economic decline was to be reversed depended in part on how it was analysed and in part on the political, economic and financial constraints operating in the postwar world. One of the consequences of accepting defeat in 1940 was that France was excluded from all Allied planning for the postwar world. In both the United States and Britain attention had focused primarily on reconstructing an international monetary system in the belief that it was the inadequacy of the Gold Exchange Standard as set up after World War One which had been responsible for the Great International Depression of 1929–32. But contrary to the right-wing view which had blamed the crisis on an over-expansion of credit, both Harry White and J.M. Keynes, the American and British authors of what was to become the Bretton Woods system, blamed the crisis on a shortage of credit. Thus their proposed postwar monetary system was designed to

11

Table 1.4 Balance of payments for France, 1920–37 (in thousand million 1928 francs)

Year	Exports of goods and services (1)	Imports of goods and services (2)	Balance of payments on current Account[1] (3)	Gold movements[1] (4)	Capital movements[2]		
					Total (5)	Visible (6)	Invisible and errors and omissions (7)
1920	12.5	40.2	−27.7	0.8	26.9	−1.3	28.2
1921	11.4	2.6	8.8	0.4	−9.2	−1.9	−7.3
1922	12.9	7.3	5.6	−0.1	−5.5	2.8	−8.3
1923	11.8	7.1	4.7	0.0	−4.7	−5.1	0.2
1924	12.6	2.4	10.2	0.2	−10.4	3.2	−13.6
1925	15.3	6.9	8.4	0.0	−8.4	3.1	−11.5
1926	16.2	7.0	9.2	0.0	−9.2	3.8	−13.0
1927	12.8	5.0	7.8	2.8	−10.6	−19.2	8.6
1928	14.6	5.0	5.7	−6.1	0.4	−4.6	5.0
1929	17.6	13.2	4.4	−8.5	4.1	8.9	−4.8
1930	16.7	16.4	0.3	−11.5	11.2	4.4	6.8
1931	12.7	15.7	−3.0	−18.5	21.5	−5.7	27.2
1932	5.4	11.7	−6.3	−17.0	23.3	20.9	2.4
1933	7.1	10.0	−2.9	1.0	1.9	2.6	−0.7
1934	6.6	7.9	−1.2	−1.5	2.7	0.3	2.4
1935	6.3	6.7	−0.4	15.0	−14.6	1.8	−16.4
1936	6.2	9.0	−2.8	20.7	−17.9	0.4	−18.3
1937	6.7	10.7	−4.0	6.5	−2.5	2.3	−4.8

Source: L. Rist, P. Schwob, 'Balance des paiements', Revue d'Economie Politique, vol. I, January–February 1939, pp. 548–49
Notes: [1] Plus = export; minus = import.
[2] Plus = import; minus = export.

allow countries with balance of payments difficulties to borrow from an international fund rather than be forced either to devalue, deflate or increase levels of protection. The fund which was to become known as the International Monetary Fund (IMF) was to provide credit on a short-term basis only. Longer-term credit needed to promote economic development or structural adjustment was to come from a separate fund which was to become known as the International Bank for Reconstruction and Development (IBRD).

But for the financial experts who had rallied to de Gaulle in London, the inadequacies of the Gold Exchange Standard were far greater than either Keynes or White acknowledged. For Hervé Alphand and André Istel, the authors of a French monetary plan,[5] the collapse of the system between 1929 and 1931 was not due to a shortage of international credit but rather to the absence of any international institutional machinery to regulate structural problems in the international economy. What they advocated was some machinery which would regulate both production and trade across capitalist and communist countries, developed and underdeveloped countries, to prevent the sort of overproduction which had occurred in the 1920s, and which had in their view destabilized the international economy. While this strategy reflected, in part, de Gaulle's vision of postwar France as a bridge-builder between East and West and caretaker of the Third World, it also drew upon the plans of the French minister of commerce, Etienne Clémentel, for world-wide controls over raw material supplies and prices after 1918.[6]

Unlike the Keynes and White plans which called for the creation of a central fund but differed over the size of the overdraft facilities provided by it, the French plan did not consider large capital contributions to be essential to the operation of postwar financial settlements. It envisaged that each country would register an agreed exchange rate for its currency and guarantee its value to all countries holding it. This guarantee would take the form of providing collateral such as gold, foreign exchange, approved securities or raw materials of between 10 and 30 per cent of the value of its currency held by other monetary authorities. To guard against the inflationary implications of such a scheme the French plan suggested that the foreign exchange holdings of a country experiencing inflation should be sterilized rather than be used to support domestic credit expansion. The French plan was thus intended to provide the liquidity necessary for higher levels of trade and to guard against the risk of currency depreciation. The operation of the system was to be supervised by an international clearing office, although this was not considered essential. The rules of the system would enable countries such as the Soviet Union, where trade and exchange movements were state-controlled, to participate without having to abandon these controls. However, such was the reality of de Gaulle's position that, apart from a brief mention in the New York Times, the Alphand–Istel plan, like the earlier Clémentel plan, was ignored entirely.[7]

PLANNING UNDER VICHY

For the technocrats drafted into the planning body, the Délégation Générale à l'Equipement National (DGEN) set up by Vichy in 1941, the causes of the international depression were not essentially monetary but were to be found in the excessive specialization within the international economy. Such specialization had worked in their view for a brief period in the nineteenth century when the gap between developed and underdeveloped economies had been greatest. But the process of economic development in the rest of the world, accelerated by import substitution during the First World War, had narrowed this gap, leading to over-production in the 1920s. From this interpretation it followed that the future for France lay in restructuring its economy in order to reduce its dependence on international trade. This was to be achieved not through an increase in protection as in the 1930s but through a planned investment programme designed to promote the competitiveness of the economy of the entire French Union. Under this programme industry was to be restructured in order to increase the production of energy and finished manufactures so that France would occupy both ends of the production chain in international trade. Agriculture was to be expanded in order to reduce food imports and expand exports.[8]

Over the course of 1943 the planners compiled a crude industrial balance sheet to assess the state of French industry and the targets for investment. It emerged from this that one of the most fundamental weaknesses of the French economy was considered to be its relatively low provision of energy. As far as the planners were concerned the fact that France was the largest importer of coal in the world did not in itself explain why other forms of energy, particularly electricity and oil, had not been more developed. The Vichy planners aimed to expand the production of all forms of energy in France as a means of improving the competitiveness of manufacturing industry. Thus coal production was to be increased from 47.5 million tonnes in 1938 to 60 million tons over a ten-year period. Almost half of the electricity produced in 1938 had come from coal-fired power stations. The plan was to expand the production of hydroelectricity since the marginal cost of this form of electricity was less than that derived from coal. Over the ten years of the plan the consumption of electricity was estimated to rise 45 per cent above the 1939 level. This was to be accounted for mainly in electrifying the railways, expanding the provision of trolleybuses, increasing the output of aluminium and magnesium as well as electrically produced steels and expanding the consumption of heavy industry, but even more by increasing domestic consumption through a greater adoption of electric lighting and all the new domestic appliances in which French production lagged far behind that of other countries. The other main source of energy was fuel oil, almost all of which had been imported before the war. The planners aimed to develop research for French sources, especially in Aquitaine, as well as developing refineries in France.

The shortage of coal, particularly coking coal, had meant that France had exported iron ore in order to import coke and coking coal in the past. This had reduced the potential size of the French steel industry, which had implications for French heavy industry in general and for France's strength as an industrial and military power. In the future the Vichy planners recommended that France should expand its steel industry and export steel, or better still finished goods, in order to import coke. And in order to economize on coke it should produce more electric steel and Martin steel which used low-grade French coal rather than Thomas steel which, using the phosphoric iron ore from Lorraine, was more dependent on imported German coal.

But a larger steel industry would not solve the problem of the chronic inefficiency of the French steel-using industries, particularly the mechanical and electrical industries. The sheer number of them meant, it was argued, that they could not benefit from economies of scale, could not undertake research and could neither compete with foreign imports nor form cartels to keep them out. This was true for agricultural machinery and electrical construction machinery but above all for machine tools. One problem was that the machine tool industry was opposed to making any changes in its structure or in the organization of its markets.[9] Aware that the sort of protection which it had enjoyed in the 1930s would not be acceptable in the postwar world it was advocating as early as 1943 that it should enjoy indirect protection through discriminatory public purchasing.[10] It was to try to overcome this sort of resistance, and make these industries competitive, that the Direction of Mechanical and Electrical Industries (DIME) in the Ministry of Industrial Production investigated the possibility of forming a postwar customs union first with Belgium and then with the Netherlands. The idea was motivated more by a recognition of the inadequacy of Vichy's machinery of economic controls than by a belief in the benefits of a customs union.

Under the Vichy regime the French state had developed a set of instruments of control which gave it unprecedented powers to intervene in the economy. As well as macro-economic controls over prices and wages designed to curb inflation the state also developed a whole range of selective controls which gave it the power to impose a direction on the economy. The Ministry of Armaments was transformed into a large Ministry of Industrial Production, which controlled a new central office for allocating industrial products, the Office Central de Répartition des Produits Industriels (OCRPI). Organization committees were then set up in each industry with responsibility for submitting requirements to the OCRPI and then for allocating goods.

There were various kinds of organization committee. In diversified industries such as the textile industry a general organization committee was set up for the whole industry with subcommittees for each branch. In a well-integrated industry such as that of steel only one organization committee was needed. Power in the committees usually rested with the biggest firms who were usually members of the main cartels or trade associations. Medium-sized and small businesses were generally not represented and labour was excluded entirely. Very often the same people represented the industry or branch in both the organization committees and the OCRPI.[11]

While this machinery may have been effective in managing the conditions of penury which existed under the occupation it was of little use to the state in trying to modernize industries in which small and medium-sized firms predominated – a prime example of which were the mechanical and electrical industries. It was for this reason that the larger market and greater competition which a customs union would generate held some appeal.

In a very detailed survey in which the mechanical and electrical industries were divided into seven groups, the one group which it was felt would benefit from a customs union was that which had not been protected in the past and which had faced no competition. The industries in this group, which represented just 6 per cent of the total, included clocks and watches, agricultural machinery, and machines for the textile, chemical, graphic, plastics and food industries. On the other hand, it was calculated that the machine tool industry, as well as metalworking and 10 per cent of the electrical industry, would suffer from the formation of a customs union unless they had been protected to a similar degree in Belgium and the Netherlands, since much of the trade would be within the customs union. The industries for which the level of the common external tariff would be critical since they had faced no competition from Belgium and the Netherlands were the car industry and manufacturers of optical and precision instruments, ball-bearings and weighing machines. But for all the other industries it was felt that the formation of a customs union would make little or no difference.[12] For this reason it was clear that detailed discussions with Belgium and the Netherlands were needed before any conclusions could be drawn.

In the first two years after the war investment levels of between 25 and 30 per cent of national income were considered to be necessary in order to begin the task of restructuring and reconstructing the French economy. These levels were also thought to be possible without encountering the sort of social problems experienced under the first Soviet five-year plan when investment was 30 per cent of national income, although it was recognized that consumption and living standards in France would have to fall. 'Work, economize and save' was to be the slogan of postwar France. In order to avoid the monetary collapse which had occurred after the First World War the franc was to be overvalued in relation to other currencies to make imports as cheap as possible.

16

Table 1.5 Investment in industry (planned under the Tranche de Démarrage)
(in millions of 1939 francs)

Energy:	solid fuels	950
	electricity	7,150
	fuel oil	2,210
	gas	840
Iron and steel		3,175
Other mineral and metallurgical industries		494
Construction material		1,415
Building and public works		1,749
Mechanical and electrical industries		5,074
Textiles and leather		1,822
Paper		420
Chemical industry		3,525
Food processing and refrigeration		2,047
Others		1,836
Total		32,707

Source: Min. Ind. 830589(5), Papiers Bellier, 'Plan d'équipement national. Tranche de Démarrage'

The Vichy planners estimated that 16 per cent of all industrial investment in the first two years after the war should go to the mechanical and electrical industry. The breakdown of all industrial investment in the Tranche de Démarrage is set out in Table 1.5.

The DGEN and the Tranche de Démarrage were retained by Mendès-France, the minister of national economy in de Gaulle's provisional government, to serve as the basis for planning the postwar economy. But the social and political climate of post-liberation France had been so altered by the French Resistance as to make the plan seem quite inappropriate.

THE LEGACY OF THE FRENCH RESISTANCE

The most immediate and enduring legacy of the Resistance for postwar France was the programme for social and economic reform agreed by the Conseil National de la Résistance (CNR) in March 1944. This programme, which became known as the 'Resistance Charter', had as its immediate objective an intensification of the struggle for national independence, thereby reflecting the concern of the Soviet Union for a second front to be opened in the west, and as its longer-term objective the preservation of that independence after the war. It was behind these goals that all the resistance groups, political parties and unions which had formed the CNR in May 1943 rallied.

National independence was defined not only in conventional foreign policy terms but in terms of domestic economic policies. Thus the state itself was to be liberated from the economic and financial monopolies to which, in the view of the French Left, it had been subservient. To this end natural monopolies such as energy and power were to be nationalized as well as the main sources of credit and insurance. This would then facilitate the expansion of national production for which a plan was to be drawn up after consultation with all those involved in the production process. Similarly women's subservience was to be ended by giving women the vote for the first time.

Social reforms included the contractual right to work and to leisure, a guaranteed minimum standard of living and the restoration of trade union liberties abolished by Vichy, backed up by a comprehensive system of social security. Agricultural workers were to enjoy the same rights and conditions of employment as those working in industry. This was to be achieved mainly through a pricing policy based on that of the National Wheat Office set up by the Popular Front government in 1936. And finally all these political, economic and social rights were to apply not only to metropolitan France but throughout the countries of the French empire.[13]

The fact that all shades of political opinion outside Vichy subscribed to this programme of action made the CNR charter a unique document in French history.[14] It was of course a compromise between different political views which had had to undergo five drafts between July 1943 and March 1944 before a consensus could be reached. But its significance rested on the fact that it did present a consensus between all the major political parties outside Vichy. Whereas de Gaulle had wanted to exclude the political parties from the CNR on the grounds that they had compromised themselves by voting overwhelmingly in favour of the armistice and in giving full powers to Marshal Pétain, it was Léon Blum who insisted that their exclusion would result in the CNR being dominated by the views of the communist party – the only party not to have voted for the armistice since it was illegal at the time, and the only party to have retained its organization within the Resistance.[15]

Léon Blum, writing from Riom where he had been imprisoned by Vichy for his part in causing France's defeat in 1940, argued that France's weakness stemmed from two factors. One was the unrepresentative nature of right-wing political parties which enabled them to pursue disastrous economic policies with impunity. The other was the divisions on the French Left which could be overcome only through a continuation of the wartime alliance between the western Allies and the Soviet Union. Only in that way, Blum claimed, would the French communist party 'cease to be a foreign sect within the nation' and cooperate fully in promoting economic recovery and social democracy. But Blum's proposal that this could be achieved by integrating the Soviet Union into a European federation, when taken up subsequently by the Socialist Action Committee in the Resistance, was rejected by the communist-dominated Resistance group, the *Front National*.

Indeed no other major group or political party supported the socialist proposal for forming a European federation after the war.

The communists did, however, come round to the view that the postwar economy could be planned even if ownership remained largely in private hands apart from a small number of key sectors including the utilities, transport and credit. The liberals in the resistance proved to be much more ambivalent about adopting a system of economic planning after the war. Their main channel of communication was a small but influential study group set up in 1942 under the name of the 'comité des experts' which changed its name subsequently to the 'comité général d'études' (CGE) to give it greater credibility as a representative group.[16] Never numbering more than nine people, most of them academics, they published a report on postwar economic policy in October 1943. The main thrust of the report was that although the economy would have to be reconstructed according to a plan, the decision as to whether planning should be retained in the longer term as a system must be based on its success in the period of reconstruction. As far as the CGE was concerned neither the experience of the economy in the interwar period nor popular opinion offered any clear guidelines about how the economy should operate once it had been reconstructed.

It seemed clear to it that a planned or directed economy was desired by certain large industrialists who had tasted political power as directors of Vichy's organization committees. Equally, civil servants in the ministries of Agriculture, Industrial Production and Supply as well as a large number of engineers, experts and trade unionists were in favour of a planned economy. On the other hand, most people working in medium- and small-scale industry and agriculture, as well as artisans, hoped for a return to economic liberty, but they were at a disadvantage in that unlike those in favour of a planned economy they were not organized as a group.

René Courtin, the author of the report, considered that the main mistake in the 1930s had been the restriction of economic activity and the protection and insulation of national markets. He recommended that both these policies should be reversed in the postwar period if France was not to slip further behind the United States and the Soviet Union. However, to expose the French economy to open competition from the United States would either prevent its reconstruction or else lead to such a level of indebtedness as to jeopardize France's political as well as economic independence. To avoid such an outcome, he advocated a clear regulation of international relations in the period of reconstruction. Courtin listed the options. They ranged from French participation in a west European group, a continental European one, one combining the European and African continents, one combining western Europe and the United States or simply an international one. For sentimental and political reasons he thought that an economic and monetary union with other devastated west European countries would be mutually beneficial, but he doubted that such a union could be achieved if each of the economies were planned unless the plans could be closely coordinated. He also recognized that Belgium, Holland and Luxembourg were linked more to Britain than to France.[17] Nonetheless this idea of forming a customs union with neighbouring states in western Europe was to be taken up by de Gaulle as part of his policy towards the defeated Germany.

NATIONAL SECURITY ISSUES

The questions of political and economic theory which divided the liberals from the socialists and communists also played a role in creating the differences of opinion over how to create future national security. But on that issue there was another divide, between the socialists who argued that the problem was systemic, and de Gaulle and the French communists who argued that it was caused by German aggression and aggressiveness. Where the problem was seen as systemic the solution lay in some form of collective security arrangement which would check the power of the nation state. Where it was considered to have been caused by Germany the solution was to weaken Germany by creating an entirely new state formed out of the Ruhr and the Rhineland, and to include that new state in some sort of customs union with France, Belgium, Luxembourg and the Netherlands.[18]

The idea of forming a customs union seems to have originated in the discussions between the Belgian and Dutch governments-in-exile in London in July 1943. On learning of these Jean Monnet developed the idea that the proposed customs union could be extended to include France, the most industrialized parts of Germany in the Ruhr and the Rhineland, and perhaps Italy.[19] By forming an area which was rich in the raw materials needed for heavy industry and thereby depriving the rest of Germany of them, the customs union was designed to strengthen France both economically and strategically. On that basis it appealed to de Gaulle. But whether it would actually strengthen the French economy was not so certain. Unable to undertake the sort of study then being carried out by Vichy, Jean Monnet asked the League of Nations to undertake a study of the economic effects of customs unions in the postwar world. Without specifying any particular group of countries he argued that the countries most likely to form a customs union were in Europe where complementary economies existed in close proximity to each other.[20]

In January 1944 the proposal which the Comité Français de Libération Nationale (CFLN) actually made was to form a customs union with Belgium and Luxembourg, but not with the Netherlands on account of the competition which its inclusion would entail for French agriculture. However, to imagine that the Belgians would abandon or postpone their customs union discussions with the Dutch in favour of forming a customs union with France was wholly unrealistic. In many respects France posed as much of a threat to the independence and integrity of the Belgian state as Germany did. On the other hand as defeated nations they had much in common. What was finally agreed as a compromise was that the governments of Belgium, France and the Netherlands would sign an agreement committing them to consult with each other on how they were going to reconstruct their economies, and set up a tripartite council for this purpose on 20 March 1945.[21] But they reached no agreement on the future of Germany.

De Gaulle's subsequent attempt to win support for his policy towards Germany from Britain also met with failure. Immediately after his government was officially, and belatedly, recognized by Britain and the United States in October 1944, de Gaulle invited Churchill and Eden to Paris to discuss his plans for western Europe. There it was explained to him that since Britain's main preoccupation was with defence, any close association with the weak and defeated countries of western Europe would undermine British security and for that reason could not be countenanced. On the other hand, because Britain feared the early withdrawal of American forces from continental Europe after the end of the war, leaving Britain alone with the Soviet Union, Churchill proposed that France be given a zone of occupation in Germany and a seat on the European Advisory Commission. This was subsequently accepted by Stalin on condition that the French zone be carved out of the British and American zones.[22]

The participation of the Soviet Union in the war and in planning the postwar settlement provided France with an opportunity which had been missing in 1919 to revive the nineteenth-century alliance with Russia in order to encircle Germany. However, when de Gaulle and Bidault, his minister for foreign affairs, went to Moscow in December 1944 to explain the French proposals for Germany they were given no commitment of support on the specific details. Nevertheless, a treaty of alliance was concluded and much was made of France's historical role as a bridge between East and West. The reality was that France was excluded from both the Yalta and Potsdam conferences to decide the future of Germany and left with no more than a veto over Allied policies arising from those conferences.

Very little had been achieved, therefore, either in implementing lessons drawn from the defeat or in achieving national security by the summer of 1945. France had been given a zone of occupation in Germany but was excluded from the Allied conferences which drew up the principles governing the occupation. The French government had signed an agreement with the governments of Belgium, Luxembourg and the Netherlands setting up a tripartite council but this council was a purely consultative body with no provision for reaching a common policy on the future of Germany. De Gaulle's government, while sharing the concern of the modernizers within

Vichy to arrest fifteen years of national economic decline by implementing a national investment plan, was divided over where the resources would come from and therefore had no plan to implement. The French Resistance had agreed a set of social and economic principles to govern policy in the postwar period but of what use were principles without policy? Mendès-France, minister for national economy, favoured a policy of austerity in order to preserve French independence provided that the sacrifices were spread equitably and that German resources contributed to French reconstruction. But the majority of the government, in the light of the Resistance Charter, feared the social and also the political consequences of such a policy. The dilemma which the government faced was that a policy which favoured consumption over investment would not address the country's chronic economic problems or meet French security needs, but neither the balance of payments nor the level of reserves permitted an increase in both consumption and investment.

NOTES

1 H. Rousso, 'L'Economie: pénurie et modernisation', in J.P. Azéma and F. Bédarida (eds), Les Années noires (Paris, 1993).
2 A.N. 80AJ 13, Archives de M. Bou.
3 Barry Eichengreen and Charles Wyplosz, 'The Economic Consequences of the Franc Poincaré', in E. Helpman, A. Razin and E. Sadka (eds), Economic Effects of the Government Budget (Cambridge, Mass., 1988) pp. 257–86.
4 K. Mouré, Managing the Franc Poincaré. Economic Understanding and Political Constraint: French Monetary Policy (Cambridge, 1991).
5 Hervé Alphand was the former French financial attaché in Washington and former head of French trade agreements in Washington. André Istel was the former financial adviser to the Reynaud ministry and one of the negotiators of the Franco–British financial agreement of 1939.
6 François Duchêne, Jean Monnet. The First Statesman of Interdependence (New York, 1993), pp. 35–40. An interesting discovery by Duchêne is that Clémentel was a personal friend of Jean Monnet's father and brought Monnet into his staff during the First World War, presumably for that reason.
7 New York Times, 9 May 1943.
8 Min. Ind. 22345 Plan décennal; also A.N.307 A.P.124, Papiers de Raoul Dautry; also Min. Ind. 830589/11 'Vues sur le commerce extérieur le l'empire en fonction du plan décennal d'équipement', study presented by Louis Delanney, March 1944.
9 Philippe Mioche, Le Plan Monnet. Genèse et élaboration 1941–1947 (Paris, 1987), p. 232.
10 Min. Ind. 850589/11, Papiers Bellier, note, 2 June 1943.
11 F.R.C. Archives of the Foreign Economic Administration, R.G.84, Box 800, report by R.H. Bowen.
12 Min. Ind. 830589(11), Papiers Bellier, 'Etude des répercussions sur les industries mécaniques et électriques françaises d'une Union Douanière France–Belgique–Pays-Bas'.
13 Claire Andrieu, Le Programme commun de la Résistance. Les Idées dans la guerre (Paris, 1984).

14 M. Margairaz, *L'Etat, les finances et l'économie. Histoire d'une conversion 1932–1952* (Paris, 1991), p. 738.

15 Léon Blum, *A L'Echelle humaine* (Paris, 1945); translated into English as *For all Mankind* (London, 1946).

16 Diane de Bellescize, *Les Neuf Sages de la Résistance. Le Comité général d'études dans la clandestinité* (Paris, 1979).

17 A.N.F[1a] 3733, 'Rapport sur la politique économique d'après-guerre', CGE, 1943.

18 Raymond Poidevin, 'René Mayer et la politique extérieure de la France, 1943–1953', *Revue d'Histoire de la Deuxième Guerre Mondiale*, no. 134, April 1984.

19 Pierre Gerbet, *Le Relèvement 1944–1949* (Paris, 1991), p. 30.

20 V.Y. Ghebali, *La France en guerre et les organisations internationales 1939–1945* (Paris, 1969), p. 223.

21 R.T. Griffiths and F.M.B. Lynch, 'L'Echec de la Petite Europe: Le Conseil Tripartite 1944–1948', *Guerres mondiales et conflits contemporains*, no. 152, October 1988.

22 A.W. DePorte, *De Gaulle's Foreign Policy 1944–1946*, (Cambridge, Mass., 1968), pp. 66–74.

2

NEGOTIATING AMERICAN AID

If the idea of reconstructing the French economy according to a national investment plan commanded widespread support within de Gaulle's provisional government the question of where the resources for that plan would come from did not. Since the level of official reserves was clearly inadequate to cover the costs of reconstruction there were three other potential sources. One was Germany, although the lack of support outside France for de Gaulle's policy towards Germany made that seem an unlikely option. The second was to raise the resources from within the French economy itself by depressing consumption, as the Vichy plan advocated, and the third was to borrow from the world's leading creditor, the United States.

Pierre Mendès-France, who was the person given responsibility for drawing up a national investment plan when de Gaulle appointed him as minister for national economy in his first provisional government, favoured the second option. Drawing on both the Soviet five-year plans and the Vichy plans Mendès-France advocated giving top priority to the reconstruction of heavy industry. After that resources were to be channelled into intermediate industries, construction and housing and finally into consumer goods industries. The consequences for French people, as Mendès-France freely admitted, were that living standards would not regain their 1938 level 'for a long time', food rationing would have to continue and the 40–hour week, introduced by the Popular Front government, would be suspended. But in his view such austerity was preferable to abandoning French independence by borrowing from the United States.

Mendès-France considered that French people would accept these sacrifices provided that the burden was shared equitably, that the nationalizations demanded by the Resistance were carried out immediately and that the French effort was supplemented by reparations from Germany.[1] But Mendès-France had not reckoned with the national mood of post-liberation France. His recommendation that wages should be frozen until production had recovered was ignored in the euphoria of liberation when wage increases of 40 per cent were granted. Similarly, his proposed currency reform, which was to reduce the money in circulation whilst penalizing the

Vichy black marketeers, was less acceptable than the voluntary methods proposed by Pleven, minister of finance.

In view of the collapse of the political Right all parties in the government, except Mendès-France's own party, the Radicals, were trying to win that part of the peasant vote which had previously supported the Right. Since it was the peasants who had prospered most from the wartime black market Mendès-France's proposal ignored the reality of post-Vichy politics. When he resigned in the aftermath of the defeat of his monetary reform proposal both his economic plan and the institutional arrangements for implementing it went with him. The Ministry of National Economy was then fused with the Ministry of Finance and all talk of drawing up a national plan for reconstruction was postponed until the war had ended and the state of the economy could be assessed.

THE LEND-LEASE AGREEMENT WITH THE UNITED STATES

This distinction between the war economy and the postwar one which underpinned the provisional government's attitude to the national investment plan was not shared by Jean Monnet. With his experience of helping to organize and coordinate the Allied war effort in both the World Wars Monnet was well placed to see the similarities between the effort to mobilize scarce resources for war and for postwar reconstruction. As early as 1943, when de Gaulle gave him responsibility for supply and reconstruction within the CFLN, Monnet was involved in drawing up import programmes to enable France to contribute to the Allied war effort, within the framework of the lend-lease agreement.

When lend-lease had been introduced in 1941 it was as a mechanism for the United States to assist the British and later Allied war effort without contravening the terms of the Johnson Act.[2] It was to be strictly a wartime measure. However, late in 1943 the possibility emerged that the United States might extend the credit facilities of the lend-lease act under a new clause, 3(c), in order to turn lend-lease into an instrument of postwar aid. Since this overturned the basis on which Congress had accepted the act in 1941 there was no certainty that this change would be possible politically. Nevertheless, Roosevelt suggested it to Stalin during the Teheran Conference in November 1943. It was Roosevelt's hope that the experience of the wartime alliance with the Soviet Union might result in its return to the international community. To facilitate Soviet participation in the international monetary system he suggested that the credit facilities of the lend-lease act could be used to provide American aid for Soviet reconstruction. At that stage Stalin projected Soviet needs at between 1 and 4 thousand million dollars. Not only would Soviet participation strengthen the international system, the breakdown of which many in the United States felt was indirectly responsible for the Second World War, but with British cooperation it would also provide a balance of power in Europe to contain the threat posed by Germany, thereby addressing the direct cause of war. The irony was that if the changes in lend-lease legislation were made, they would be made in pursuit of a policy which made France irrelevant to the future security of Europe as well as marginal to the operation of the international monetary system.

The United States had signed an agreement with the CFLN in 1942 in preparation for the Allied invasion of North Africa. Under its terms the United States provided all military supplies on a lend-lease basis but civilian supplies had to be paid for out of the proceeds of American troop expenditure. When the agreement was renewed one year later, the Americans insisted that the French provide reciprocal aid in the form of goods, such as graphite and mica from North Africa, in return for military supplies. All civilian supplies still had to be paid for in dollars.[3]

Whereas most of the military equipment came from the United States, under the terms of the agreement France had to provide reciprocal aid to both Britain and the United States. This meant that France would incur dollar debts but sterling credits. Unknown to the French this was the precise reason for the change in the agreement. The Foreign Economic Administration (FEA), which had been set up in 1943 to prepare and coordinate American foreign economic policy in the postwar world, feared that Congress would not agree to extending lend-lease into peacetime so leaving Britain with a huge burden of debt and with no means of covering it. For this reason it was seen to be necessary to give Britain as much assistance as possible during the war, but not such as to enable it to pursue a policy independent of, or indeed contrary to, American interests after the war. So the FEA's plan was to use the agreement with France to build up Britain's debts with France, in addition to those which Britain already had with countries in the Sterling Area. Since France would in turn be indebted to the United States it would have to import from Britain in the first instance. This would give Britain a chance to establish a foothold in the markets of France and its colonies free from American competition, which would compensate it partially for the loss of some of its own colonial markets to the United States.[4]

One worry with this strategy though was that it might push Britain into forming a customs union with France and the smaller west European countries, which it was known that France favoured. This would have the effect of dividing Europe into two competing blocs, led by Britain and the Soviet Union, which could undermine Roosevelt's hope of creating a one-world multilateral system. It might also create an economic bloc powerful enough to be independent of the United States in the postwar world. Shephard B. Clough, the historian, in his capacity as wartime adviser to Roosevelt, felt that a smaller west European customs union which excluded Britain would not be contrary to American interests. He considered though that it would serve French interests less well than a larger trading area since a European customs union would be dominated by German industry.[5]

The decision to discount France was not shared by the US State Department or by the British government. Uneasy about the political and economic consequences of relegating France to the ranks of a minor European power, the State Department felt that, as one of the most protected economies in the 1930s, France with its empire had a central role to play in laying the basis for the transition to a liberal international economic system. Shortly after the Teheran Conference, Jean Monnet was told unofficially by Dean Acheson, at that time the assistant secretary of state, that France would also be eligible for postwar aid if it signed a lend-lease agreement with the United States.[6]

On the eve of the Normandy Landings the United States had to decide whether it would provide goods on lend-lease to enable France to assist the Allied war effort or make the French pay out of their reserves as the British had had to do initially for military supplies. Roosevelt decided to extend the existing arrangements with the CFLN and provide goods to metropolitan France on lend-lease. A document agreed by the State Department, the Treasury and the FEA, and signed by Roosevelt was given to de Gaulle and Alphand when they visited Washington in July 1944. This stated that the United States would provide France with goods necessary for the war of liberation on a lend-lease basis but all civilian goods including those under the Military's Plan A programme designed to prevent disease and unrest would have to be paid for in dollars.[7] It was in response to this that the CFLN set up an Import Committee, headed by Jean Monnet, to draft French requirements for the war effort. Mindful of Acheson's advice in 1943 that credit facilities might be available for goods supplied under lend-lease but which had a postwar utility, Monnet viewed the programme as the first step in reconstructing the French economy. In August 1944 he drew up two import programmes – one was a list of emergency supplies to supplement the Military Plan A programme in the first six months after liberation and the second was an 18–month programme covering the period from December 1944 to June 1946, the assumed duration of the war with Japan. This included goods necessary for the war effort but which had an obvious postwar utility as well.[8]

Both plans had to be revised to take account of the state of the French economy after its liberation but it was not until February 1945 that the United States finally signed the lend-lease agreement. The delay was mainly due to divisions within the American administration over its postwar policy. Morgenthau, secretary to the Treasury, in his concern to win British support for his plan for the pastoralization of Germany after the war, came to an informal agreement with Churchill at the Quebec Conference in September 1944. Whereas the US Treasury had previously insisted that Britain would receive lend-lease only when its official gold and hard currency reserves had fallen below 1,000 million dollars, Morgenthau was now prepared to relax this restriction and to agree to British demands for more generous treatment under lend-lease. Lord Cherwell, paymaster general and Churchill's personal adviser, who accompanied Churchill to Quebec, saw another advantage in supporting the US Treasury's plan for Germany. This was that Britain would be able to take over German export markets estimated to be worth about 400 million dollars per year. With these two inducements Churchill agreed to consider but not necessarily support the Morgenthau Plan.[9]

If the United States was going to give more lend-lease to Britain this weakened the case for signing an agreement with France. Indeed when the results of an Anglo-American fact-finding mission to France in September 1944 confirmed that the extent of war damage was slight, Roosevelt decided to postpone signing the lend-lease agreement. The findings of what was known as the Weir–Green Mission were that the only sectors in France to have suffered any significant damage were the car and tyre industries and therefore that France could contribute chemicals and textiles to the Allied war effort immediately without lend-lease.[10]

Unaware of this change in American policy Monnet revised his import programmes to take account of the economic conditions in France and of the priorities of the new provisional government. As the government saw it France had to choose between first satisfying the needs of civilians by importing food and consumer goods or satisfying the needs of industry by importing machinery and industrial raw materials. Put another way France had to choose between social peace or economic independence. Mendès-France, as we have seen, favoured importing investment goods in the first instance in order to conserve French foreign exchange holdings and French independence, whereas Paul Giacobbi, minister for supply and production, feared the social consequences of depressing food rations below the levels experienced under the occupation. The choice in Monnet's view was unnecessary, since provided that France signed a lend-lease agreement it could import both food and investment goods.[11]

The revised plan was presented to the Supreme Headquarters of the Allied Expeditionary Forces (SHAEF) and to the representatives of the Anglo-American civilian agencies meeting in four-party committee on 20 November 1944. It was then referred by them to the Combined Chiefs of Staff for formal transmission to the Combined Shipping Adjustment Board for shipping clearance. But given Roosevelt's decision to postpone signing a lend-lease agreement with France indefinitely, no action was taken to give shipping authorization. This meant that the French economy was operating with even fewer imports than under the occupation. On 2 January 1945 Monnet sent a long letter of protest to the new secretary of state, Edward Stettinius, pointing out the urgency of the French economy's need for imports to enable it to contribute to the war effort. His case rested on the fact that since liberation the French economy had been deprived of those imports from eastern Europe which, however small, had contributed to the

functioning of the economy during the occupation years. Thanks in particular to food imports from eastern Europe rations had been held at a level of
about 1,300 calories per day, and clothing had not been requisitioned. But
since September 1944 the effects of the contraction of imports together with
the general exhaustion of stocks and the disruption of the transport network
by Allied bombing had brought the economy to a virtual standstill.[12] Food
imports in 1944 were just 3 per cent of the 1938 level compared with 47 per
cent in 1941. With the French economy operating at such a low level of
activity its contribution to the Allied war effort was well below its potential.

With the Ardennes offensive proving to be much more protracted than
the Allies had estimated, the full contribution of France to the Allied war
effort became more necessary. But even then it was only the British government's request that France be given a zone of occupation in Germany and
the French government's conclusion of a Treaty of Alliance with the Soviet
Union in December 1944 which finally forced Roosevelt to settle the issue
with France. And it was clear that when the American government signed
the lend-lease agreement with France on 28 February 1945 it did not
represent any fundamental change in American policy towards France or
in its perception of France's role in European affairs.

The lend-lease agreement was similar in many respects to those signed by
Britain and the Soviet Union. Under article 7 the French government
agreed that conditions would be established which did not hinder trade
between the two countries but which would encourage mutually beneficial
economic relations between them and improve world economic relations.
Under the same article the French promised to eliminate all forms of
discrimination in international trade and to reduce tariff and other customs
barriers at the end of the war. The American President retained the right to
withhold supplies if he considered that their delivery was not in the national
interest, and at the end of the war France would be obliged to return those
articles not used or destroyed. The exception to this was those goods
ordered under section 3(c) of the agreement. While these goods were
specifically for the war effort they were intended also to contribute to
French reconstruction after the war.

The 18-month civilian programme which Monnet had drawn up in
December 1944 was analysed and dissected in great detail and despite
Monnet's schemes and efforts, all services and supplies which were solely
for reconstruction purposes were eliminated. This included all the demands
for air transport. The rest of the items were put into two separate lists. The
first list consisted of food, short-life goods and services, which were to be
provided on a lend-lease basis until the end of the war and then according
to the provision of section 3(c) on credit at an interest rate of 2.375 per cent
over thirty years beginning 1 July 1946.[13] This came to 1,675 million
dollars. The second list consisted of long-life investment goods necessary
for the war effort but which would also benefit the French economy when

the war ended. For this reason the American government insisted that they be paid for in their entirety on the basis of 20 per cent down payment and 80 per cent on credit at an interest rate of 2.375 per cent over thirty years beginning 1 July 1946. The total value was 900 million dollars. The French counterpart of American lend-lease was an agreement on reciprocal aid. However, while the American aid took effect from the date of the lend-lease agreement, namely 28 February 1945, the French part of the bargain was back-dated to 6 June 1944. This part of the agreement caused some irritation, particularly to Monnet, but in general the government was satisfied. As René Pleven, the minister of finance, pointed out, until then France had been paying for its civilian imports from the United States in gold. Now it had to make a down payment of 180 million dollars for goods in category two and even if the war ended before France had received any goods in category one, the total debt would be no more than 2,395 million dollars, repayable over thirty years.[14] This satisfaction was not shared by the American Congress. The following month it altered the terms of section 3(c) of the lend-lease act to prevent its use for postwar reconstruction. This meant that when the Belgian government signed a lend-lease agreement in April 1945 it did so under the stricter conditions which were to govern American policy in the postwar world.

This world arrived sooner than expected when the Americans decided to drop the atomic bomb on Japan. When that brought the war to an end the Americans abruptly terminated lend-lease. Between April and July 1945 the French services in Washington had tried to place the maximum possible orders in the United States. These totalled 1,100 million dollars by the time lend-lease ended, of which half had been requisitioned but no contracts drawn up. For these the United States agreed, in September 1945, to grant an Export–Import Bank credit of 550 million dollars conditional upon an exchange of notes on commercial policy which was satisfactory to the American government.[15] For the other half, for which contracts had been drawn up, it was proposed that no payment would be made for goods supplied by 2 September 1945 and the remainder would be paid for under the terms of section 3(c) of the lend-lease agreement. This came to about 480 million dollars.[16]

The significance of the lend-lease agreement for France was that at the end of the war it was to receive goods necessary for reconstructing its economy to the value of over 1,000 million dollars. These were to be paid for over a thirty-year period at a low rate of interest. Although the scale of the imports was less than half that agreed at the end of February 1945 and left France with the problem of financing the imports needed for reconstruction, the financial situation was not as critical as in Britain. France had not been obliged by the United States to run down its official reserves of gold before benefiting from lend-lease, as Britain had, and some provision was made for financing imports after the abrupt termination of lend-lease. On the other hand the British government had voluntarily rejected the credit arrangements of section 3(c) in the hope of negotiating more favour-able terms with the United States at the end of the war.[17]

The lend-lease programme which had been drawn up in France with a view to meeting some of the needs of the postwar economy was based on very inadequate knowledge of the state of the economy after the second wave of hostilities. The task of collecting this information and making policy recommendations was assigned by Pleven, not to the planning organization within his Ministry of Finance and National Economy but to a prewar body, the Conseil National Economique (CNE). This was a tripartite group which had been set up in 1925 to advise on economic policy.[18] It had been and was to remain entirely powerless. Thus the report which it produced in September 1945 was a purely advisory document.

The report endorsed the conclusions reached by the Vichy planners about the backwardness of the French economy but differed from them in its recommendations for dealing with the problem. It acknowledged that in some respects the economy was in a very much worse state than when the 'Tranche de Démarrage' had been published in May 1944. In particular the damage and disruption of the entire transport network was a major obstacle to the functioning of the economy. But unlike the experience in the First World War the major industries had not been destroyed. The problem stemmed not from the war but from the lack of investment in the 1930s. One consequence of this was that French industry was using machine tools whose average age was 30 years compared with 8 in Britain and 5 in the United States. But whereas the Vichy planners had called for the adoption of the Soviet model of rapid and forced industrialization the CNE argued that, because of a labour shortage in agriculture and because of the large number of old people in the French population, imports of food would have to take priority over imports of investment goods. This meant aban-doning the policy of agricultural protection and financing food imports either out of French reserves or from reparations from Germany and postponing investment until consumption needs had been met.[19] Subse-quent calculations which were to show the inadequacy of French reserves pointed to the need for reparations to solve the external payments problem.

At the end of August 1945 French reserves of gold and hard currency totalled 2,151.8 million dollars, compared with over 3,000 million dollars in 1938. A very provisional estimate of private French assets held abroad put them at 3,000 million dollars of which 800 million dollars were in sterling and 1,000 million dollars in other non-convertible currencies. Those held in dollars were protected under American bank secrecy rules. As against this, import needs in 1946 for consumption and excluding investment were projected at 2,910 million dollars. These imports were first screened exten-sively and then divided by the Ministry of Finance and National Economy into the monetary areas of supply in order to calculate their foreign exchange implications. Trade with the Dollar Area had to be settled entirely in gold. Under the terms of the Anglo-French financial agreement of March 1945 one-third of the French trade deficit with the Sterling Area had to be paid for in gold although it was recognized that when the agreement was renewed the terms might not be so generous. Trade with continental Europe was settled under the terms of bilateral agreements and, in the case of Portugal and Switzerland, this required a partial settlement in gold.

The trade deficit with the Dollar Area in 1945 was expected to total about 777 million dollars. On top of this France needed about 160 million dollars to settle the 1945 payments agreement with Britain and 9 million dollars to settle trade with continental Europe. As against this total receipts in gold and dollars in 1946 were expected to be no more than 600 million dollars. This left a deficit of 346 million dollars which would have to be drawn from the gold reserves.

A decision would then have to be taken as to how much of the remaining reserves, totalling 1,800 million dollars, could be used to finance imports in 1946. If reserves were reduced to 1,000 million dollars then 600 million dollars could be spent in the Dollar Area and 200 million dollars in the Sterling Area. Canada had offered a loan of 200 million dollars and Argentina one of 100 million dollars.

Imports from continental Europe would depend on the availability of goods in Europe and in France and it was estimated that these would total about 235 million dollars. Altogether this would mean that imports in 1946 would be as shown in Table 2.1.

Table 2.1 Forecast of imports into France in 1946 (in million dollars)

Continental Europe	
Switzerland	60
Sweden	25
Belgium	45
Holland	15
Norway and Denmark	16
Portugal	4
Spain	50
Others	20
Total	235
Sterling Area	400 (perhaps 600)[1]
Dollar Area	$\begin{cases} 300^2 \\ 600^3 \end{cases}$
Overall total	1,535 (1,735)[1]

Source: Min. Fin. B 33015, Direction du Trésor, 11 September 1945
Notes: [1] If the 1946 payments agreement with Britain was the same as that of 1945.
[2] From credits from Canada and Argentina.
[3] Excluding investment goods to be financed from an Export–Import Bank loan.

When compared with the original estimates of 2,910 million dollars it was clear that large reductions would have to be made in some programmes. Table 2.2 sets out the original programme with some of the proposed reductions.

Table 2.2 French import programme for 1946 (million dollars)

Area	Original demands	Reductions
(a) *Metropolitan France*		
Industrial products		
Paper	55	
Wood	110	40
Fancy goods	6	
Fuels	107	10
Coal	126	0
Tar	15	
Other products	86	
Steel	304	100
Chemicals	258	25
Textiles	273	50
Leather	18	
Total	1,358	
Food and agriculture	600	large
Merchant marine	3	
(b) *North Africa*		
Cereals	84	0
Other agricultural products	58 ⎫	100
Industrial products	269 ⎭	
	411	
(c) *Colonies*		
Indochina	152 ⎫	25
Others	136 ⎭	
(d) *Freight*	250	50
Overall total	2,910	

Source: Min. Fin. B 33015, Direction du Trésor, 11 September 1945

The Ministry of Finance and National Economy argued that no reductions could be made to the import programmes for coal, on which an expansion of economic activity depended, nor on imports of cereals into North Africa, on account of the increase in population there. Indeed it calculated that if more coal could be imported to expand industrial production generally, this would provide an incentive for peasants to increase food production, with significant savings on imports of food and steel.[20]

In the interwar period France had depended on coal imports for up to one-third of its needs and for some qualities of coal, particularly coking coal for the steel industry, the degree of dependence had been much higher. Traditionally Britain and Germany had been its major suppliers. At the end of the war the disruption to the transport network and to coal mines were recognized to be the two major problems impeding the recovery of all the economies of north-western Europe. A joint Anglo-American investigation calculated that the countries of north-western Europe would need to import a minimum of 30 million tons of coal between 1 June 1945 and 30 April 1946 to stimulate their economic recovery. Britain, the United States and South Africa would between them be able to export no more than 5 million tons leaving 25 million tons to come from Germany. On the basis of the report drawn up by Potter and Hyndley, President Truman issued a directive to the zonal commanders in Germany making the export of this quantity of coal a priority – to be achieved regardless of the consequences to Germany and irrespective of plans for other industries or the needs of the German economy. General Clay, commander-in-chief of the American army in Germany, objected that the programme would 'increase cold, hunger and human distress in excess of that apparently necessary to make the German people realize the consequences of the war which they caused.'[21]

The British who had assumed sole control over the Ruhr mines on 17 July 1945, when the North German Coal Control replaced the Anglo-American Combined Coal Committee, doubted the feasibility of implementing Truman's coal directive. The people who were actually engaged in managing coal production in the Ruhr considered that general economic rehabilitation of the entire Ruhr area was a precondition for raising coal production and exports.[22] In principle though, the British agreed that the policy of stimulating German production in order to relieve western Europe's acute shortage of coal was the only one possible. But in order to prevent exports of German coal from securing a permanent foothold in those European markets which had previously been supplied by Britain, the British wanted German coal to be sold at world market prices. If it was agreed that German coal would be supplied as reparations, and the British wanted to restrict this to the first two postwar years, then the difference between the world market price and the price paid to the German colliery could go into the reparations account of the recipient country. Once coal production had regained its prewar levels in Britain and western Europe the British wanted to reduce German coal production to synchronize it with the availability of British coal for export.[23]

But whereas Britain had a long-term objective of being the primary supplier of the French market, as it had been before 1914, the immediate objective of France was to import as much coal as possible from Germany and as cheaply as possible. After Truman's coal directive it placed more hope in the United States than in Britain to help it achieve this objective.

AN AMERICAN LOAN

Observing the situation in France at this time the American Office of War Mobilization and Conversion concluded that the French government really had no idea how to formulate a long-term economic strategy which would prepare the economy for participation in the one-world liberal order anticipated in the Bretton Woods Agreement.[24] Staff from the American embassy in Paris explained this policy inertia in terms of the conflicting pressures from left- and right-wing forces within the coalition government, and from the high level of military expenditure which dominated policy. In August 1945 60 per cent of French textile production and 50 per cent of timber output was going to the French army.[25]

Since it was the American intention to hold an international conference sometime in 1946 to agree a set of rules governing trade and employment policies, the State Department wanted to secure the agreement of a number of key countries in advance of that conference. Discussions with Britain which had begun in March 1945 then became part of the postwar financial negotiations between the two governments designed to wind up lend-lease and determine Britain's credit needs for postwar reconstruction. Early in September 1945 the State Department discussed with Jean Monnet the possibility of opening similar negotiations with France sometime after the French elections scheduled for October 1945.[26] It was the American hope that these elections, which were the first since 1936, would end the uneasy coalition of communists, socialists, Christian democrats and radicals which had been governing France since September 1944. The intention was to use the occasion to secure a more binding commitment from the French government than under the lend-lease act, to undo the trade restrictions which had been developed during the 1930s and the war. It was the State Department's fear that unless such agreements were reached with a large number of countries as soon as possible, these restrictions would become permanent.

However, in the October elections for a constituent assembly in France votes were fairly evenly divided between the three main parties, the communist, socialist and MRP. The communist party, with 26 per cent of the vote, emerged as the largest party. Rather than concede to its demands to control the key ministries of Foreign Affairs and Defence, de Gaulle gave it control over four economic ministries – National Economy, Industrial Production, Armaments and Labour. For this reason the Americans doubted the ability of the French government to honour any commitment which it would make to the principles of free trade, in return for a dollar loan. Jefferson Caffery, the American ambassador to France, now advised that the negotiations be postponed.[27]

This prompted a number of developments in France. Although the economic ministries were controlled by communists, committed to the permanent use of economic controls including controls over trade, there was equally strong support for dismantling many of those controls as the economy recovered and for participating in the new liberal world order promoted by the United States. Not only did many in France agree with the United States that the breakdown of the international system in the 1930s had been the major factor contributing to the Second World War, but they held American isolationist policy responsible for the breakdown of that system from 1929 onwards. For Monnet the change in American policy offered the greatest hope for securing peace in the postwar world.[28] This view was shared by Pleven, the minister of finance, and Bidault, the minister for foreign affairs, who pushed for an exchange of notes with the United States in November 1945 committing France to pursuing a liberal commercial policy.

Although the United States refused to set a date for the loan negotiations, the Ministry of Foreign Affairs asked Monnet at the end of November 1945 to prepare the statistical back-up on which the French case for a loan was to be based. This was the direct origin of the small planning body which de Gaulle set up at Monnet's insistence at the beginning of January 1946.[29]

The French Ministry of Finance also took the decision to devalue the franc, thereby enabling the government to register a par value for it with the International Monetary Fund and to sign the Bretton Woods Agreement. This marked the end of a policy based on the deliberate overvaluation of the franc which had been pursued since liberation in the hope that it would exert deflationary pressure on domestic prices and wages. By the summer of 1945 it had become clear that the policy was not working. In June 1945 controlled prices in France were 2.5 times the 1939 level and prices on the black market were very much higher. This compared with an increase of 30 per cent in the United States and of 70 per cent in Britain. Wages had risen over the same period in France by about 2.3 times their 1939 level.[30]

In spite of mounting pressure from both the Bank of France and the Bank of England[31] to devalue and stabilize monetary conditions in France, Pleven was reluctant to take such an unpopular step before the elections in October 1945.[32] When the government finally devalued the franc and ratified the Bretton Woods Agreement in December 1945 it did so on the understanding that the franc would not become convertible into gold until equilibrium in the balance of payments on current account had been reached without the need for greater trade controls. It was estimated that this could be achieved under the five-year transitional period specified in the Bretton Woods Agreement, but only if the French government received a loan from the United States to assist it in reconstructing the French economy. This did not include the 550 million dollar loan finally granted by the Export–Import Bank in December 1945 to cover the purchase of goods ordered under section 3(c) of the lend-lease agreement.[33]

It was de Gaulle's sudden resignation as president in January 1946 which altered the foreign policy situation. In the political upheaval

Table 2.3 Export–Import Bank credit of US $550 million

Sector	Million dollars	% of total
Food	235	42.7
Energy		
Coal	27	
Petrol	43	
Total	70	12.8
Raw materials		
Textiles	40	
Leather	2	
Rubber	11	
Paper	7	
Wood	8	
Metals & Minerals	30	
Chemical Products	26	
Total	124	22.5
Investment goods		
Agriculture	22	
Transport	19	
Reconstruction	3	
Total	44	8
Freight	77	14
Overall	550	100.0

Source: MAE-A, 194–5, 15 April 1947

which followed, the French socialist party refused the invitation of the communist party to form a coalition government without the MRP. Léon Blum had explained to Caffery several months earlier that he felt the differences between the communists and the socialists to be so great as to render joint action impossible.[34] He now announced that he was going to make a trip to Washington to explain that France 'had not gone Red'.[35]

This decision made it difficult for the United States to continue postponing the loan negotiations. Indeed the State Department could see a number of political advantages arising if, as a result of combining the loan negotiations with Blum's visit, support for the socialist party in France increased at the expense of the communist party. But Bidault and the French Foreign Ministry, located in the Quai d'Orsay, saw Blum's visit in a different light. Since the socialist party did not support the official French policy towards Germany, they feared that Blum would make concessions on Germany in return for a loan, that he would barter France's 'future security with momentary easing of [their] financial difficulties'.[36]

The main interest of the United States in the loan negotiations was, as it had been from the start, to secure French support for their proposals for setting up a more liberal international trading order. These had been published as a White Paper in December 1945. Since many in the commercial section of the State Department felt that a mistake had been made in not tying a number of conditions to the Export–Import Bank loan of 550 million dollars in December 1945,[37] they wanted to use the loan negotiations to secure French support for the White Paper without committing themselves to asking Congress for a loan in return. This meant that a loan to France would have to come out of the resources of the Export–Import Bank.[38]

These had been increased from 700 million dollars to 3,500 million dollars to bridge the gap between the end of lend-lease and the operation of the International Bank for Reconstruction and Development. By March 1946 the Export–Import Bank had an unused lending power amounting to 1,900 million dollars. Of this 1,000 million dollars were earmarked for a loan to the Soviet Union, while China was also to be assisted with 500 million dollars. Furthermore, as the National Advisory Council on International Monetary and Financial Problems (NAC), which had been set up in July 1945 to coordinate American foreign lending policy, realized, if the United States made a loan to the Soviet Union without making one to China, it would destroy the tenuous unity existing in China. The consequences could be as serious if a loan were made to France and not to China.[39] This meant that if the loan to the Soviet Union were to go ahead France could receive no more than 400 million dollars. This led Harry White, the American author of the Bretton Woods Agreement, to question the viability of the whole loan programme. The level of destruction and economic disorder in Europe was very much greater than had been envisaged in 1943 and he argued that if the United States were to assist the Soviet Union this would extend the transitional period for European countries during which they could retain controls on currency and trade from the five years specified in the Bretton Woods Agreement to ten years.[40] Nevertheless, the consensus in the NAC was that the loan to Britain should be the only one put before Congress in 1946, on the grounds that Britain was a special case in view of its importance in world trade. But because of the uncertainty over the loan to the Soviet Union it was agreed that France would not be told at the outset of the limitations on the size of the loan, or that it might not be granted except as an Export–Import Bank loan.

This created the impression in France that the loan negotiations might take the form of the British negotiations and entail the same concessions. This would mean an early end to exchange controls on current payments, the relaxation of trade preferences within the French Union and support for the principles of trade liberalization embodied in the American White Paper. It was on this basis that the Monnet Plan, which under the title of the Plan de Modernisation et d'Equipement came into existence in January 1947, was first drafted.

In February 1946 a tariff policy commission was set up to investigate how levels of tariff protection could be reduced in order to honour French commitments to the United States. Its results revealed that the motor vehicle industry had enjoyed the highest levels of tariff protection in the 1930s and had also suffered the greatest damage during the war. Because of the restricted size of the domestic market, exports were considered crucial for the future success of the industry. Yet one of the problems which it faced was that the price of steel, a major component of vehicle manufacture, was more expensive in the domestic market than in the export market because of the way in which the International Steel Cartel had operated.

A precondition for exposing the French motor vehicle industry to greater competition was seen to be freer trade in steel. The French steel industry, though, argued that it was not competitive because of the price and quality of French coal and the restricted size of the domestic market. It showed no willingness to abandon either protection by tariff or cartel arrangements which it claimed were essential in order to regulate markets during recessions.

Agriculture, which had also been highly protected in the 1930s with tariffs ranging from 30 to 50 per cent on both cereals and meat, was confident that the French parliament would never approve tariff reductions. However, if, as was suggested, tariffs could be reduced without consulting parliament, then it was argued that metropolitan agriculture should no longer have to face competition from the French colonies and that their agriculture should be made complementary. The one industry which had enjoyed little tariff protection, but considerable protection by quotas, in the 1930s and which felt quite confident about the future was textiles, with the exception of clothing. But the textile industry was extremely dependent on imported cotton from the United States and wool from Australia, while contributing little foreign exchange in return since most of its exports were to the rest of the Franc Area.[41]

What the results of the tariff policy commission revealed was that for it to be acceptable to French industry and agriculture the reduction of tariffs would have to be accompanied by the retention of quotas and cartels and involve a reorientation of trade within the Franc Area. But since the American White Paper on 'Proposals for the Expansion of World Trade and Employment' specifically proscribed cartels and the use of quotas for protective purposes, this made the case for a loan from the United States to assist in the restructuring of the French economy all the more necessary to overcome domestic political resistance. Moreover, since the American

White Paper made no reference to the free mobility of labour which, in the French view, would be necessary if German industry were to be reduced to the levels under discussion by the Allies at that time, this was seen to mean that the Americans were not committed to the permanent restriction of the level of industry in Germany.[42] This made a loan to restructure the French economy necessary in order to secure French defence against Germany.

Because the Monnet Plan and the subsequent medium-term plans were eventually to attract so much attention as the archetype of reformed capitalism, of the postwar mixed economy and the distinctive contribution of France to economic policy-making, it is worth emphasizing here how the Monnet Plan emerged from the welter of other proposals for reconstructing the French economy and how closely it was shaped by the circumstances of the reconstruction and the way they changed.

The first version of the Monnet plan was drawn up in haste in order to demonstrate France's need for further American aid in the negotiations to wind up lend-lease. It was designed to show how such aid would be used to enable the French economy to achieve a balance in its external payments by 1950 without the need for further protection or foreign aid. Since the major bottleneck impeding economic recovery at that time was coal, another purpose of the plan was to demonstrate the French economy's dependence on coal imports. As Monnet explained to the Council of the Plan at its first meeting on 16 March 1946, 'the development of our industrial capacity, and of steel in particular, would be impossible if we were not assured of regular supplies of at least 20 million tons of coal annually from Germany'. France had imported 7 million tons of coal from Germany in 1938 out of total imports of 22 million tons. The Council of the Plan subsequently recommended that the peace treaty with Germany should stipulate that France would receive 20 million tons of coal from the Ruhr for twenty years.[43]

THE BLUM–BYRNES NEGOTIATIONS

The negotiations for a loan opened on 25 March 1946 and lasted until 28 May 1946.[44] During those nine weeks various technical committees set up by the American National Advisory Council examined the statistical basis of the French plan. The case for increased coal imports was emphasized from the outset. The plan aimed to restore the 1938 level of industrial production by the end of 1946, provided that sufficient coal was available. After that, on the assumption that the labour bottleneck could be overcome, industrial production was to rise by 25 per cent to match the 1929 level by the end of 1949. It was then to increase by a further 25 per cent in 1950. When production equalled the 1929 level imports were to be lower and exports the same as in that year. This was to be achieved by restructuring the French economy, while it was being reconstructed. The total cost of this process was calculated by estimating the replacement cost of capital destroyed during the war and adding it to the cost of replacing that part of the capital remaining which was considered obsolete as a result of insufficient investment in the 1930s – provided that it conformed to the plan. Investment and consumption levels were then forecast as well as the proportion of each which would have to be imported. Then, on the assumption that exports would recover gradually until they regained their 1929 level by 1949, the overall payments deficit was calculated.

The first thing that the Americans questioned was the size of the investment programme. Given that the industrial capacity existed to achieve the 1938 level of production they persuaded the French to postpone the non-productive part of the programme, namely the reconstruction of private dwellings, until after 1950, and to substitute American surplus property for some new investment. This brought the total of almost 40,000 million dollars down to 12,000 million dollars, less than a third of the original. However, since only about 5 per cent of the planned investment was to come from capital imports such a reduction did not make much difference to the potential current account deficit. This was estimated at 6,973 million dollars for the total period from 1946 to 1949.

To meet this the French thought that they could raise 1,300 million dollars by requisitioning foreign assets which were privately held in the United States, 80 million dollars from Belgian gold taken by Germany during the war, 20 million dollars from new gold production and finally 607 million dollars from official reserves. This would still leave 1,200 million dollars in the reserves which Monick, the governor of the Bank of France, argued was the minimum necessary to secure confidence in the franc and to back the trade of the entire Franc Area. This left 4,186 million dollars which the French claimed that they needed to borrow in order to implement the reconstruction plan. It was an enormous sum: over four times the size of the loan earmarked for the Soviet Union.

As far as the United States was concerned, one of the key questions raised by the French investment programme was whether the French economy would be able to sustain the rate of capital formation required by the programme. The investment programme was designed to absorb 18 per cent of national income over the period 1946–49, leaving 82 per cent available for consumption. French national income, however, was forecast to increase from 92 per cent of the 1938 level in 1946 to 132 per cent in 1949, which was approximately the 1929 level. But due to the high rate of investment and despite an import surplus, consumption was to rise more slowly, from 88 per cent of the 1938 level in 1946 to 115 per cent in 1949, which was only 90 per cent of the 1929 level. And it was the doubt that French people would be willing to postpone any significant increase in consumption, and the belief that French governments would be unable to maintain effective controls, which most concerned the Americans. But such

Table 2.4 French estimate of investments necessary for the restoration, modernization and extension of French productive capacity (in thousand million 1938 francs)

Industries	Restoration	Modernization and expansion	Total	Percentage of investments provided by imports
Coal Mines	0	30	30	6
Electrical production and distribution	0	40	40	9
Fuel	9	9	18	14
Private and public buildings and public works (including deferred maintenance)	360	280	640	0.5
Maritime harbours	10	5	15	5
Transport and communications				
(a) Railways	70	25	95	4
(b) Inland waterways	4	2	6	4
Merchant marine	13	7	20	40
Road transport	30	20	50	0
Farm equipment	10	117	127	4
Steel industry	2	14.5	16.5	25
Mechanical and electrical industries	15	15	30	25
Textile industries	0	13	13	14
Miscellaneous	7	23	30	4
Colonies	0	53.5	53.5	17
Total	530	654.5	1,184.5	
Stocks	80	0	80	
Deferred maintenance	81	0	81	
Overall	691	654.5	1,345.5[1]	

Source: MAE A 194–5, Special Table 19, 28 March 1946
Note: [1] 38,484 million dollars at an exchange rate of 1 dollar = 34.95 francs in 1938.

doubts did not affect their commitment to the objectives of the plan. Indeed, they realized that if only a minimum programme of industrial investment were achieved, consumption in 1946 and 1947 would probably be slightly higher than under the Monnet Plan. But the situation in 1949 would be extremely serious when France would have a national income marginally above the 1938 level and be forced to bring its foreign payments into balance with exports only slightly above the 1938 level and a heavy service burden for foreign reconstruction loans. French industrial productivity would still be lower than prewar, they thought, and much lower relative to that of the United States.

Another problem identified by the Americans was the slow rate of recovery planned for French exports and the fact that the target for 1949 was to be no higher than 1929. In both respects they felt that French plans compared most unfavourably with those of Britain and cast some doubt on the French government's commitment to the principle of expanding world trade. The slow rate of recovery of French exports also undermined the French case for replacing Germany as the main industrial power in continental Europe. But the Americans did accept the French argument that they were receiving a smaller proportion of their prewar coal imports from Germany than were Belgium and Luxembourg, the second largest market for German coal, and that France should receive more coal in 1947.

Harry White, the American author of the Bretton Woods Agreement, estimated that with more coal from 1947 onwards domestic production could increase more quickly than predicted and exports could rise by as much as 500 million dollars in 1947 and 250 million dollars in 1948. If this coal came from Germany rather than the United States this would also lead to a dollar saving, since German coal was 10 dollars per ton cheaper than American coal. The Americans also thought that the French could save on the price of their cotton imports from the United States if they negotiated a bulk-purchasing arrangement. Another way to reduce the payments deficit was to transfer ships from the United States, where there was a surplus, to France. Altogether, according to American calculations, the savings on imports and freight charges came to over 2,000 million dollars. This, together with an expansion of exports, if the French adopted a more aggressive export policy, reduced the French deficit from over 4,000 million dollars to little over 1,000 million dollars.[45]

When the NAC Top Committee met on 25 April to conclude the final negotiations William Clayton, assistant secretary of state for economic affairs, emphasized that France as well as Britain formed the key to the whole western European situation. Nonetheless his proposal that France should receive 750 million dollars from the Export–Import Bank was rejected on the grounds that the United States would be very magnanimous to provide even five hundred pounds in comparison with what they could give to the rest of the world. E.M. Bernstein, a former 'Morgenthau planner', however, supported Clayton's view that France and Britain would have to replace Germany as the suppliers of European industrial needs although he recognized that the Monnet Plan objectives provided little evidence that this would be possible. Henry Wallace, secretary of commerce, thought that 650 million dollars was the very minimum even to initiate the French recovery programme. William McChesney Martin, representing the Export–Import Bank, complained that the bank had not had sufficient time to consider the French loan because the State Department was pushing it for 10 May as Blum had asked. He refused to vote on the loan. Nevertheless, by a majority of three to two it was decided to lend

Table 2.5 Imports for consumption in the Franc Area
(in million dollars at 1946 prices)

	Actual 1929	*Actual* 1938	1946	*Forecast* 1947	1948	1949
Agriculture and food supply						
Cereals	90	16	275	20	20	15
Sugar	25	8	25	15	15	15
Colonial foods	32	23	20	20	20	20
Oil seeds	68	44	70	50	50	50
Miscellaneous (incl. tobacco)	200	80	79	50	25	25
Total	415	171	469	135	130	125
Energy						
Coal	172	175	164	220	220	240
Petroleum	105	155	60	134	124	116
Electricity	–	–	–	28	30	30
Total	277	330	224	382	374	386
Raw materials and producer goods						
Ores and metals	79	85	60	115	135	150
Non-metallic minerals	23	13	3	15	15	20
Steel	22	8	90	–	10	10
Chemicals	71	67	206	125	150	150
Rubber	14	20	25	15	25	30
Textiles	480	230	180	280	300	350
Leather, hides and skins	49	27	20	20	20	30
Paper pulp	43	31	31	20	30	40
Wood	58	21	44	90	90	90
Miscellaneous	200	7	44	40	40	80
Total	1,039	509	703	720	815	950
Finished products						
Machinery	64	43	–	45	50	50
Chemicals	–	8	–	5	10	10
Rubber	80	5	–	5	5	5
Textiles	27	26	–	–	5	5
Miscellaneous	35	40	–	3	6	6
Gems and pearls	61	18	–	5	10	10
Total	267	140	–	63	86	86
French overseas territories	320	270	600	300	325	350
Overall	2,318	1,420	1,996	1,600	1,730	1,897

Source: MAE-A 194–5, Special Tables 101 and 102

France 650 million dollars and to "dress it up" to appear more than one thousand million dollars. This was to be done by giving the French a loan to buy American surplus property and to cover those goods imported under section 3(c) of lend-lease, and not included in the Export–Import Bank loan in December 1945.

The original value of the surplus property was 1,398 million dollars which the United States wanted to dispose of in bulk as it had done with Britain at 30 per cent of the original cost for army equipment and 10 per cent of the original cost for air equipment. With dollars so scarce the French objected to using them to buy such things as 40,000 jeeps, 450,000 blankets, 620,000 towels and 1,000 light vessels which were not a priority. In one instance concerning the sale of a pipeline in the Rhône, after many months of negotiations during which the French refused to meet the American Army's price of 2.5 million dollars, the Army dismantled the pipeline at a cost of 300 thousand dollars to sell it as scrap. Such cases were not to be repeated, so when the French insisted on buying only those items vital for their reconstruction, such as rolling stock, the Americans refused even to classify the rolling stock as surplus and sold it independently. The French were then forced to pay 300 million dollars for surplus property which the Ministry of Finance valued at no more than 175 million dollars and to accept credits for the purpose.

The Americans displayed greater generosity in the lend-lease settlement. In return for 2,409 million dollars of supplies under lend-lease they accepted the 844 million dollars already paid by the French in reciprocal aid, with no further payment. Of the debts contracted by the French under section 3(c), 359 million dollars were to be written off and the remaining 420 million dollars were to be repaid at 2 per cent interest over thirty-five years. The British had been given the same rate of interest but the repayment had been extended over a fifty-year period. The Americans justified this different treatment of Britain by explaining that the British had contracted a war debt of 14,000 million dollars with their dominions which would weigh heavily on their postwar economy. In comparison, the French debt of 420 million dollars was largely for goods imported after the end of the war which, although not part of the imports required by the Monnet Plan, nevertheless had contributed to French recovery.

It took two weeks of hard bargaining with the Export–Import Bank for the French to have any say over how the loan of 650 million dollars would be spent. The Export–Import Bank at first insisted on financing only those investment goods which they deemed necessary for reconstruction, whereas the French also needed to buy raw materials and food for current consumption. As a major concession the bank finally agreed to a compromise whereby the contracts for investment goods which had already been accepted under the bank loan of 550 million dollars in December 1945 but not delivered were to be financed under the second loan under discussion. This left 267 million dollars of the first loan to finance current consumption and 193 million dollars of the second loan to pay for raw materials and charges incurred in respect of past services.

At the last moment another argument developed which caused Blum to delay his departure. The French were under the impression that the American government was going to commit itself formally to back a French request for a loan from the International Bank for Reconstruction and Development. To announce the near certainty of receiving at least 500 million dollars from the International Bank in 1947 would, Blum felt, make his mission to Washington appear more successful than it in fact had been. But the American government refused to give such a statement of intent.[46]

The agreement consisting of nine separate documents was finally drawn up in Washington on 28 May 1946. In addition to the loan of 650 million dollars from the Export–Import Bank and a loan of 720 million dollars for surplus property and goods not provided under direct lend-lease, the French had to buy seventy-five liberty ships at 40 million dollars. In return the French agreed to the American proposals on international trade which were to be submitted to the United Nations trade conference later that year. They also agreed to draw up new *ad valorem* tariffs which would not increase protection above the prewar levels, to abandon the prewar policy of protection through import quotas, except when needed to safeguard the balance of payments, to restore trade with the United States to private channels, and to abandon their price equalization procedure. This procedure which had been instituted by decree on 13 August 1945 subsidized exports and taxed imports in order to compensate for the over-valued franc. It was modelled on a practice set up in 1940 to combat the opposite problem.[47]

That the French accepted these conditions in return for a modest loan was seen by some British commentators as proof that the planners were looking for some sort of external constraint to enable them to abandon the social reform programme of the French Resistance.[48] To the Quai d'Orsay the failure to win American support for the French policy towards Germany was evidence that France had sacrificed its independence, and in particular its security, in return for the dollar loan.[49] What it does reveal is that the crux of the French problem was not a severe dollar shortage without which the French economy could not function nor the investment plan be implemented. The singularly generous lend-lease agreement which the provisional government had signed with the United States not only left French reserves intact but provided credit through to the end of 1945. It then remained a political question how those reserves would be used in 1946 and beyond. What France faced was a specific bottleneck in coal and coke supplies caused mainly by the collapse of German production and exports. It was this problem which was undermining French economic recovery and the investment plan. Truman's coal directive issued in June 1945, although recognizing the problem, had not managed to resolve it.[50] Without a solution French economic recovery and independence was indeed compromised. It was not a case of France sacrificing its independence in return for a dollar loan but of trying to negotiate the terms for regaining its independence.

THE FAILURE OF A MISSION?

Although Blum's mission was a political failure for the socialists who lost seats in the June 1946 elections both to the communists and the MRP, it was not seen as a failure for the plan. Indeed on the assumption that more coal would be available from Germany in 1947 than had been envisaged in the spring, Robert Schuman, the new minister of finance, agreed with the Americans that both production and exports could be expanded more rapidly than originally estimated, and he revised the balance of payments figures accordingly.

Table 2.6 Original and revised import programmes of supplies 1946–50
(in million dollars)

Imports	1938	1946[1]	1946[2]	Year 1947[1]	1947[2]	1949	1950
Metropolitan France							
Food and agriculture	150	469	450	135	180	125	110
Energy							
Coal	222	164	110	220	185	240	225
Electricity	2	–	10	28	8	30	4
Petroleum products	81	60	75	134	97	116	121
Raw materials							
Steel	7	90	50	–	46	10	–
Minerals and metals	101	63	140	130	133	170	175
Chemical products	134	206	175	125	196	150	240
Textiles	450	180	350	280	464	350	530
Leather and skins	27	20	20	20	30	30	40
Construction materials	10	6	–	8	–	–	8
Timber	18	44	28	90	25	90	40
Paper	53	31	36	20	50	40	49
Other raw materials	20	69	15	55	18	110	18
Finished products	140	–	155	63	150	86	160
Total	1,415	1,396	1,620	1,300	1,590	1,547	1,720
Overseas territories	170	600	340	300	260	350	310
Overall	1,585	1,996	1,960	1,600	1,850	1,897	2,030

Source: Ministère des Finances, *Inventaire de la situation financière 1913–1948* (Paris, 1946)
MAE-A 194–5, Statistics for Washington
Notes: [1] Original; [2] Revised.

Similarly, the changes made to the investment projections during the loan negotiations were now incorporated into the plan. Thus in November 1946 when the CGP drew up its general report to present to the government it outlined six priority sectors in the plan: coal, steel, cement, electricity, railways and agricultural machinery. The plan was then automatically approved by an all-socialist 'interim' government led by Léon Blum, in January 1947. It was approved at a time when France was facing a crisis in its coal imports which threatened both the production and export targets on which the plan was based. However, the formation of the Bizone in January 1947 meant that the United States now added Britain's economic and financial concerns in the Ruhr to its own concern to promote French reconstruction using German coal resources.

The two concerns, as Britain had been pointing out since the war, seemed incompatible. However, the State Department's fear was that to ignore French needs until those of Germany had been met would have fuelled social unrest and benefited the French communist party and ultimately the Soviet Union. In the context of the growing Cold War the United States devised the Marshall Plan as a way of promoting the recovery of both France and Germany and thereby stabilizing political conditions in Europe.

Table 2.7 Original and revised export programmes (in million dollars)

Exports	1938	1946[1]	Year 1946[2]	1947[1]	1947[2]
From metropolitan France					
Food and agriculture	150	–	90	–	95
Coal	10	–	6	–	6
Minerals and metals	132	35	50	70	68
Timber and construction material	17	–	6	–	9
Mechanical and electrical goods	75	30	63	50	320
Textiles	214	150	125	300	400
Leather and skins	49	–	12	–	22
Art and designs	60	–	25	–	30
Chemical products	81	25	80	50	110
Other industrial products	28	–	28	–	30
Other goods	74	–	30	–	30
Total	890	330	515	600	1,120
From overseas territories					
Food	76	–	15	–	30
Phosphates, iron ore⎱			35		45
Other raw materials⎰	114	50	45	150	30
Total	190	50	95	150	105
Overall	1,080	380	610	750	1,225

Source: Ministère des Finances, op. cit. MAE-A 194–5, statistics for Washington, p. 646.
Notes : [1] Original; [2] revised

Table 2.8 Estimates of French balance of payments, 1946–49 (in million dollars)

	Results 1945	Estimates[1]	1946[2]	Estimates[1]	1947[2]	Estimates[1]	1948[2]	Estimates[1]	1949[2]
Receipts									
Exports and additional receipts	30	450	670	750	1,225	1,200	1,600	2,000	2,000
Interest and arrears	4	350 }	120	50 }	60	30 }	40	20 }	30
Allied troop expenditure	100	120 }	–	–	–	–	–	–	–
Tourist expenditure	–	10	25	150	150	300	275	350	300
Payments on old debts	52	–	–	–	–	–	–	–	–
Miscellaneous	10	10	–	10	–	10	–	10	–
Total	196	940	815	960	1,435	1,540	1,915	2,380	2,330
Payments									
Imports of supplies	1,773	2,557[a]	1,960	1,600	1,850	1,700	1,900	1,800	1,950
Imports of investment goods		650	350	750	760	750	590	250	300
Freight		250	295	220	145	240	75	320	60
Non-commercial settlements	220	586	275	520	257	300	307	300	323
Total	1,993	4,043	2,880	3,090	3,012	2,990	2,872	2,670	2,633
Deficit	1,797	3,103	2,065	2,130	1,577	1,450	957	290	303
Financing the deficit with existing means	1,797	1,972	1,985	405	945	405	505	5	105
New resources needed	–	1,131	80	1,725	632	1,045	452	285	198
Public assets left at end of year	1,807	1,200	–	1,200	–	1,200	–	1,200	–

Sources: [1] MAE-A 194–5, Statistics for Washington and [2] Ministère des Finances, op. cit.
Note: [a] of which 277 million dollars applied to deliveries made before 30 June 1945 and 320 million dollars to orders under the 1945 programme.

NOTES

1 Pierre Mendès-France, *Oeuvres complètes. Vol. II. Une Politique de l'économie. 1943–1954* (Paris, 1985), pp. 55–72.
2 Under the Johnson Act passed in 1934 all countries which had not repaid in full their debts to the United States incurred during the First World War were excluded from any further borrowing from the United States.
3 A.N. F^{60} 921, note for de Gaulle, 21 October 1943.
4 F.R.C. R.G. 169, Box 1069, FEA, W. Woolston to E. Dietrich, 19 August 1944.
5 F.R.C., Foreign Post Files, R.G. 84, E.S. Clough, 'French Postwar Economic Problems'.
6 A.N. F^{60} 921, Monnet to Mendès-France, 26 April 1944.
7 J. Dougherty, *The Politics of Wartime Aid* (Westport, 1978), p. 175.
8 A.N. F^{60} 896, Monnet to Comité économique interministériel, 28 July 1944.
9 Alan P. Dobson, *The Politics of the Anglo-American Economic Special Relationship 1940–1987* (London, 1988), p. 39.
10 Dougherty, op. cit., p. 179.
11 A.N. F^{60} 909, Debate in Conseil économique interministériel.
12 A.N. F^{10} 5623, Monnet to Stettinius, 2 January 1945.
13 T.L., Clayton Papers, office files, France, 5 March 1945.
14 A.N. F^{60} 898, Accords Prêt-Bail, 19 February 1945.
15 U.S.T., N.A.C. Meeting No. 4, 27 September 1945.
16 A.N. F^{60} 918, meeting in Ministry of National Economy, 24 October 1945.
17 L.S. Pressnell, *External Economic Policy since the War. Volume I. The Post-War Financial Settlement* (London, 1986), pp. 252–53.
18 J. Jackson, *The Politics* op. cit., pp. 20–21.
19 A.N. F^{60} 901, report from Ministry of National Economy, 3 September 1945. Also Min. Fin. 5A 19.
20 Min. Fin. B 33015, Direction du Trésor, Programmes d'importation de 1946, 11 September 1945.
21 S.D. RG 165, 463.3, Box 221, Clay to McCloy, 6 September 1945.
22 FRUS 1945, Conference of Berlin, vol. 1, p. 608. Truman Papers, Briefing Book, paper no. 418.
23 PRO T 236/279, E. Griffith (Ministry of Fuel and Power) to E. W. Playfair (Treasury), 15 June 1945.
24 F.R.C. Office of War Mobilization and Conversion. R.G. 250, Box 17613, memo, 7 September 1945.
25 N.A.U.S. F.W. 851.50/9–445, memorandum written by L. Malony, R. Eldridge and I. White, 17 August 1945.
26 N.A.U.S. 851.51/9–1045, Acheson to Labouisse and White, 10 September 1945.
27 Foreign Relations of the United States, 1945 vol. IV, Europe, p. 773.
28 A.N. F^{60} 918, meeting in Ministry of National Economy, 24 October 1945.
29 Philippe Mioche, 'Le Démarrage du Plan Monnet: comment une entreprise conjoncturelle est devenue une institution prestigieuse', *Revue d'histoire moderne et contemporaine*, July–September 1984.
30 N. Buchanan and F. Lutz, *Rebuilding the World Economy* (New York, 1947), pp. 139–41.
31 P.R.O.T. 236 1893, Cobbold to Eady, 28 June 1945.
32 N.A.U.S. 851.51/9–2245, Caffery to Byrnes, 22 September 1945.
33 N.A.U.S. 851.51/9–2445, Monnet to Clayton, 24 September 1945.
34 N.A.U.S. 851.50/6–2545, Caffery to Byrnes, 25 June 1945.
35 N.A.U.S. 851.50, Caffery to Byrnes, 23 January 1946.
36 J. Dumaine, *Quai d'Orsay (1945–1951)* (London, 1958), p. 52.

37 N.A.U.S. 851.50/1–1046, Merchant to McVey, 10 January 1946.
38 U.S.T., N.A.C. Meeting No. 13, 21 February 1946.
39 U.S.T., N.A.C. Meeting No. 16, 20 March 1946.
40 N.A.U.S. 851.51/2, White to Acheson, 11 February 1946.
41 MAE–A–10–13, GATT. 1, March 1945–April 1946, 16 January 1946.
42 Min. Ind. 830589, 11 Papiers Bellier, note from Beaurepaire, 19 January 1946.
43 *L'Année politique, 1946*. Catherine de Cuttoli-Uhel, 'La politique allemande de la France (1945–1948). Symbole de son impuissance?', in R. Girault and R. Frank (eds), *La Puissance française en question 1945–1949* (Paris, 1988).
44 Accounts of these negotiations can be found in Gérard Bossuat, *La France, l'aide américaine et la construction européenne 1944–1954* (Paris, 1992), M. Margairaz, op. cit., and Irwin M. Wall, *The United States and the Making of Postwar France 1945–1954* (Cambridge, 1991).
45 T.L., Treasury File, Box 129, Fred M. Vinson Collection 6. France Meetings, April–June 1946. Also U.S. Treasury File, Records of National Advisory Council R.G. 56, and MAE-A 194–5.
46 MAE-A 194–5.
47 Min. Fin. B. 33015, note by Briand, 22 August 1945.
48 T. Balogh, 'French Reconstruction and the Franco–US Loan Agreement', *Bulletin of the Oxford Institute of Statistics*, vol. 8, nos 8 and 9, 1946.
49 Annie Lacroix-Riz, 'Négociation et signature des accords Blum–Byrnes (octobre 1945–mai 1946) d'après les archives du Ministère des Affaires Etrangères', *Revue d'Histoire Moderne et Contemporaine*, July–September 1984.
50 John Gimbel, *The Origins of the Marshall Plan* (Stanford, 1976), pp. 30–34.

3

FRANCE AND THE MARSHALL PLAN

THE 1947 CRISIS

Signs of an impending crisis in France were identified by William Clayton, the American secretary of state for economic affairs, as early as March 1947.[1] At that time it was feared that France faced two major problems. One was a potential shortage of coal caused by a drastic cutback in exports from Britain and from the British occupation zone in Germany, which it was anticipated would lead to a sharp drop in industrial production. The second was an imminent shortage of wheat both in France and on the world market which looked like being as bad as at any time during the war. The coal problem threatened to be all the more severe in view of the optimistic forecasts of German coal exports made in Washington during the Blum–Byrnes negotiations. Quite unforeseen was the crisis in the British coal industry which resulted in no coal at all being exported to France in December 1946. A special visit by Blum, who was then the prime minister of an all-socialist interim government, produced a mere 100 tons of coal in January 1947 compared with 122,100 tons in January 1946.

Then in February 1947 exports of coal from the Ruhr declined dramatically to little more than 1,000 tons. This led to a diplomatic onslaught on the United States to resolve the question of German coal exports at the Council of Foreign Ministers meeting in Moscow in March–April 1947. The result was an agreement known as the Moscow Sliding Scale for coal which was to link coal exports to coal production in the Rúhr. When coal production in the three western zones of Germany reached 280,000 tons per day, the proportion exported was to be 21 per cent, rising to 25 per cent when production reached 370,000 tons per day. France was to get a 28 per cent share of these exports, which it was estimated would mean a maximum of 370,000 tons per month by the end of 1947.[2]

The French communist party saw little reason for the government to be pleased with the sliding scale agreement since it fell far short of the 1 million-ton target of monthly coal imports which France had argued was needed if the Monnet Plan was to be implemented. A more serious objection voiced by Maurice Thorez, the communist party leader, was that the agreement would mean the abandonment of the French thesis that the Ruhr had to be placed under international political control in order to prevent future German aggression.[3] Indeed Hervé Alphand, the director of the economic section of the Quai d'Orsay, in discussions with the British, had already conceded the fundamental point that French interests in the Ruhr could be served equally well through a form of control which fell short of the political detachment which the French had been demanding. What provoked this concession was the fear that after the formation of the Bizone in January 1947 the British and the Americans were preparing bilaterally to revise the level of industry permitted there above the level agreed by the four occupying powers in March 1946. The most immediate implication for France of such a revision would be that Ruhr coal would be retained in the Bizone for the benefit of German industry rather than be exported to France to assist French reconstruction.[4] The overriding concern of both the Quai d'Orsay and the planners was thus to secure an agreement on German coal exports before the British and Americans revised the level of industry in the Bizone.

If this concern was met then, as Monnet explained, France would be able to join the British and Americans in opposing Soviet demands for reparations to be taken immediately out of current production as well as from fixed capital.[5] But even with the Moscow Sliding Scale agreement coal exports from the Ruhr continued to fall well below the requirements of the French economy. In order to minimize the effects on industrial production the French government increased its imports of coal from the United States. In 1947 they were more than twice as large as in 1946. In view of the great dollar savings which the Americans had argued during the Blum–Byrnes negotiations could be made on coal imports in 1947 this had serious implications for the French balance of payments.

It was a heavy price to pay for only a small increase in total coal availability over the year 1946, leaving that total, as Table 3.1 demonstrates, still well short of the prewar figure and short of what was needed to sustain the planned increase in manufacturing output. As the table also shows the shortfall compared to prewar was entirely in imports from Europe.

The crisis in agriculture, which was apparent by February 1947, was caused by a sharp reduction in the area sown under winter wheat and a severe frost which destroyed much of that wheat. The problem had implications for the balance of payments since, it will be recalled, the planners had forecast that agricultural output would have regained its prewar level by 1947 so that food and agricultural imports would be almost 60 per cent less than in 1946. In view of the global shortages still prevailing in wheat the minister of agriculture himself went to Washington in February 1947 to try to negotiate last-minute wheat deliveries.[6] He succeeded in getting 362,000 tons for the period until June 1947. This was less than the 500,000 tons needed to maintain daily bread rations at 250 grams, 50 grams below the

Table 3.1 Coal availability in France, 1938–47 (in million tons)

	1938	1946	1947
French production	47.6	49.3	47.3
Imports from			
USA	0	5.2	12.0
GB	6.5	0.7	0.005
Germany	7.2	3.4	3.1
Belgium	4.9	0.4	0.6
Holland	2.1	0.03	0.1
Poland	1.6	0.6	0.5
USSR	0.09	0	0
Turkey	0.1	0	0
Czechoslovakia	0.07	0.01	0.03
Morocco	0.05	0.02	0.09
Indochina	0.2	0	0
Others	0.02	0	0
Total imports	22.8	10.4	16.5
Total availability	70.4	59.7	63.8

Source: G. Pilliet, Inventaire économique de la France, 1948 (Paris, 1948)

existing level. Over the year as a whole the quantity of cereals imported from the United States was less than in 1946 but, because American wheat prices had more than doubled, France spent 62 million dollars in 1947 compared with 45 million dollars in 1946 and compared with the 20 million dollars planned.

In view of the critical shortage of wheat, both in France and in the international market, the planners advised as early as February that daily bread rations should be cut immediately to 250 grams.[7] It was not until the end of April though that Prime Minister Paul Ramadier acted on this advice and made this cut. This unleashed a wave of strikes which, for the first time since the war, were supported by the communist party and resulted in the dismissal of the communist ministers from government.

That Ramadier was acting under instructions from Washington in order to prepare the ground politically for the Marshall Plan has long been an allegation of the French Left. Clearly the trigger for the strikes at the Renault factory at Billancourt was the reduction in the daily bread ration. We have seen how Ramadier postponed taking this unpopular decision until after the Moscow Council of Foreign Ministers meeting in March–April 1947. It is entirely plausible that he did so in order to strengthen the French negotiating position on Germany. Once an agreement on German coal exports had been reached with the British and the Americans the usefulness of maintaining links with the Soviet Union and therefore with the French communist party declined. When the Soviet Union refused at Moscow to support the French claim to annexe the Saar, the need to reorientate French foreign policy seemed confirmed. It was therefore to further French policy in Germany that Ramadier acted as he did, even if his dismissal of the communist ministers fitted well into the new strategy for Europe then being developed in the United States.[8]

Although the unforeseen imports of coal and wheat from the United States in the first half of 1947 help to explain the deterioration in the current account position they explain only part of the payments crisis which prompted French acceptance of Marshall Aid. Another contributory factor was that the loan of 250 million dollars granted by the International Bank for Reconstruction and Development (IBRD) in May 1947 was only half the amount hoped for in 1946. It will be recalled that the conclusion of the Blum–Byrnes negotiations was delayed when the French attempted to secure American support for a loan of 500 million dollars from the IBRD. Even when this support was not forthcoming the French government remained unrealistically confident that its request for a loan of that amount would succeed. Given that the total lending capacity of the bank was only 700 million dollars at that time,[9] the French were fortunate to receive as much as 250 million dollars.

However, if we compare the current account position in 1946 and 1947 with the forecasts made in July 1946 it would seem that in spite of the problems mentioned so far, the forecasts were actually reasonably accurate (See Table 3.2). What Table 3.2 disguises, though, is the great imbalance in the payments with each monetary area and the high proportion of exports to countries with which France had signed bilateral payments agreements.

In 1946 exports to these countries accounted for 61 per cent of all exports and in 1947 for 62 per cent, whereas imports accounted for 26 per cent and 33 per cent respectively. While France was closing the payments gap with these countries as well as with the Sterling Area in 1947, the gap with the Dollar Area was increasing. The large import surplus which the French ran

Table 3.2 French balance of payments on current account, 1946–47 (in million dollars)

| | Year | | | |
| | 1946 | | 1947 | |
	Actual	Forecast	Actual	Forecast
Exports	452.8	670	1,040	1,225
Imports	1,980.0	2,310	2,492	2,610
Invisibles (net)	−521.6	−425	−223.7	−192
Total	−2,048.8	−2,065	−1,675.7	−1,577

Sources: Ministère des Finances, *Inventaire de la situation financière (1913–1946)* (Paris, 1946); Institut National de la Statistique et des Etudes Economiques (INSEE) 'La Balance des payements de la Zone Franc', *Bulletin Mensuel de Statistique. Supplément*, January–March 1953

with their zone of occupation in Germany compounded their dollar shortage. This was because the French had accepted an American demand at the Potsdam Conference that most exports from Germany should be paid for in dollars.[10] In the first nine months of 1947 their trade deficit with their zone in Germany amounted to 58 million dollars.[11]

The overall payments problem stemmed from the fact that even if France were to revert to its prewar position of running a surplus with Britain and much of western Europe, because of the payments problems of these countries it would not be able to convert this surplus into dollars to finance its imports from the Dollar Area.

The American offer of Marshall Aid, made conditional upon European governments cooperating with each other in a joint recovery plan, offered a solution to both the French and western Europe's payments problem in the medium term, once the terms for aid had been internationally agreed. But the long political wrangle to reach that agreement meant that Marshall Aid did not flow until the summer of 1948. The offer therefore did not alleviate France's immediate dollar shortage, which had become so severe by August 1947 that the government was obliged to suspend all imports from the Dollar Area apart from the vital necessities of wheat and coal.

Even these were threatened when in September 1947 the Bank of France first discovered that almost the entire gold reserve, which had fallen to 445 million dollars, was already committed by the government in payments agreements. Not only had the Ministry of Finance issued import orders without consulting with the bank but the Fonds de Stabilisation had been using the gold in its possession to buy three-month Treasury Bills. While this was permitted by the wartime decree of 29 February 1940 it undermined the original intention of the Popular Front government, which had created the fund in 1936, to protect the exchange rate of the franc.[12]

And although 200 million dollars of the Export–Import Bank loan had not been spent by August 1947, the bank was initially unwilling to release it for imports for consumption rather than investment. Bread rations which had been reduced from 300 grams to 250 grams per day in April 1947 were

Table 3.3 French trade and payments by monetary area (in million dollars)

	Year					
	1946			1947		
	D	S	B	D	S	B
Exports	79.2	97.8	275.8	109.6	285.7	644.7
Imports	1,068.7	390.6	520.7	1,242.8	431.9	817.0
Balance of trade	−989.5	−292.8	−244.9	−1,133.2	−146.2	−132.3
Balance on current account	−1,356.8	−290.8	−401.2	−1,395.7	−57.9	−222.1

Source: INSEE, Bulletin Mensuel de Statistique. Supplément, January–March 1953
Notes: D = Dollar Area; S = Sterling Area; B = Bilateral Agreement countries.

reduced again in August 1947 to 200 grams, which was lower than at any time during the occupation. Indeed total consumption as a proportion of net national output was lower in 1947 than in 1946. The United States, fearing that the consequent social unrest would strengthen support for the communist party and thereby weaken support for the Marshall Plan, rushed an emergency 'interim aid' programme through Congress. This totalled 328 million dollars of which 111 million dollars was for imported wheat and 116 million dollars for American coal.[13]

At the same time, though, the American Treasury refused to cooperate with the French government to disclose information about the assets held in the United States by private French citizens. In spite of threats from Monnet that the French government would bring back its communist ministers the information remained secret.[14] Income from this source totalled only 95 million dollars in 1947 instead of the 400 million dollars hoped for.

As a result of these fairly *ad hoc* arrangements to finance imports until Marshall Aid began to arrive in 1948 the predicted economic crisis did not materialize. Industrial production fell in some sectors, particularly coal mining, metal production and construction, in November and December 1947, but this was due to a record number of strikes, largely protesting against the Marshall Plan, rather than to a downturn in the economy. By April 1948 industrial production was 17 per cent above the 1938 level.

THE ECONOMIC EFFECTS OF MARSHALL AID

Of the many interpretations of the impact of the European Recovery Programme advanced by historians the most challenging is the claim that it changed the way in which the capitalist system operated in western Europe; that it replaced the zero-sum game which had dominated prewar politics with a system which enabled the economy to grow. The investment necessary for growth was no longer to be at the expense of wages and living standards but was to be financed through higher labour productivity.[15] This was the essence of the New Deal which Hogan claims that Marshall Aid brought to Europe.[16] In theory Marshall Aid allowed levels of both investment and consumption to rise. Investment then led to higher labour productivity which in turn led to higher incomes. The battle against communism in western Europe was to be won by providing increasing prosperity for the working class and thereby reconciling it to the American form of liberal capitalism. This reformed capitalist system would be free from the cyclical fluctuations caused by imbalances between supply and demand since increases in supply would be matched by rising demand. Say's law would at last come true.

It is central to the argument based on the 'politics of productivity' that investment did lead to higher labour productivity, out of which higher wages could be paid, and not to higher unemployment. In France productivity levels, measured in terms of output per man hour, rose at an unprecedentedly high rate across most branches of activity in the period 1949–62, with the greatest increases being in electricity, gas, chemicals and agriculture.[17] The fact that this was the story across western Europe is usually attributed to the process of catching up with the technological leader, the United States, and to the transfer of labour from low productivity sectors to high productivity sectors as part of that process. Marshall Aid became the mechanism both for transferring the new technology and for ensuring that such investment would not be at the expense of consumption. The result, it is claimed, is that Marshall Aid started a process of economic growth which in terms of its high rates and duration was without precedent in recent European history.[18] These claims have not gone unchallenged, particularly with respect to the West German experience.[19] But in France, where the debate has been dominated by the Cold War, it is the political consequences of American aid, particularly the perceived loss of an independent foreign policy, which has commanded attention, leaving these wider issues unexplored.[20]

France was the second largest beneficiary of Marshall Aid next to the United Kingdom and the largest recipient if indirect aid in the form of drawing rights is included. (Direct aid was for the finance of imports from the Dollar Area while indirect aid was for imports from other countries in the OEEC.) Although in absolute quantity more aid was allocated to importing consumption goods, relative to their share in the total of prewar imports certain categories of investment goods were disproportionately favoured in Marshall Aid deliveries and this by deliberate action on the part of the French government.

Even though most of the goods imported with Marshall Aid were for current consumption it was many years before living standards in France had regained their prewar level. While wage rates and consumption levels did increase it was not until as late as 1956 that the purchasing power of an unmarried workman in Paris regained its level of 1938.[21] On the other hand, a father of five working outside Paris was almost 30 per cent better off by 1949 than in 1938 but this was due to the extension of social security in the form of more generous family allowances rather than the result of his higher productivity. And he was in any case much less likely to have been a communist voter.[22] In effect, therefore, Marshall Aid was used to achieve the modernization of certain sections of French manufacturing, which in other circumstances might have been both economically and politically more difficult.

Depending on what is included as investment goods the calculation of how important they were in the total imports financed by Marshall Aid varies. ECA calculated that until the end of 1950 French imports of machinery and machine tools accounted for 22 per cent of the total.[23] Alan

Milward estimated that machinery and vehicles accounted for 21.1 per cent of all ERP shipments in 1949 and 38.8 per cent in 1950.[24] According to an official French calculation three-fifths of the investment goods imported under the Marshall Aid programme until the end of 1950 were for three sectors of the economy: steel, mechanical engineering and air transport.[25]

In any consideration of the question of catch-up in terms of the acquisition of American technology it would be difficult to demonstrate the economic benefits which accrued from the acquisition of new and used American aircraft. The question is more open in the case of steel and mechanical engineering, the other two main beneficiaries of investment goods under the Marshall Plan. Indeed, it is arguably that in helping to modernize the French steel industry Marshall Aid made its most important contribution to French reconstruction. Not only did it help to restore the competitiveness of the steel industry, and by extension much of French manufacturing industry, but it was central to laying the basis for the political settlement between France and Germany in the form of the Schuman Plan.

THE MODERNIZATION OF THE STEEL INDUSTRY

The French steel industry emerged from the war relatively unscathed. Although output in 1945 was only 26 per cent of that of 1938 the capacity existed to produce 12 million tons of finished steel. The major limiting factor was coke and coking fines from the Ruhr, on which trade the steel industry in 1938 had depended for 63 per cent of its needs. This meant that the rate at which the French steel industry recovered was dependent to a considerable extent on the rate of recovery of German coking coal production and exports. This in turn was determined partly by decisions taken by the Allies about the level of industry to be permitted in Germany and the speed at which that level was to be reached.

The French government saw its responsibility for dealing with this problem extending far beyond the sphere of traditional international diplomacy. The steel industry occupied a position of strategic importance in the economy, not only because of its role in armaments production but because it was a basic material in a large number of manufacturing industries, and particularly in the key growth industries of motor vehicles and home appliances. Without a guaranteed supply of inputs the planned expansion of output could not be ensured. It was not, however, only a question of quantity; price was equally important. The price of steel, therefore, was influential in determining the competitiveness of much of French manufacturing industry. Steel inputs into the four largest automobile firms accounted in 1951 for 28 per cent of their production costs.[26]

The price of steel for most of the interwar period was fixed not only by the market but by agreement among steel producers. The first European steel cartel formed in 1926 resulted from the desire of the German steel industry to prevent any further loss of domestic market share to French steel exporters who were capitalizing on the falling value of the franc. It was supported by the French steel industry which wanted to consolidate its export gains before the franc was stabilized *de facto*. The cartel agreement set controls on steel production in member countries and on exports from France, Luxembourg and the Saarland to Germany. But the agreement did not survive in this form when the demand for steel slumped after 1929. Because the larger producers in France and Germany were less dependent on the export market than their competitors in Belgium and Luxembourg they chose to exceed their production quotas as set by the cartel. In the French case the steel industry then lobbied the government to impose quantitative restrictions on steel imports. This was to enable it to increase its prices on the domestic market and reduce them on the export market. Faced with such a situation the small steel producers agreed to accept an arrangement which was much less favourable to them than that of 1926, but which at least avoided the threat of dumping in third markets by the larger producers. It was for this reason that the cartel formed in 1933 no longer regulated domestic production but confined itself to sharing the export market. The agreement enabled the French steel industry to maintain its high price on the domestic market and thereby shield itself from the worst effects of the depression. But in the absence of competition and in the face of declining demand it was under no pressure to change or modernize its structure in any way.

In 1932 a control body, the Comptoir Sidérurgique de France (CSF) was set up to allocate shares of the domestic market among the main steel firms. These were based initially on the production statistics of the late 1920s and remained unchanged for a five-year period. Agreement between firms was obtained by setting up equalizing funds between the main products and between the domestic and export markets, thus reducing still further the pressure to modernize and increasing the extent of protection.

The only time in the whole interwar period when an opportunity for modernizing the steel industry for the benefit of the entire economy may have existed was in the period between the end of the First World War and the formation of the steel cartel in 1926. On the eve of the First World War the output of crude steel in Germany, at 17.6 million tons, was almost four times that of France. Between 1914 and 1918 whereas Germany produced 70.5 million tons of crude steel France managed a mere 9.5 million tons.[27] The return to France of the major steel producing area of Lorraine as part of the peace settlement was not sufficient to assuage official French fears, particularly those of the ministries of Foreign Affairs and Industry, that the French steel industry was too small relative to that of Germany. But in view of the fact that before the war 90 per cent of steel production had been sold on the domestic market the steel producers, with some exceptions, were fearful that, were they to expand production, the domestic market would not be able to absorb the increase, leaving them with surplus capacity. The solution proposed by some of the French banks was to rationalize the steel industry in order to concentrate production on high-quality steel which could supply both foreign and domestic markets.

Whereas the French banks, unlike their German counterparts, had played no part in financing the development of the steel industry in the nineteenth century they saw an opportunity to change this after 1918. In view of the financial difficulties in which many steel firms found themselves the Banque de Paris et des Pays-Bas expected to be approached for help. This led it to draw up a series of proposals between 1922 and 1926 for reorganizing the steel industry in return for a loan. These proposals included closing down some works in order to concentrate production in three large groups in the north and east of France which would specialize in producing high-quality steel.[28]

But nothing was done since the falling value of the franc encouraged steel exports and enabled the steel firms to remain independent of the banks. Once the steel cartel had been formed the opportunity for rationalization and concentration disappeared.

By 1938 the gap in production between the French and German steel industries had widened considerably and it was to continue to widen during the war years. Not only that but, as the Vichy planners estimated, the productive capacity of the French steel industry had also declined relative to world capacity in the ten years after 1929 by as much as 50 per cent. Its relative position in Europe had deteriorated as well. Whereas in 1929 the French steel industry had accounted for 17 per cent of European steel production, by 1938 it accounted for no more than 10.7 per cent. Nor was this decline due to technical factors. The Vichy planners calculated that the production of 1 ton of finished steel required 6 tons of iron ore and 4 tons of coal. Given that one of the main sources of iron ore in western Europe was in Lorraine, technical considerations alone, they argued, would have dictated that France should have been a major producer of steel, with a productive capacity well above 12 million tons. One of the reasons why it was not was that France had to export iron ore in order to import coke and coking coal. This led the planners to recommend a series of measures designed to reduce the proportion of coke to ore required in steel-making. These included modernizing the blast furnaces and expanding the production of Siemens–Martin and electric steel which used scrap as an input, rather than Thomas steel which used a high proportion of ore. Altogether it was estimated that France could save up to 13 per cent of its 1939 coke consumption and 12 per cent of its coal consumption in these ways. And to meet the estimated growing postwar demand in western Europe for finished steel the planners concluded that the French steel industry would have to be rationalized in order to encourage much greater specialization.[29]

The Vichy planners did not tackle the question of how these plans were to be implemented though, particularly if they were not supported by the industry itself. Preliminary consultations after the war revealed that the industry was as concerned as in the past with the risk of overproduction caused by fluctuations in demand. Its solution was to return to some form of cartel.[30] But this spelt disaster for the steel-consuming industries for whom the steel cartel had meant high domestic prices. For the left-wing members of the Resistance the answer to this was to nationalize the steel industry.[31]

Although this proposal had the support of Mendès-France as minister of national economy in 1945, it was not implemented. Among the reasons given at the time were that the running of the industry was too complex for it to be transferred to the state while the essential cooperation with private steel firms in Belgium, Britain and the Ruhr could be undermined if the industry was nationalized in France.[32] The following year Monnet made it a precondition for the implementation of his Modernization Plan that no further nationalizations should take place, on the grounds that even the discussion of them deterred private investment.[33]

Steel was nevertheless selected following the pattern of all the earlier proposals for economic reconstruction as one of the priority sectors of Monnet's plan to modernize the French economy. In considering the future of the steel industry Monnet and his planners drew upon many of the arguments made by the DGEN in Vichy. They aimed to expand steel production to 10 million tons by 1949, which was equivalent to the maximum output of the interwar period achieved in 1929, then to increase it to 12 million tons in 1951 and subsequently to 15 million tons. The plan, taken in conjunction with the restrictions imposed on the level of industry permitted in Germany in March 1946, would mean that the centre of heavy industry on the European continent would move from Germany to France. Because the industry already had the capacity to produce the target of 12 million tons, the first limiting factor to be overcome was the supply of coke.

What the Monnet Plan called for was therefore not an immediate expansion of capacity but a more rational utilization of existing capacity. It advocated regrouping some of the 177 steel firms into 12 larger units each with an average capacity to produce 1 million tons of steel annually. It also called for the installation of two continuous wide-strip mills. These mills were an American invention of the 1930s which greatly reduced the cost of producing the thin sheet steel used in making motor vehicles, office equipment and the new generation of consumer durables for which demand was expanding rapidly. By the beginning of the Second World War there were three of these mills in operation in the United States, each producing 1 million tons, as well as a small one in Dinslaken in Germany.[34] Mendès-France had hoped that the French could take the German one as reparations but it went to the Soviet Union instead.[35]

The cost of this investment alone was high. Out of a total of 70,000 million francs specified in the Monnet Plan for investment in the steel industry between 1947 and 1953, 21,000 million francs was for the wide-strip mills alone. And since they would have to be imported from the United States it represented a large slice of the remaining French dollar reserves. In view of the cost the Monnet planners recommended installing the first wide-strip mill as a matter of top priority and deferring the second one until the other modernization projects in the steel industry had been undertaken.[36] None of the existing steel firms had either the steel-making capacity to justify, or the financial resources to undertake, such an investment. However, two firms in the north of France, Denain–Anzin and the Forges et Aciéries du Nord et de l'Est put forward a proposal in February 1946 to the Ministry of Industrial Production suggesting that they would merge to form one company if they were allowed to place an order for a wide-strip mill in the United States. This was the origin of the new company called USINOR which was finally set up in July 1948.[37]

Less than two weeks later a group of firms in Lorraine led by de Wendel proposed forming a partnership known as the Société Lorraine de Laminage Continu (SOLLAC) in order to install the wide-strip mill in Lorraine. It would have been the more obvious location given that 67 per cent of the steel produced in 1938 had been produced in Lorraine, compared with 19 per cent in the north. Yet the Ministry of Industrial Production favoured USINOR on account, it has been suggested, of its smaller degree of dependence on Ruhr coke and its stronger financial position.[38]

The American offer of Marshall Aid was a mixed blessing. On the one hand, it provided a possible source of finance for one or both of the wide-strip mills, but, on the other hand, since it presaged the upward revision of the level of industry in the Bizone it increased the fear of overproduction facing the French steel industry. The French government had never doubted that a central purpose of the Marshall Plan was to revive the German economy. But initially it harboured the illusion that Allied policy towards Germany would continue to be determined by the four-power Allied Control Council and that France could continue to exert a veto by remaining in control of its zone in Germany.[39] The Soviet rejection of Marshall Aid was greeted with some incredulity in Paris since it was not the intention of either the French or the British government to surrender sovereignty in return for aid.[40] However, shortly after the sixteen European countries which had accepted the American offer of aid had convened in Paris to form the Committee for European Economic Cooperation (CEEC), the French heard unofficially of the American and British decision to raise the level of industry in the Bizone. This decision was confirmed in the four-year programme submitted by the Bizonal authorities to the CEEC in August 1947.

The four-year programme set out figures for production, imports and exports for the Bizone over the period 1948–51 which were to be included in the total submission for aid from CEEC. What most concerned the French was that exports of coke from the Ruhr were scheduled to be lower in 1948 than in 1947. This, Monnet argued, would enable German steel production to rise whilst curbing any increase in French steel production.[41] The Monnet Plan's target of producing 12 million tons of steel by 1951 would have to be reduced as a consequence by two or three million tons, thereby confirming the French communist party's allegations that Marshall Aid was designed to promote the recovery of the German economy at the expense of the French.

The only concessions which the French could secure were that the Moscow Sliding Scale for coal would be extended to include coke and that in the likely event that no agreement was reached on Germany at the four-power Council of Foreign Ministers meeting in London later that year, the western Allies would set up an international authority in the Ruhr. This would consist of representatives of the United States, Britain, France, the Benelux countries and Germany and would have the power to allocate the output of coal, coke and steel between German internal consumption and exports.[42] The more precise powers of this authority were not to be specified until the nature and powers of a new German state had been agreed.

Throughout 1948, during the three stages of the London Conference which met to determine these powers, the French lost ground on every issue. The new German state was to have a unitary national assembly elected by universal suffrage rather than chosen indirectly by Länder parliaments as the French wished. It was left open whether the powers over investment, management and development of the Ruhr industries would devolve to the new International Authority for the Ruhr, as the French wanted, to the Military Security Board or to some other body. Whereas the French wanted to retain a limit on the level of steel output in Germany the Americans advocated the removal of all restrictions.[43]

This uncertainty gave the French no guarantees at all that the limits set on German steel production would be retained. Indeed, all the evidence pointed to the contrary. Since the summer of 1948 an American mission had been in Germany studying the ways in which German steel production could be increased to the 10.7 million tons decided by the Bizonal authorities in the summer of 1947. This paved the way for the Economic Cooperation Administration (ECA) to appoint a committee, under the chairmanship of the industrialist George Humphrey, to consider the logic and justification for continuing the policy of dismantling German steel plant when at the same time the ECA was financing new investment in the German steel industry. In December 1948 it was known unofficially that the committee was recommending the retention of 167 plants in Germany in order to increase output.[44] What would be left of French policy towards Germany or of the Monnet Plan in France if the remaining controls on the German steel industry were to be lifted at a time when French steel output had reached only 7.3 million tons, less than 75 per cent of capacity? Furthermore if the German steel industry were to import a wide-strip mill with Marshall Aid, as General Clay and the American army in Germany were advocating, the German steel industry and German manufacturing industry would not be dependent on importing the steel made by the wide-strip mills in France as the French planners had intended.[45]

Yet in March 1948 the French Ministry of Industrial Production had recommended that SOLLAC's proposal to install a second wide-strip mill should be abandoned on financial grounds.[46] Since then the demand for steel, particularly in Germany, had soared. How could France argue against the installation of a wide-strip mill in Germany if the French government was not even supporting the plan to install a second one in France? The only way to rescue French policy towards Germany was to import the second wide-strip mill with Marshall Aid.[47] The ECA supported SOLLAC's bid which was in fact to be the largest single project financed by the ECA in the world. A total of 55 million dollars was allocated to cover the cost of a continuous hot-strip mill, a blooming mill, two cold mills and all the ancillary facilities.[48]

But if the installation of a second wide-strip mill at SOLLAC succeeded in postponing the day when Germany would get one (it was not until 1955 that the Thyssen firm was to acquire its own) it nevertheless exacerbated other problems. Since it would mean that the French steel industry would have a capacity for producing steel sheet far in excess of French needs for some years, and since every other country in western Europe with a steel industry was also installing at least one wide strip mill, it created the risk of surplus capacity and revived the idea of regulating it through cartel agreements. The expansion of capacity also increased the French industry's dependence on imported coal and coke. Although some of the investment undertaken within the context of the Monnet Plan was to reduce the relative dependence on coal and coke any expansion in steel output would increase it in absolute terms.

The correlative dependence of the Ruhr steel industry on iron ore from Lorraine had been in steady decline throughout the interwar period as the Ruhr had turned increasingly to the richer ores in Sweden instead. What was needed in France on both foreign and economic policy grounds was some mechanism which guaranteed to the French steel industry access to the Ruhr coal and coke on equal terms with the German steel industry and which stabilized the market for steel without undermining the interests of the manufacturing industry in the process. The solution proposed by Monnet in the Commissariat au Plan was to dismantle all barriers to the free movement of coal, iron and steel between France and the Federal Republic of Germany and to set up a supranational High Authority to regulate investment and production in these sectors. Since this would ensure continued supervision over the Ruhr the proposal appealed to Prime Minister Robert Schuman on foreign policy grounds.

And although it represented a much more limited form of integration than that being advocated with increasing vehemence by the United States it nonetheless was welcomed by them. While no European country, except perhaps Sweden, was excluded *a priori* as long as they accepted the terms set out by Monnet, it was not merely coincidental that it was the members of the International Steel Cartel of 1926 which formed the European Coal, Iron and Steel Community, together with Italy and the Netherlands, on account of their plans to expand their domestic steel production.[49]

This is probably the most striking way in which the Modernization Plan was shaped by the changing circumstances of reconstruction and in this case extended its reach to shape the reconstruction of much of western Europe. Without the considerable help given to the French steel industry under the Marshall Plan it is doubtful whether modernization and rationalization on the scale undertaken would have been achieved. A repetition of the 1920s experience is more plausible. The installation of the two wide-strip mills in France re-created a degree of interdependence between the steel industries in France and Germany which made the Schuman Plan a viable economic as well as political solution to the problems at the heart of Europe. The initial hostility of the French steel industry to the proposed European Coal, Iron and Steel Community was overcome when the French government agreed to reduce the size of the steel firms' debt to the state by one-third, to offer a number of tax concessions and to tackle finally the transport problem alleged to have afflicted the Lorraine steel industry for over 100 years by canalizing the Moselle in order to make it more navigable.[50]

The high import cost of the continuous strip rolling mills which Marshall Aid financed was thus only the core of the modernization problem in the steel industry and achieving the start of that modernization turned out to have dramatic consequences for European reconstruction as a whole and American involvement in it. It could fairly be said, especially when the importance of the Coal, Iron and Steel Community to the European peace settlement is taken into account, that in no other single field was Marshall Aid used to such a universally beneficial purpose.

MARSHALL AID AND THE FRENCH MACHINE TOOL INDUSTRY

Although more dollars were allocated to buying machine tools than for modernizing the steel industry their use was spread over a wide range of industries. Indeed the one industry which did not benefit was the French machine tool industry itself – an industry which the planners had held up as exemplifying French economic and technical backwardness.

According to a survey carried out in 1943 there were 500,000 machine tools in France with an average age of 25 years. They were produced in small workshops catering for a local highly specialized market. The industry itself blamed the situation on French government policy during and after the First World War. To meet the huge increase in demand the government had imported 80,000 machine tools from the United States during the war. As far as the French industry was concerned the government then compounded the problem by importing a further 60,000 machine tools as reparations from Germany after the war. These imports catered for the growing mass market in machine tools and established a reputation which the French industry was unable to challenge. As a result the French machine tool firms continued to cater for the smaller specialist domestic market.[51]

Rather than repeat after the Second World War what they considered was a policy error, the organization committee for machine tools under Vichy advocated that the French machine tool industry should be allowed to meet the needs of French industry during the period of reconstruction – even if this meant that reconstruction would take longer. While this found favour with a Vichy government anxious to reduce the French economy's dependence on imports, it was rejected by the Ministry of Industrial Production in de Gaulle's postwar government. Yet the Ministry of Industrial Production's counterproposal, known as the Plan Pons, after its author, a high-ranking Polytechnician in DIME, was rejected by the professional organization of the machine tool industry. The plan called for 140,000 new machine tools to be made in France, 40,000 to be imported and 85,000 to be taken or recovered from Germany.

When the Monnet Plan was being drafted, the representatives of the machine tool industry who sat on the Modernization Commission recommended that 215,000 new machine tools should be made in France over a five-year period in order to reduce the average age of the French stock to 8 years. Criticizing the industry for its blatant protectionism, Monnet disbanded the Modernization Commission and set his own targets. Interestingly these were much closer to those of the Modernization Commission than to those of the Plan Pons. Monnet called for 200,000 new machine tools to be made in France and 50,000 to be imported, largely because the idea of taking machine tools from Germany as reparations had been abandoned. Although estimates of the number actually taken vary it did not exceed 25,000. As Table 3.4 indicates, the number of machine tools produced in France over the six-year period 1947–52 fell well below that put forward by Monnet and was almost 60,000 less than that proposed by the Modernization Commission for a five-year period. Had it not been for the 75 million dollars spent importing machine tools under the European Recovery Programme on top of those imported before it began, French industry would have been saddled with out-of-date machine tools for much longer.

Table 3.4 Production, imports and exports of machine tools in France (in units)

Year	Production	Exports	Imports
1938	15,900	4,150	4,450
1945	8,550	650	2,900
1946	16,050	1,300	25,150
1947	24,500	2,200	16,200
1948	27,800	4,250	8,250
1949	23,200	7,150	6,900
1950	28,150	8,950	7,800
1951	25,000	11,800	10,650
1952	28,900	9,550	10,200

Source: Adapted from Annuaire Statistique de la France, on the basis that the average weight of 1 machine tool was 2 tons. See P. Mioche, 'Les Difficultés', op. cit., p. 3

In terms of the total investment in the French economy over the period of the European Recovery Programme the value of investment goods imported with dollar aid was but a tiny fraction. Any further analysis of the contribution to French modernization of specific imports would not detract from such a conclusion. What is clear is that the contribution of Marshall Aid to French reconstruction was qualitative rather than quantitative. Without it it is most unlikely that investment on such a scale would have been undertaken in the steel industry. It would have exceeded the financial capability of the steel firms themselves as well as the political capability of the government to devote such an amount of scarce dollars to one industry and one which remained in private hands. But without that investment in the steel industry the political settlement with West Germany in the form of the Schuman Plan would have been inconceivable on economic grounds alone.

Over the whole period 1945–January 1953 American aid to France in one form or another totalled 10,901 million dollars.[52] Over the same period reparations from Germany totalled 716,000 million francs or 2,046 million dollars. When compared with the French estimate of the damage caused during the Second World War, 98,000 million dollars, or of Germany's part in it, 92,300 million dollars, then American aid plus German reparations represented between 13 and 14 per cent of that damage. After the First World War German reparations to France covered one-third of the estimated damage. Of course after the First World War France had to repay debts incurred with the United States during the war which reduced the net value of reparations, whereas after the Second World War war debts were largely written off by the United States.

Nevertheless, in global terms aid and reparations covered a smaller proportion of wartime damage after 1945 than they had after 1918. Yet economic recovery was both speedier and more durable after the Second World War. The argument that the most valuable reparations after the Second World War consisted neither in fixed capital nor current production

Table 3.5 Use of counterpart funds to promote production
(dollar equivalents in millions of dollars)

Industry	France	% of total
Electricity, gas and power facilities	724.5	76
Transportation, shipping and communications	281.3	36
Agriculture	203.9	33
Coal mining and other mining and quarrying	340.2	75
Primary metals, chemicals and strategic materials	195.1	59
Machinery	10.4	6
Light industry	10.8	17
Petroleum and products	11.7	53
Technical assistance	–	–
Other and undistributed	157.4	35
Total	1,935.3	50

Source: William Adams Brown and Redves Opie, *American Foreign Assistance* (The Brookings Institution, Washington, DC, 1953), p. 237

but in hidden transfers of human capital[53] is refuted by French historians. Not only were living conditions much less attractive in France than in the United States but French employers were unwilling to share their industrial secrets with German scientists or to provoke discontent among their own employees, it is argued.[54] However plausible that view may be on a general level, there were clearly important exceptions to it. It has been shown for example that the interest of French chemical firms in the German chemical industry was strong enough to overcome any such opposition and resulted in close cooperation between French and German engineers in the reconstruction of plant.[55]

Where historians are more in agreement is in explaining the greater success of the post-1945 reconstruction, compared with post-1918, in terms of the double use made in France of Marshall Aid.[56] Not only was Marshall Aid used to finance imports of investment and consumer goods but the counterpart in French francs was used to subsidize investment under the Monnet Plan which, in the three years between the end of the war and the arrival of Marshall Aid, had been financed through a high rate of domestic price inflation. It was in this sense that Marshall Aid was considered to have saved the Monnet Plan. What it fails to explain is why the French needed foreign aid to cover a domestic deficit.

NOTES

1 Ellen Clayton Garwood, *Will Clayton: A Short Biography* (Austin, 1958), pp. 115–18.
2 US Department of State, *Germany 1947–49. The Story in Documents* (Washington, DC, 1950), pp. 481–82.

3 PRO FO 371 67676, Clarke to Warner, 25 April 1947.
4 PRO FO 371 64243, meeting at Massigli's house between Alphand, Massigli, Harvey, Hall-Patch, Turner and Burrows, 19 February 1947.
5 PRO FO 371 66779, meeting between Monnet and Hall-Patch, 2 March 1947.
6 Irwin M. Wall, op. cit., p. 64.
7 AN 80AJ 266, note from J. Bustarret, 18 February 1947.
8 For a more detailed development of this point see Irwin M. Wall, op. cit., pp. 66–73.
9 Robert W. Oliver, *International Economic Cooperation and the World Bank* (London, 1975), p. 232.
10 C. Buchheim, *Die Wiedereingliederung Westdeutschlands in die Weltwirtschaft 1945–58* (Munich, 1990); M. Roseman, 'Division and Stability: recent writing on post-war German history', *German History*, vol. 11, no. 3, 1993, pp. 364–89.
11 Gouvernement militaire de la zone française d'occupation en Allemagne, 'Direction Générale de l'économie et des finances, *Bulletin Statistique*.
12 B.D.F., Délibérations du Conseil Général, no. 139, 1948, Projet de lettre au Ministère des Finances, 15 January, 1948.
13 T.L. Truman Papers Official File, Box 1273, Clark Clifford to Truman, 15 October 1947.
14 F.J.M. AMF 12/2/1, note from Guindey, 26 September 1947.
15 C.S. Maier, 'The Politics of Productivity: Foundations of American International Economic Policy after World War II', in P. Katzenstein (ed.), *Between Power and Plenty: The Foreign Economic Policies of Advanced Industrial States* (Madison, 1978); C.S. Maier, *In Search of Stability: Explorations in Historical Political Economy* (Cambridge, 1987); C. S. Maier and G. Bischof (eds), *The Marshall Plan and Germany* (New York and Oxford, 1991); D. Ellwood, *Rebuilding Europe. Western Europe, America and Postwar Reconstruction* (London, 1992).
16 M.J. Hogan, op. cit.
17 L.A. Vincent, 'Population active, production et productivité dans 21 branches de l'économie française 1896–1962', *Etudes et Conjoncture*, no. 7, July 1963.
18 M. Abramovitz, op. cit.; C. Feinstein, op. cit.
19 W. Abelshauser, 'American Aid and West German Economic Recovery: A Macroeconomic Perspective' in Maier and Bischof (eds), op. cit.
20 G. Bossuat, op. cit.; A. Lacroix-Riz, *Le Choix de Marianne* (Paris, 1985).
21 M. Perrot, 'Données statistiques sur l'évolution des rémunérations salariales de 1938 à 1963', in *Etudes et Conjoncture*, no. 8, August 1965.
22 P. Williams, *Politics in Postwar France* (London, 1955), pp. 55–59.
23 M. Margairaz, op. cit., p. 1177.
24 A.S. Milward, *The Reconstruction of Western Europe, 1945–51* (London, 1984), p. 103.
25 A.N. F^{12} 1180, J. Gabory, 'Trois années du Plan Marshall', December 1950.
26 J. Chardonnet, *La Sidérurgie française. Progrès ou décadence?* (Paris, 1954), p. 13.
27 B.R. Mitchell, *European Historical Statistics 1750–1970*, abridged edition (London, 1978).
28 E. Bussière, 'The Evolution of Structures in the Iron and Steel Industries in France, Belgium and Luxembourg: national and international aspects, 1900–1939', in E. Abe and Y. Suzuki (eds), *Changing Patterns of International Rivalry. Some Lessons from the Steel Industry* (Tokyo, 1991).
29 Min. Ind. IND 830589(11), DGEN, March 1944.
30 MAE A-10–13, GATT, 1 mars 1945-avril 1946, 16 January 1946.
31 Philippe Mioche, *Le Plan Monnet*, op. cit., p. 250.
32 A.N. F^{12} 10063, note from the general secretary at the Ministry of Industrial Production, 13 March 1945.

33 F.J.M. AMF 5/2/10 'Position que peut prendre le plan dans la politique économique et financière française', 5 November 1946.

34 D. Burn, *The Steel Industry 1939–1959. A Study in Competition and Planning* (Cambridge, 1961), p. 80.

35 P. Mioche, *Le Plan Monnet*, op. cit., p. 251.

36 'Premier rapport de la Commission de Modernisation de la Sidérurgie', November 1946.

37 J. Chardonnet, op. cit., p. 216.

38 P. Mioche, *Le Plan Monnet*, op. cit., p. 251.

39 F.J.M. AMF 14/1/2, note for the President, 17 July 1947.

40 AN 80 AJ 266, draft memo, 1 July 1947.

41 F.J.M. AMF 14/1/10, 'Relèvement des niveaux de l'industrie allemande', 18 August 1947.

42 A.S. Milward, *The Reconstruction*, op. cit., p. 74.

43 ibid., p. 161.

44 ibid, p. 148.

45 A.N. 81A3 171, letter to the Steel Control Group, Düsseldorf, 17 May 1951.

46 Matthias Kipping, *L'Amélioration de la competitivité de l'industrie française et les origines du Plan Schuman*, unpublished mémoire (Paris, 1992), p. 34.

47 F.J.M. AMF 22/2/1, Alphand to Schuman, 29 November 1948.

48 Min. Fin. B10927, 'Aid to France'.

49 MAE Série EU Europe Généralités, note, 25 May 1950.

50 P. Mioche and J. Roux, *Henri Malcor, Un Héritier des maîtres de forges* (Paris, 1988), p. 281.

51 P. Mioche, 'Les Difficultés de la modernisation dans le cas de l'industrie française de la machine outil, 1941–1953', *EUI Working Paper*, no. 85/168, 1985.

52 A.N. 80 AJ 13, Archives de M. Bou.

53 Tom Bower, *The Paperclip Conspiracy: The battle for the Spoils and Secrets of Nazi Germany* (London, 1987).

54 Marie-France Ludmann-Obier, 'Un Aspect de la chasse aux cerveaux: les transferts de techniciens allemands en France: 1945–1949', *Relations internationales*, no. 46, summer 1986.

55 R. Stokes, *Divide and Prosper. The Heirs of I. G. Farben under Allied Authority 1945–1951* (London, 1988).

56 Jean-Pierre Rioux, *La France de la IVᵉ République* (Paris, 1980).

4

FINANCING INVESTMENT UNDER THE MONNET PLAN

In the first report of the Monnet Plan submitted to the Council of the Plan in November 1946 it was estimated that the total cost of reconstruction and new investment which the French economy could sustain between 1947 and 1950 was 2,250,000 million francs, equivalent to just over the estimated size of the national income in 1946. Of this, 49 per cent represented the repair of war damage, which the government was legally committed to finance in full. In addition investment in modernizing the recently nationalized coal and electricity industries was to account for a further 9 per cent of the total. The only year for which the planners attempted to itemize investment and the sources of finance was 1947. The itemization was based on a calculation of how investment had been financed in the first half of 1946. As Table 4.1 indicates more than 43 per cent of the actual total investment in 1946 had come from public funds, but the forecast for 1947 was that this proportion would fall to less than a third, in the expectation or hope that private savings would increase and be channelled into planned investment.

The precondition for an expansion of private savings was thought to be that the government would bring inflation under control. Apart from two

Table 4.1 Actual and planned investment and sources of financing in the modernization plan, 1946–47 (thousand million francs)

| | Jan-June 1946 (actual) | | 1947 (planned) | |
	Total	% of total	Total	% of total
Self-finance	20–25	11–13	70	15–16
Public funds	80	43–44	140–50	31–32
Private savings	83	44–45	240–50	53
Total	183–88		450–70	
National income (estimate)[1]	2,000		3,200	

Source: Commissariat Général du Plan de Modernisation et d'Equipement, Rapport général sur le premier plan de modernisation et d'équipement, novembre 1946–janvier 1947 (Paris, 1947)
Note: [1] for 1946 as a whole.

brief periods in the interwar period prices had been rising steadily in France throughout the twentieth century. Even though French people were spared the violence of the inflation in Germany and eastern Europe of the early 1920s the apparent persistence of inflation in France profoundly affected people's attitude to saving. Not only did it depress the general level of private savings but it encouraged particular forms of saving – most notably the hoarding of gold. This is easily explained since savings placed in the form of gold in 1914 were worth 110 times the equivalent savings placed in government bonds at 3 per cent interest by 1947.[1] While it was difficult for the authorities to measure the extent of such hoarding since most of it was not declared in order to escape taxation it was thought to be in the region of 2 million million francs by 1950,[2] which was the equivalent of about one-quarter of the national income in that year.

Because of the considerable financial gain to be made from hoarding gold rather than holding government bonds successive governments found it increasingly difficult to cover their expenditure through voluntary methods. Nor was it easy for them to substitute public saving in the form of increased taxation for private saving. With 36 per cent of the French labour force still employed in the agricultural sector by the end of the Second World War, and increasingly demanding support from the state rather than contributing to it, and only 22 per cent employed in the manufacturing sector, the potential for raising direct taxes on income was limited. On the other hand, if indirect taxes were raised the fear was that this would lead to an increase in prices and would fuel inflationary pressure. At the same time the demands on the government were greater than ever, and not merely because of the immediate problem of physical reconstruction.

As in Britain the experience of economic depression followed by war had changed popular expectations of the role of the state in the economy and society. France participated in the wave of reforms which produced the welfare state, the nationalization of the credit, energy and transport infrastructure and a public commitment to full employment and higher living standards, including a higher relative level of income for the agricultural sector. But in France, where four years of occupation had placed the country on the brink of civil war, the pressure on the postwar state to re-establish its legitimacy was even greater. This explains the uniquely generous compensation treatment given to those who had suffered damage during the war. Under a law passed at the end of October 1946 the state promised to repay the full cost of repairing this war damage, setting a maximum of 20 per cent for depreciation and obsolescence. And on top of that, as we have seen, in January 1947 the government accepted the Monnet Plan for modernizing the French economy, a plan which was based on stimulating a higher level of public and private investment than France had experienced since the 1920s.

The need for investment in the private sector after a decade of depression was incontestable. What was much less certain was the ability of the private sector to finance investment from its own resources. The effect of war and occupation on the economy had been varied. Those sectors which were not dependent on imported supplies and which managed to evade controls and to trade on the black market were in a fairly liquid if exhausted condition after the war. But for the rest of the economy the only way that investment could be financed was through external borrowing. This effectively meant that the private sector would be competing with the greatly increased public sector for credit, when there was no indication that the long-run rate of inflation which had deterred savers from contributing to public finances would drop; quite the contrary indeed, since the nationalization programme presaged increases in public expenditure, as did the government's other additional commitments.

The Monnet Plan was thus intended to deal with the direction of public investment in the long-run context of declining private investment and the weakness of the French capital market. It was to do this by generating an increase in both public and private investment and directing both towards the appropriate targets. In the light of France's historical experience this was indeed a daunting task. The basic sectors of coal, electricity, steel, cement, agricultural machinery and transport were to receive priority in terms of the allocation of scarce goods using the controls inherited from the war and the Vichy period. This evidently gave them a favoured position with potential investors, public or private. But no satisfactory provision was made initially to ensure that the basic sectors would have the financial resources to undertake the investment planned.

Eventually investment in the sectors targeted by the Modernization Plan amounted to 38 per cent of total investment over the period 1947–52.[3] But this was hardly the result of sticking to the plan's first forecasts. As we have already seen the plan was subject to the buffeting of changing international circumstances and the alteration to meet these circumstances had as great an effect on the way in which it dealt with investment in general as they had on the detailed planning for the steel industry.

The rate of inflation in 1946, when the investment targets were first set, was 64 per cent. While there was no doubt that such a high rate of inflation owed much to the way in which the war and occupation had been financed, the fact that the inflation rate in 1946 was higher than in 1945 pointed to other factors as well. The main source of inflation was the size of the public debt, which had quadrupled over the period 1939–44 in order to pay first for the war and then for the occupation levies imposed by Germany. As a result the money supply increased by 250 per cent. That official prices rose by 'only' 180 per cent was due to the draconian controls placed on wages, which rose by 63 per cent over the same period. The deterioration in living standards was even more marked than this gap would suggest since prices on the black market, which escaped the official price index, were very much higher. For people with something to sell there was a happy coincidence between withholding goods from the Vichy authorities and by extension from the German war economy and making a handsome profit by selling on the black market. Estimates of how much money was made in this way vary. What is known is that people preferred to hold their money in the form of banknotes rather than in easily identifiable bank deposits. The volume of banknotes increased by over 300 per cent while bank deposits increased by 147 per cent.[4]

While it did not know the precise details of the monetary situation in France the CFLN in Algiers understood the danger which such a mass of liquid purchasing power posed for the future. But it was torn between the desire to reverse the most glaring injustices of the Vichy regime and the need to maintain tight controls over the economy in order to prevent the situation from deteriorating any further. Mendès-France, whom de Gaulle had appointed commissioner for finance in the CFLN in Algiers, favoured compulsory measures to bring inflation under control and to punish those who had benefited from the occupation.[5] His proposed measures, which were most unpopular, included blocking wages until production had recovered and then confiscating ill-gotten gains through a currency reform.[6] In the euphoric days of liberation wage rises averaging 40 per cent were granted across the country. De Gaulle then chose to appoint a liberal as minister of finance and to appoint Mendès-France to the Ministry of National Economy.

The new minister of finance, Aimé Lepercq, decided to tap into this mood of national euphoria by launching a liberation loan which he hoped would reduce some of the inflationary pressure. At 3 per cent interest the loan brought in 164,000 million francs which was equivalent to almost 18 per cent of the war-related debt.[7] In November 1944 the franc was devalued by 13 per cent against the dollar. Although this left the franc hugely overvalued the new exchange rate was supported by the Allies as a short-term measure to help reduce the inflationary pressure in France still further before a realistic rate was registered to mark France's formal ratification of the Bretton Woods Agreement. It also limited the purchasing power of the Allied troops stationed in France.

After Lepercq's sudden death in a car crash de Gaulle appointed another liberal, René Pleven, to succeed him. Pleven too did not favour Mendès-France's proposal for a currency reform with blocking and confiscation. His own scheme, which de Gaulle supported, was for a simple exchange of banknotes which he argued would be of greater benefit to the economy. On one level it would provide the state with fairly comprehensive information for taxation purposes. Those people who preferred not to disclose this information would lose anyway. It would also encourage savers to put their banknotes into bank accounts or Treasury bonds, Pleven argued, simply to avoid the physical inconvenience of exchanging them. In terms of these rather limited objectives the currency reform was judged to be a success.[8] The estimated value of banknotes not exchanged was 36,500 million francs.

This revival of traditional public debt procedures combined with the issue of new currency notes, relying on public enthusiasm and support for the restoration of the Republic, avoiding the draconian nature of currency reform in Germany, the less draconian reform in Belgium, or the deliberate inflationary debasement of the old currency as in Hungary, at first achieved a measure of success. Savings in banks and postal accounts rose from 33 per cent of the total money supply in April 1945 to 47 per cent in July. Subscriptions to Treasury bills reached almost 100,000 million francs by July.[9]

However in the last quarter of 1945 public fears about the terms of the bill nationalizing credit and the expected devaluation of the franc to accompany French ratification of the Bretton Woods Agreement led to a panic and a rush to withdraw savings. The so-called nationalization of credit, discussed more fully below, arose from proposals written into the CNR charter. The terms of the bill presented to the National Assembly at the beginning of December 1945, in confirming the state's insistence on its overriding role in reconstruction, upset the delicate balance between public and private investment which had been preserved by the initially cautious policy of the Ministry of Finance. Banknotes, as a proportion of the total supply of notes plus deposits, reached 62 per cent – a very high proportion particularly in comparison with Britain and the United States where it was 22 per cent and 17 per cent respectively.[10] At the same time subscriptions to private shares and to public loans declined, causing the Treasury to increase its borrowing from the Bank of France. This was fixed by law at 100,000 million francs and the fear in the Ministry of Finance was that this limit would already be reached in the first six months of 1946 unless the government cut its current expenditure and eased fears about the extent of its nationalization programme.

After the first wave of spontaneous nationalizations in 1944 which affected the Renault car firm and Charbonnages du Nord, the nationalization of credit was the first nationalization bill to be presented to the Constituent Assembly at the end of 1945. It was inspired by a view commonly held in left-wing circles in the 1930s that a 'wall of money' had blocked economic reforms in France. The refusal to devalue the franc before 1936 and the flight of capital which occurred after the victory of the Popular Front government seemed to provide ample proof of this. But the only change made by Léon Blum's government to the financial power structure was to change the statutes of the Bank of France. This change was designed to include all the shareholders in the decision-making process rather than the 200 principal shareholders reputed to hold the strings of power in France.[11]

De Gaulle included the nationalization of credit in his speech in March 1945 in which he listed the sectors which were to be nationalized. But he did not specify whether that meant some or all of the country's financial institutions. Between March and 2 December 1945, when the final text of the nationalization bill was presented to the National Assembly, the precise details were shrouded in the greatest secrecy. It is said that Pleven, who was minister of finance throughout this period, even typed the bill in his own house.[12]

Under the bill the government divided banks into three categories, deposit banks, business banks and medium-term credit institutions, and proposed that only the four largest deposit banks, the Crédit Lyonnais, the Société Générale, the Banque Nationale pour le Commerce et l'Industrie and the Comptoir National d'Escompte as well as the Bank of France should be nationalized. In addition a new body, the Conseil National du Crédit (CNC), was to be set up to 'recommend to the Ministry of Finance all measures designed to encourage bank or savings bank deposits, to discourage the hoarding of currency, to promote the use of deposit money and to mobilize liquid funds in the general interest'. It was also to be consulted by the Ministry of Finance regarding the general credit policy with a view especially to the financing of reconstruction and of the plan for the modernization of the national economy and of import and export plans.[13]

Deposit banks were banks which received from the public deposits at sight or for a period of not more than two years. They could not hold participations amounting to more than 10 per cent of the capital of enterprises other than banks, financial institutions or building societies necessary for the conduct of their business. In no case could the total amount of such participations, including firm subscriptions to issues of shares, exceed 75 per cent of their own resources. Exceeding this limit, as well as any employment of their deposits in participations on property investments, was forbidden unless authority was given by the Deposits Committee of the CNC.

Business banks were banks whose main activity consisted of taking and managing participation in firms which existed already or were in the course of formation and of opening credits without limitation as to period in favour of public or private firms. Business banks could not invest in firms any funds other than those originating from their own resources or from deposits fixed for a period of at least two years or subject to at least two years' notice. Long- and medium-term credit institutions were institutions whose main activity consisted of opening credits for a period of at least two years. They could not receive deposits for a shorter period unless authorized by the Medium-term and Long-term Credit Committee of the CNC.

The legislation was the outcome of vigorous criticism of the banking system in the 1930s as one cause of the low levels of investment and the economy's feeble performance. This criticism had not only come from the communists and socialists, although the new law did pander to their views. The tasks of reconstruction in the full sense seemed so overwhelming that opinion across the political spectrum could be found in favour of greater direction of investment, and it was this that the legislation was mainly intended to achieve. Although this was indeed a problem, an even greater one was the inability to mobilize resources for investment generally. This meant that there was a misfit between the legislation and the problem to be solved. In fact the new laws made it harder at first to mobilize capital, by increasing the suspicions and fears of savers and investors.

While there was unanimous support in the National Assembly for natio-nalizing the Bank of France and setting up the CNC the rest of the bill fell far short of the reforms demanded by the Left. Since the left-wing parties held a majority in the Constituent Assembly de Gaulle feared that their rejection of the entire bill, which would take it to a second reading, would have disastrous consequences for people's confidence in the financial in-stitutions. To avoid this it was suggested that the Constituent Assembly should approve the bill in the form in which it was presented by the government and leave the question of which banks, in addition to the four deposit banks, should be nationalized to the CNC to propose at a subsequent date. This suggestion was accepted; the Bank of France and the four main deposit banks were nationalized but then as expected the Con-stituent Assembly, with insufficient time before the referendum on the constitution in May 1946 to debate the bill to nationalize coal and to reopen the question of extending the nationalization of credit, gave priority to the nationalization of coal.[14]

The successful completion of this 'nationalization of credit' enabled the government to ratify the Bretton Woods agreement at the end of December 1945 and to register a par value for the franc with the International Mone-tary Fund. This required a further devaluation of the franc. Once again it was deliberately overvalued in order to reduce the inflationary pressure in the economy. The dollar rate was reduced from 49.63 francs to 119.1 francs. But the damage to public confidence had been done and the chances, always slender, of financing the ambitious scope of reconstruction without drastic changes in the operation of public finances, other than this attempt to give the state a greater measure of influence over that part of the banking sector with which most of the population dealt, now seemed to have gone.

To British or American readers this nationalization of the deposit banks might seem a more drastic measure than it probably did at the time to the French. It is true that where the French population kept their money in banks they did so in the deposit banks with their extensive branch net-works. But such bank accounts, and the use of cheques for payment, were much less developed habits in France than in Britain or the United States. As Jean Bouvier explains, so great was the French people's distrust of the banks that in the 1930s the banks became the 'victims of a veritable social allergy'.[15]

Although the legislation arose from a long dissatisfaction with the inter-war years and the determination that reconstruction should remedy it, it was hard to see it as threatening the safety, much less the earning power, of people's bank deposits. Their earning power compared to other forms of saving was pretty miserable anyway. Nor was the legislation likely to be particularly effective in steering bank deposits towards the particular reconstruction targets specified by the state, as was soon to be demonstrated in practice. The episode is mainly significant for the way it revived the social and financial anxieties which had burst out under the prewar Popular Front government and so dissipated the initial goodwill towards the liberation government, replacing it with financial suspicions whose origin lay as much in recent history as in current events. And that, of course, was the biggest threat to achieving the ambitious goal of reconstruction, because the fundamental problem was not the capacity of the state to direct investment but the pervasive shortage of all investment arising from the long-run deficiencies of the capital market.

This was made much worse by the government's cheap money policy, which was intended to make the investment task lighter, but actually deterred savers from placing their funds in government paper. Since the outbreak of the war the government had pursued a policy of low interest rates mainly to reduce its own cost of borrowing. This had been continued after the war. Until December 1946 the discount rate of the Bank of France was 1.625 per cent and the rate of return on bonds fluctuated between 3.6 per cent and 4.6 per cent. Even after a couple of increases, implemented with the greatest reluctance, the rates were 2.5 per cent and almost 7 per cent respectively by the summer of 1948. In view of the very high rates of inflation in these years, real interest rates were strongly negative.[16]

Table 4.2 illustrates the gap between inflation rates and interest rates. Until 1953 inflation rates were higher than the interest rates, including those on government bonds. Expectations that inflation would be brought

Table 4.2 Major financial statistics

Year	Bank of France discount rate	Deposits in savings banks (thousand million francs)	Retail prices (% change) (1938 = 100)
1945	1.63	269.5	38
1946	1.62	292.1	64
1947	1.91–2.42	308.5	60
1948	2.56–3.06	398.0	58
1949	3.0	487.5	11.3
1950	2.72	617.8	11.2[1]
1951	2.79	692.8	17.0[1]
1952	–	839.0	11.8[1]
1953	3.50	1,028.0	−1.2[1]

Sources: INSEE, Annuaire Statistique, 1951; INSEE, Mouvement Economique 1944–1957; J.-P. Patat and M. Lutfalla, op. cit.
Note: [1] 1949 = 100

down to a level nearer to the return on savings could not have been high by late 1946, in spite of repeated government assurances that this was a policy objective; and the increasing demands on the public purse, as reconstruction was overlaid by modernization, were evident to all citizens.

The ineffectiveness of these interventions in the banking system was shown at once. At its first meeting on 1 February 1946 the only recommendation which the CNC felt able to make, until the Monnet Plan had been drawn up, was to advise banks not to finance stock building in order to force goods on to the market.[17] But it was extremely difficult for banks to do this since they had no means of knowing whether a firm which wanted credit for investment had previously used its own resources to build up stocks as a hedge against inflation.[18] It was a fairly obvious problem to which neither the government nor the banks themselves had an answer. Guidance from the central bank was more positive, but proved equally difficult to implement in practice.

In preparing for the postwar period the main concern of the Bank of France had been to ensure that the banking system would be able to meet the vastly increased demand for credit anticipated after the war. Central to its considerations was the desire to avoid the mistakes made after the First World War. The major innovation then had been the agreement of the Bank of France to rediscount commercial bills representing credit granted by the commercial banks to industry. These loans were normally for one year but could be renewed and frequently were. But the system was basically unsatisfactory for industry since it was having to borrow short term to finance medium- or even long-term investment. In an attempt to improve the situation several banks joined together to set up institutions which could provide medium-term loans to industry. One such example was the 'Union pour le crédit à l'industrie nationale' formed by the Crédit Lyonnais and the Comptoir National d'Escompte in 1919. But the experiment did not work. Due to their limited resources these institutions found themselves displaced once the capital market reopened after Poincaré's financial stabilization of 1926. After that the demand for bank credit slumped.

By 1932 the liquidity ratio of French banks was as high as 38 per cent whereas before 1914 it had never risen above 9 per cent. As a consequence of their lack of investment in French industry the banks concentrated their activity in interbank lending and in dealing on the national and international money markets.[19] One positive result was that French banks emerged relatively unscathed from the depression which caused such havoc in the banking systems of many other countries.

In 1944 the Bank of France agreed that it would accept bills for discount which were drawn at not more than three months in order to mobilize loans for up to five years on condition that such credit was for investment. And to ensure that it was indeed for investment rather than consumption or stock building four separate signatures were required, including those of the

Crédit National and the Caisse des Dépôts et Consignations. Since these two institutions, both set up in the aftermath of the First World War, had substantial resources, the Bank of France expected not to be asked to rediscount the bills.[20]

The first signs that the National Credit Council would not be able to ensure the financing of the Monnet Plan were evident by the third quarter of 1946. In July the government had invited representatives from trade unions, farm organizations and industrial employers to a major conference at the Palais-Royal in Paris in an attempt to resolve simultaneously the pressures on wages, costs and prices. Since the 40 per cent wage increase granted at liberation, wage increases had remained consistently below price rises. By July 1946 the index of wages (1938=100) was 332 whereas retail prices had risen on the same basis to 576.[21]

The outcome of the Palais-Royal conference was a 25 per cent increase in wages and a 50–60 per cent increase in agricultural prices. This had the effect of increasing the demand for credit. The banks responded to this demand by discounting their Treasury bills directly at the Bank of France and doing so at a faster rate than the government was able to issue them. As a result, between the second and third quarters of 1946 the banks were giving less credit to the public sector than to the private sector.[22]

At the same time the fixed interest bonds launched in July 1946 by the Crédit National at 3 per cent interest and guaranteed by the state to finance the repair of war damage failed to win enough subscribers. Wilfrid Baumgartner, the director-general of the Crédit National, a public bank set up in 1919 to facilitate reconstruction loans, blamed the fact that only 30,000 million francs out of a total of 40,000 million had been subscribed on the competition from the recently nationalized firms. Instead of issuing shares these firms had now to issue bonds yielding between 4.5 and 5 per cent interest which Baumgartner felt was crowding out the market for Crédit National bonds.[23]

The basic problem seems to have been the fact that in a period of rapidly rising prices, and with no confidence in the government's ability to contain the rise, people were reluctant to subscribe to fixed interest bonds, and the pressure was first felt on those with a lower interest rate. Thus when in January 1947 the government tried to borrow over 100,000 million francs to finance long-term investment in the nationalized industries it succeeded in raising only 17,600 million, which casts much doubt on Baumgartner's argument.[24] The argument nevertheless did represent a popular conviction that the demand for finance for the nationalized industries would lead to the crowding out of other claims. It was to meet this objection that the National Assembly, when it passed the War Damage Law on 28 October 1946, placed war damage repair within the framework of the Monnet Plan and proposed the creation of a separate fund to ensure its finance.

Part of the resources for this fund were to come from the French franc counterpart of the International Bank loan expected in the spring of 1947. Anxious to secure parliamentary control over such expenditure and to distinguish it from current budgetary expenditure, Robert Schuman, as minister of finance, undertook a study of all public finance. The results published in December 1946 as the *Inventaire de la situation financière 1913–1946* was the first time since 1926 that the French were given a complete breakdown of all their public finances.[25]

In the inventory Schuman argued that if 'ordinary' state expenditure could be covered by current budgetary receipts this in itself would establish sufficient confidence to enable the 'extraordinary' expenditure of investment in the basic sectors of the plan as well as war damage repair to be covered by voluntary saving. This meant that all the government needed to do was bring its normal expenditure under control. A number of measures were outlined to achieve this ranging from a cut in the size of the civil service to reductions in price subsidies and an increase in duties on tobacco and alcohol.

But Schuman's reorganization of public finances provided no guarantee that investment in the basic sectors specified in the Monnet Plan could actually be financed. The government was now legally committed to paying for the repair of war damage, but although it formally approved the Monnet Plan in January 1947, it was not under the same legal obligation to finance modernization.

In April 1946 Monnet had recruited a young American economist, Robert Nathan, to advise the planners on this issue. Nathan was a supporter of the American New Deal and his advice drew largely on the American experience of the 1930s. Paradoxically, though, it was not to one of Roosevelt's reforms that he directed the French planners but to an institutional innovation of Roosevelt's predecessor, Herbert Hoover. This was the American Reconstruction Finance Corporation (RFC) which had been set up in 1931 to rescue American banks from collapse. Nathan suggested that the French should set up a similar public fund which could then issue loans, underwritten by the government, to the priority sectors at a rate of interest lower than that prevailing in the market. This would enable the government to adopt a tight monetary and fiscal policy, which would bring inflation under control without jeopardizing the priority investments of the Monnet Plan.[26]

For a number of reasons the American experiment was not easily transferable to France. The capital of the RFC, 500 million dollars, had come out of a budget surplus. Furthermore, it had actually made loans at interest rates higher than those in the market to guarantee that the federal government would not be competing with private financial institutions. Demand for credit had been lower than it was likely to be in France. The RFC had to report to Congress at monthly and quarterly intervals but it did not have to disclose either the names of borrowers or the amounts of individual loans.[27] The French government by contrast was running a large budget deficit and it was extremely unlikely, in the prevailing political climate, that loans could be made to private industry without any form of public scrutiny. But the fundamental obstacle to implementing Nathan's recommendation was that the French public did not have enough confidence in the government's ability to control inflation to subscribe to such a fund. Where then would the capital come from?

It was a question which French officials argued over for months.[28] François Bloch-Lainé, at that time *directeur du trésor* in the Ministry of Finance, did not rule out deficit financing provided that the deficit was used for investment rather than current budgetary expenditure. But he suggested a number of additional sources of capital. These included the proceeds from the heavier taxation of capital gains and of luxury consumption, the franc counterpart of gold and foreign exchange holdings in the Exchange Stabilization Account and finally reparations. These funds would then be channelled through an enlarged 'caisse d'amortissement'[29] which would be responsible for all loans to nationalized industries and to priority industries in the private sector. It would cover the needs of both the repair of war damage and modernization. The new fund, which he called the 'caisse autonome de la reconstruction et de l'équipement' would represent parliament, the administration and the main economic interest groups and would itself be responsible for securing guarantees on all loans. This would have the advantage, he claimed, of not having to get parliamentary approval for every separate loan made to private industry.[30]

The greatest criticisms of Bloch-Lainé's scheme came from within the Ministry of Finance itself. First, the suggestion that parliament might be bypassed in allocating funds to private industry was found unacceptable. Second, it was felt that if loans were made to healthy private industries, this would be interpreted as a step towards their nationalization while if loans were made to unprofitable industries it could cause scandals. The sources of finance suggested by Bloch-Lainé were also criticized for being altogether illusory, as in the case of reparations, or too uncertain. And finally it was felt that these loans would be inflationary unless they served to increase the availability of consumer goods. And this of course was not their primary purpose.[31]

It was one of Monnet's planning team, Paul Delouvrier, who argued that the only non-inflationary means of financing planned investment was by increasing taxes. These additional taxes of about 200,000 million francs should be ear-marked for specific purposes, he suggested, and placed in several funds. By using current Treasury resources to finance investment under the plan the government was losing the means of putting pressure on parliament to make the necessary fiscal effort, according to Delouvrier.[32] But his suggestion found little resonance in the administration.

Monnet himself objected to the idea of one fund being set up to cover the needs of both reconstruction and investment in the basic sectors, and to it being placed under the control of the Ministry of Finance. His preference was for a separate fund to be set up to finance the plan to which private savers would be asked to subscribe. Since they would know exactly where their savings were going this would increase their confidence and willingness to subscribe, he argued. Schuman was sceptical that private financial institutions would agree to cooperate with the state in financing investment since he felt that they would interpret it as the first step towards their nationalization and he was equally sceptical that the public would agree to nationalized industries borrowing from the fund, since this would remove them from the control of the Ministry of Finance.[33]

The CNC now joined in the debate to find alternative methods of financing the plan. On political grounds it ruled out the option of increasing prices in order to allow a greater degree of self-financing out of profits. Not only would this run counter to the government's policy of stabilizing prices, particularly those of basic commodities such as coal and steel, but by increasing the autonomy of individual firms it would undermine the ability of the planners to control the direction of investment. It preferred a policy based on increasing savings above the 5 per cent of national income recorded in 1946. This, the CNC suggested, could be achieved through a variety of means ranging from increasing interest rates to launching new loans, although the evidence, as we have noted, hardly seemed to support this conclusion. It was understandable that the CNC, given its origins, should have seen the main problem as the effective direction of savings, and minimized the difficulty of increasing and attracting them, tasks for other financial institutions. Indeed the only specific recommendations to emerge from its lengthy deliberations were that official scrutiny should be extended to loans of less than 25 million francs and that the planners should establish a larger number of priority sectors in order to provide more detailed guidelines for the banks. In October 1947 the CNC tightened the conditions for granting credit still further by insisting that firms should have explored every other means available from their own resources before borrowing from the banks.[34]

In spite of the general fear, expressed by Baumgartner, of crowding-out, in the first six months of 1947 while bank credit to the private sector continued to expand it was doing so at the expense of financing the public loans necessary to implement the Monnet Plan. This left the Treasury with little option but to borrow from the Bank of France or abandon the plan. Schuman's commitment to the plan inclined him to the former option. By June 1947 he was forced to ask the Bank of France to raise the ceiling on advances to the government from 100,000 million francs to 200,000 million francs and to put gold at a value of 30,000 million francs into the Exchange Stabilization Account.

Under pressure Monick, the governor of the Bank, agreed to raise the ceiling to 150,000 million francs but made any further advances subject to ratification by the National Assembly. At the same time he stressed the need for the government to pursue a more rigorous economic and financial policy in order to stem the rising prices which were contributing to the growing external deficit.[35] But as we saw in Chapter 3 Monick did not realize that the Ministry of Finance was using the franc counterpart of the reserves in the Exchange Stabilization Account to finance investment, thereby adding to the external deficit and causing the dollar crisis in September 1947.

THE COUNTERPART OF MARSHALL AID

It was as a potential solution to the domestic problem of financing priority investment that Marshall Aid was initially seen in France. There was nothing novel about the government using the franc counterpart of gold and foreign currency holdings to finance public investment. The problem was that this form of financing was inflationary and the government was reaching the limits of its domestic borrowing capacity. It was highly unlikely that France's European partners, not to mention the United States, would be more sympathetic than the French public to the government's inflationary spending policies, since they not only increased the size of the external deficit but led to a deterioration in French living standards and increased social unrest.

Opinion within CEEC was sharply divided over how the need for Marshall Aid should be calculated. The American secretary of state had attached only one condition to his offer – namely that the European recipients should cooperate with each other in assessing Europe's dollar deficit over a four-year period. At one extreme the Belgian government argued that aid should be used directly to promote dollar convertibility. This was understandable in view of Belgium's position as a net creditor in Europe and a debtor to the United States. But for the British government, which at the time was witnessing the dramatic failure of its attempt to restore the convertibility of sterling, such a policy was not a priority. As the largest debtor to the United States it was in its interests to calculate aid on the basis of each country's dollar deficit. For France the external deficit was seen as a symptom rather than a cause of the internal deficit. Yet Monnet fully recognized that the French could not make a case for dollar aid to be calculated on the basis of a country's need for the counterpart in domestic currency of that aid. It would come under pressure to bring domestic inflation under control. Far better, Monnet advised Prime Minister Ramadier, for the French government to take control of the situation itself and announce its implementation of a stabilization programme in return for dollar aid based on the external deficit.[36]

Therefore, dollar aid would be for the purpose of domestic stabilization as in the 1920s. The French delegation duly announced to CEEC its government's 'determination' to meet from current revenue all budget expenditure including military and reconstruction expenditure in 1948, with the sole exception of indemnities for war damage and financing industrial investment.[37]

But although the budget deficit was officially presented as being the main source of inflation, privately Monnet recognized that the issue was far more complex. As he saw it the domestic price level was a function of several policies, and inflation would only be brought under control if the government pursued several policies simultaneously. Thus it needed to coordinate its fiscal policy with its monetary policy as well as with its commercial, distribution, prices and wages policies. A further policy area was added as a result of discussions with René Auboin, President of the Bank for International Settlements and a former banking associate of Monnet in the 1920s. This was exchange rate policy.

Although the use of flexible exchange rates was proscribed under the rules of the Bretton Woods Agreement, Auboin argued that measures already tried in Austria, Italy and South America which were based on using the exchange rate to help stabilize domestic prices in fact conformed to the spirit if not the letter of Bretton Woods. The method recommended by Auboin entailed allowing the franc to float freely and legally in one market and fixing the rate in other markets, whilst maintaining controls over trade and capital movements.

The free exchange rate was to operate on all imports of non-essential goods from the Dollar Area while imports of essential goods from that market were to be at as high a rate as possible. Auboin suggested a rate of 190–200 francs to the dollar which would have represented a devaluation of nearly 70 per cent. Exporters would sell their dollar earnings to the Bank of France, half at the official rate and half at the free market rate and importers would buy at similar rates. Auboin expected the free rate to establish itself at the black market rate of 280–300 francs to the dollar, which existed in places like Switzerland, but then to fall as confidence revived so that it could finally be stabilized at 210–20 francs to the dollar.[38]

But Auboin also argued that before the exchange rate could be stabilized the government would have to bring its public finances into order. This would mean ending Treasury borrowing from the Bank of France, making the Exchange Stabilization Account independent of the Treasury and reforming the system of price controls and subsidies. This, Monnet finally concluded, would mean a complete reversal in his method of planning. Instead of calculating the desired level of investment and then trying to find the resources to finance it, he would have to establish as accurately as possible what the likely resources would be and then tailor the plan to fit the means available.

To do this the planners set up a Commission du Bilan National in September 1947 headed by an economist from the CGP, Pierre Uri. He faced a formidable task. National income accounting was even more in its infancy in France than in Britain, Germany or the United States. Despite its long history of state intervention in industry the official statistical service in France had had to rely on population data from the national census in order to derive the structure of production. It was not until 1938 that Alfred Sauvy was able to convince the Reynaud government to issue a decree law making the furnishing of industrial statistics obligatory. But before the new law could take effect France was at war. The conditions of scarcity under the occupation, together with the anti-liberal nature of the Vichy government, led to the collection of economic data on an unprecedented scale. For the first time planning the economy became a viable policy option. It was not until 1942 that Keynes' *General Theory of Employment, Interest and Money* first appeared in French translation. At around the same time the French statistician L.A. Vincent had begun calculating French national accounts. This work was then taken over by the Institut de Conjoncture, set up in 1945.[39]

When the Commissariat au Plan was set up the following year it was assigned the task of collecting statistics. Those assembled for the Washington loan negotiations were very rudimentary indeed and it was not until March 1947 that the CGP published its first estimation of the French National Income and that was for 1938, the last 'normal' year. Before the war the only studies of national income in France were on the distribution of income between wages, profits and rents. This was useful for fiscal purposes, but the scale of investment which was deemed necessary after the war made it crucial for the government to know whether the French

Table 4.3 Forecast of French national income in 1948 (in thousand million francs)

	1948	1st half
Resources		
GNP	4,635	2,181
Net foreign aid	289	124
Total	4,894	2,305
Claims		
Operating cost of public services	552	268
Public and private investment	968	430
Private consumption	3,739	1,806
Total	5,259	2,504
Difference between claims and resources	365	199

Source: Commissariat Général au Plan, *Estimation du revenu national français* (Paris, 1947)

would save enough to finance it or whether there would be an inflationary gap, and in which case how to close it. Much of the vagueness about how the Monnet Plan would be financed, as well as the illusory optimism once it had been drawn up that the level and direction of savings could cope with the specified investments, arose from this ignorance. In December 1947 the Commission du Bilan National presented its report which for the first time put the investment programme for 1948 in the context of the resources anticipated in that year and the competing demands on those resources. The balance sheet revealed an inflationary gap of 365,000 million francs.[40]

It was this gap which the new government formed by Schuman in November 1947 had to close. Its strategy, presented in the form of finance minister René Mayer's Stabilization Plan in January 1948, reflected not only the outcome of the calculations carried out within the Commissariat au Plan but the increased strength of right-wing parties in the new government. The results of municipal elections held in October 1947 had demonstrated a sharp fall in support for the communists, socialists and MRP, a slight increase in support for the radicals, and considerable support for de Gaulle's new party, the Rassemblement du Peuple Français (RPF), which won 35 per cent of the vote. When the communist party formally moved into opposition at the end of October 1947 it became impossible for the centre parties to govern without those right-wing deputies who had refused to support de Gaulle. This new political configuration became known as the 'third force'. Thus in Schuman's new government the radicals and Right gained ground largely at the expense of the socialists. Schuman's choice of René Mayer, a radical, reflected this shift in political power.

Mayer's Stabilization Plan was based on cutting public expenditure and increasing revenue in order to close the inflationary gap in the first six months of 1948. Most price controls were lifted in order to reduce the cost of subsidies, which in 1947 had amounted to 12.4 per cent of the budget, and to close the gap between industrial and agricultural prices. It was the government's inability to control the price of agricultural products which Mayer felt had been the root cause of the wage pressure which then had led to increases in industrial prices.[41] Where controls were retained as on the price of coal, steel, electricity and rail tariffs the prices were almost doubled. Wages, however, remained controlled. The gold market was reopened to encourage the repatriation of gold. At the same time the government issued a compulsory levy designed to penalize those who had profited most from inflation. For that reason wage earners were exempt. So too were those who accepted the option of subscribing to a loan at 3 per cent interest over ten years. Finally the government announced that all 5,000 franc notes, the note most commonly used in black market transactions, would be blocked for a period of time. The compulsory loan raised 108,000 million francs, less than the 150,000 million francs which the government hoped to raise, while the blocking of the 5,000 franc note reduced the amount of money in circulation although the effect was nullified by an increase in the velocity of circulation.[42]

Acting on the advice of René Auboin the franc was devalued against the dollar for the third time since the liberation and a free market set up for all financial transactions and tourist expenditure. Commercial transactions were carried out, not at the fixed dollar rate of 214.39 francs but at a point mid-way between the fixed and the free rate, which worked out at about 264 francs. As expected, the move was condemned by the IMF and France was denied all borrowing rights until it registered a fixed par value with the IMF again. Although the American Treasury shared this outrage this did not affect American support for France within the European Recovery Programme. And this support was considerably more important both financially and politically than that of the IMF, provided that the ECA agreed to the French request to use the counterpart in francs of dollar aid.

The final element in Mayer's Stabilization Programme was his decision to set up the two funds which had been under discussion for so long – a fund to finance the repair of war damage and a separate one to finance new investment in the Monnet Plan. Known as the Caisse autonome de Reconstruction (CAREC) and the Fonds de Modernisation et d'Equipement (FME) they were both placed under the control of the Treasury, despite the protests of Monnet who argued that the FME should be placed under the direct control of the prime minister with Monnet himself acting as its vice-president. Monnet also wanted the fund to receive two-thirds of the French franc counterpart of American aid in 1948 as well as two-thirds of the proceeds of the compulsory levy which, he said, would cover investment in the basic sectors in 1948. In 1949 he proposed that the fund should receive half the counterpart of Marshall Aid.[43] But René Mayer considered the Ministry of Finance to be a more impartial arbitrator between competing claimants than the planners who, he said, openly favoured industrial modernization, ignoring parliament's request that public funds should be allocated to agriculture as well as industry. He also announced that two-thirds of the capital levy should be used to finance the repair of war damage on the grounds that it had been sacrificed in 1947 to channel resources into modernization.

Table 4.4 Changes in the franc–dollar exchange rate, 1939–49

Date	Exchange rate (franc–dollar)
August 1939	37.8
November 1944	49.63
December 1945	119.1
January 1948	214.39 (official rate) 310 (free rate)
October 1948	264
September 1949	350

Source: Reports of the Bank for International Settlements

This left open the question of the actual use of counterpart funds. On 2 January 1948 the French government had signed a bilateral agreement on interim aid with the United States. This specified that the counterpart in francs should be used to reduce the national debt and stabilize the currency.[44] Clearly the use made of interim aid could set a precedent for Marshall Aid which was then being debated by the American Congress. As the Quai d'Orsay explained, the French wished to use the counterpart to finance investment in modernization and reconstruction but only as temporary measure until public finances were sound enough to enable the government to launch a long-term loan. Once that was achieved the counterpart would be used to repay the public debt.[45] Monnet emphasized the political advantage to the United States of being seen to be helping France to achieve economic independence by 1952, the scheduled end of Marshall Aid. By allowing France to invest the counterpart first of interim aid and then of Marshall Aid in the Monnet Plan, he argued, much of the adverse criticism of American interference in French affairs would be dispelled.[46]

The American concern was to ensure that the use of the counterpart for productive investment would actually help to reduce inflation and to restore equilibrium in the balance of payments by 1952. To exert some influence in this direction they insisted that the French government should place French francs to the value of the goods delivered under ERP into a special account at the Crédit National, even before it had sold the goods on to the French market. These French franc counterpart funds would then remain blocked in the Crédit National until the ECA gave its permission for their periodic release. In theory the ECA could withhold its permission on the grounds that the French government was not doing enough to tackle inflation. In practice it recognized how counterproductive such action would be since the French Treasury could simply resume its borrowing from the Bank of France to finance investment in the plan and the United States would be blamed for the inflationary consequences.[47] As a result the ECA tended to use its nominal control over counterpart to extract very detailed economic and financial information from the French government, often on a weekly basis, and to link the release of counterpart to the French government's policies to control inflation.[48]

Over the period 1948–52 the counterpart of American aid covered just 13 per cent of total investment in the French economy. Its contribution to the resources of the FME was very much greater, as Table 4.5 makes clear, but its importance declined after 1949. When the distribution of credit from the FME is analysed it turns out that almost 45 per cent of all loans went to the two nationalized sectors of coal and electricity. It may be said, therefore, that just as direct American aid for imports was important in solving the problem of increased investment in steel and machine tools, the counterpart of the aid by this rather complicated mechanism was important in enabling

FINANCING INVESTMENT UNDER THE MONNET PLAN

Table 4.5 Resources of the Fonds de Modernisation et d'Equipement
(thousand million francs)

Resources	1948	1949	1950	1951	1952	Total
			Year			
Counterpart of US aid	104	225.7	155.1	49	–	533.8
Loans from treasury	27.3	53.5	176.9	154.7	250.3	662.7
Exceptional levy	33	3.2	–	7.2	0.3	43.7
Own resources (interest etc)	–	0.1	21.3	33.6	45	100
Total	164.3	282.5	353.3	244.5	295.6	1,340.2
Counterpart as % of total	63	80	44	20	–	40

Source: Commissariat Général au Plan, *Rapport sur la réalisation du plan de modernisation et d'équipement de l'union française* (Paris, 1953), p. 84

the increase in investment in these two energy sectors to be accomplished. It provided a source of capital outside the normal public revenue and outside parliament's control of that revenue, while the anti-inflationary controls on its disbursement were largely fictitious unless the French themselves chose otherwise.

Table 4.6 Allocation of loans from the Fonds de Modernisation et d'Equipement, 1948–1952 (thousand million current francs)

Sector	1948	1949	1950	1951	1952	Total
			Year			
Coal	45.9	56.5	57.4	28.3	37.0	225.2
Electricity	67.1	97.3	71.7	77.5	62.5	376.1
Gas	3.4	7.0	2.1	6.0	8.0	26.5
National Rhône Company	–	–	18.0	10.7	18.5	47.2
SNCF	26.6	29.1	32.5	6.4	–	94.6
Air France	–	–	3.5	2.9	2.7	9.1
Commercial fleet	–	–	0.9	0.9	2.6	4.4
Air and seaports	–	1.3	1.1	0.6	2.0	5.0
Agricultural and fertilizer industry	6.9	14.7	29.9	29.7	29.4	110.6
Industrial and commercial firms	–	15.3	35.1	23.9	34.1	108.4
North Africa	5.1	35.8	48.8	38.2	55.6	183.5
Indochina	–	4.5	28.1	31.0	32.3	95.9
Saar	–	2.4	2.9	2.3	3.2	10.8
Agricultural loans	–	–	6.0	5.5	3.0	14.5
Others	–	–	0.8	0.5	0.6	1.9
Manufacturing industry	–	–	–	–	–	–
Tourism	–	0.7	1.0	3.0	3.4	8.1

Source: Michel Margairaz, op. cit., p. 1232

To stress their commitment to financing public investment in a non-inflationary way the French set up an Investment Commission in June 1948. This body was to coordinate all public investment expenditure to ensure that it remained within the resources available to the Treasury. Presided over by the Ministry of Finance it brought together the under-secretary of state for economic affairs, the planning commissioner, the governor of the Bank of France and the directors of the Treasury, the Budget and Economic Programmes. Spending ministries were to submit their investment programmes to it and take part in the discussion of them each year. The two guiding principles for these discussions were that investment was to be financed from the resources available without any further advances from the Bank of France and that all investment was to contribute to the goal of reaching equilibrium in external payments by 1952.

These principles also guided the planners when they revised the Monnet Plan to extend it to 1952. One of the most significant changes to the original Monnet Plan was that the entire agricultural sector was to be included as a basic sector. The Investment Commission debated the implications of this at its first meeting on 21 June 1948 when it discussed whether public money should be used to finance investment in agriculture or whether that sector, which had benefited both during the occupation and during the postwar inflation, should finance most of its investment from its own resources. Since the war public investment in modernization, as opposed to the repair of war damage, had been channelled almost exclusively into the nationalized industries. This was justified on the grounds that since it was easier for the state to control prices in these industries they had less scope to finance investment from their own resources. But it meant that those private industries which had been classified as basic sectors in the original Monnet Plan – steel, cement and agricultural machinery – had been denied public funding, while the private capital market failed to provide for their needs. The conclusion drawn by the Investment Commission was that it was the responsibility of the government to ensure the financing of investment in all the basic sectors of the plan and that the Investment Commission's task was to choose between competing claims to ensure that such investment did not contribute to inflation.[49] This meant that public funds would also have to finance investment in agriculture.

A second issue was whether the FME should make loans at interest rates lower than market rates and at different rates for different sectors or even for different firms within the same sector. Was it correct for the Monnet Plan to discriminate in this way? The issue arose in part because in the first six months of 1948 Mayer's Stabilization Plan seemed to be working and prices remained fairly stable. The gap between agricultural and industrial prices was narrowed with the abolition of many subsidies on industrial products. But the devaluation of the franc in respect to the dollar led to a rise in the price of imports which domestic producers were able to exploit. French wheat growers in particular took advantage of the higher price of American wheat on the French market to raise their own prices.

Wholesale food prices rose by 10 per cent in July 1948 which triggered off an increase in retail prices and wages. Partly owing to the political crisis which brought down two governments in July and August 1948, and partly owing to the end of the income flow from the compulsory levy, the Treasury was forced to resume its borrowing from the Bank of France. Between June and September these advances rose by 45,000 million francs, whereas in the six months between December 1947 and June 1948 the Treasury had been able to reduce its advances by 27,000 million francs. By September 1948 the Treasury was reaching the legal ceiling of 200,000 million francs set in December 1947. At the same time bank credit had been expanding steadily. Only 7 per cent of all requests had been refused or reduced under the qualitative guidelines set out by the CNC – mainly because bankers found it impossible to apply the criterion of 'national interest' to individual loans.

In September 1948 the Bank of France took advantage of a political crisis to raise its discount rate by a further percentage point to 3.5 per cent. The storm of protest which greeted this was quite startling.[50] But the only way to comprehend the importance attached to interest rates is to see it in terms of the principle of discrimination. Whereas the Ministry of Finance wanted to use interest rates to discriminate between sectors and even between firms and criticized the September increase on the grounds that it treated essential and less essential activities alike, the Bank of France was opposed to differential interest rates in principle. In the end the Investment Commission set up a separate committee which concluded that it was dangerous both to have several different interest rates operating at the same time and to set those rates below the market rate. The main exceptions were to be nationalized industries for which the interest rate was 4.5 per cent over thirty years, the two steel firms of USINOR and SOLLAC for which the rates were 5.5 per cent over twenty years and 5 per cent over forty years respectively, the fertilizer industry, for which the rate was 5 per cent, and loans to the Crédit Agricole, at 3 per cent over five years.[51] At the prevailing rate of inflation, when this decision was reached, these loans looked nearer to gifts.

Apart from interest rates the other issue which caused concern to the government which the radical Henri Queuille was finally able to form in September 1948 was the lending policy of the banks. In discussions between the government, the Bank of France and the CNC the conclusion was reached that the way in which banks financed business was itself inflationary. Two-thirds of all such financing was done with commercial bills. Because such bills lasted for less than ninety days the banks had viewed them as self-liquidating paper and thus wholly neutral in their monetary effect. The belated recognition that such bills represented bank credit which contributed to monetary inflation just as much as bank overdrafts led to the conclusion that some more effective way of controlling such credit was required than the qualitative controls imposed by the CNC in 1946.[52]

This led the Queuille government to take the unprecedented step in France of imposing quantitative controls on bank credit. These controls were, first, that in lending out new deposits banks were to be restrained by the imposition of a special reserve requirement on all increases in deposits after 1 October (until then there had been no formal reserve requirement). These reserves were to be held in cash in short-term government paper. Second, banks were to retain their current portfolio of government paper when they suffered a reduction in deposits. Third, when using the rediscount facilities at the Bank of France in order to add to their reserves, banks were to be forced to remain below a certain maximum which was to be fixed for each bank. And, finally, the prior approval procedure was to be extended to cover discounts of commercial paper above a certain figure.

The impact of credit controls on inflation could not have been great, given the return in the summer of 1948 to financing both public and private investment in the Monnet Plan from central bank advances. Indeed when the Commission du Bilan National published its second report for the second half of 1948 it concluded that credit policy was the least important factor in achieving monetary stability compared with policies on wages, prices and taxation.[53] In all these areas policy had been erratic, pursuing conflicting objectives. The way in which the investment goals of the Modernization Plan were pursued in 1948, when savings and private investment failed to come to the rescue as the original forecasts had hoped they would, was obviously inflationary. But if other major areas of economic policy had been more consistently anti-inflationary the consequence might well have been less drastic. Any such plan, however, can only operate in the given political context. An anti-inflationary wage policy was particularly difficult to envisage in view of the increasing radicalization of the labour force. The decontrol of prices had been necessitated by the growing cost of subsidies. And the increase in agricultural prices was unavoidable because of the power which agriculture had both politically and economically. The government would forget at its peril the severe wheat shortage of 1947. In this context either the objectives of the Monnet Plan would have to be abandoned, with all the implications for French living standards in the future and for French policy towards Germany which that would have, or a firmer basis for financing it would have to be sought. The planners now concluded that the only way to save the Monnet Plan was to make French people pay for it through increased taxation, as Delouvrier had recommended over a year earlier.[54]

Altogether in 1948 public investment was financed in an *ad hoc* and piecemeal manner and the government had little idea what the total would be for the whole year or what the sources of finance would be. The lack of control over public investment was symptomatic of the government's lack of control over its spending in general. Although the number of special Treasury accounts had been reduced from over 400 in 1947 to 70 in 1948 the continuing fragmentation of public spending made it virtually impossible for parliament to control it. It was parliament's increasing dissatisfaction with this state of affairs, a dissatisfaction shared by the ECA, which made the government agree to present the National Assembly at the beginning of the 1949 fiscal year with a complete programme of expenditure broken down into major categories together with the proposed income to cover that expenditure. This was known as the 'loi des maxima'.[55]

But it was a commitment which it was almost impossible to honour. The Investment Commission soon realized that it made little sense to bring the budget for investment expenditure into balance if the rest of the budget was in deficit. On the expenditure side the Ministry of Defence refused to submit its budget for defence expenditure in 1949 to the Ministry of Finance, while on the revenue side the total value of America's aid in 1949 was not known since the American and French fiscal years did not coincide. Nor was the value of the counterpart known since the Americans controlled the release of the counterpart funds.

To get around this uncertainty it was decided to divide investment into two categories, unconditional and conditional. The first category included all those projects where it could be demonstrated that additional investment would make a positive contribution to the French balance of payments by 1952. This category was to benefit from those funds which seemed certain when the budget was presented to parliament in January each year. Of course since the entire reconstruction programme would fall into the second category some other criteria had to be found to arbitrate between reconstruction and modernization. These criteria were not made explicit.

In December 1948 the Investment Commission proposed to Maurice Petsche, the minister of finance, that the budget for repairing war damage should be 270,000 million francs and that for modernization 280,000 million francs.[56] But when Petsche cut the modernization budget to 260,000 million francs on the grounds that the nationalized electricity company (EDF) could find an extra 20,000 million francs from its own resources while the overseas territories should receive a further 4,000 million francs, this was criticized immediately by David Bruce, the ECA administrator in France. Such a figure for productive investment, Bruce warned, was dangerously low if France was to increase its production as planned.

It might seem surprising, in the circumstances, that the ECA, in a year in which its concern about inflation in Europe steadily increased, should have argued in this way. But it had come to the same conclusion as the French planners that the only remedy for France's problem lay in the French government reforming its fiscal system. Such a reform, on which the release of counterpart in 1949 was to depend, would, Bruce argued, make the investment programme less inflationary.[57] If private investment from savings would not finance modernization to the extent that the French planners had hoped, public investment out of increased taxation would substitute and the increased taxation would be anti-inflationary. This depended on fiscal reform, as much as had French reconstruction after 1918, when those reforms were also postponed.

In view of the extreme unpopularity of such a measure the French National Assembly had given the government the power to pass legislation by decree. Despite this freedom the reforms enacted in December 1948 were even less ambitious than those passed in the First World War. Confined to taxes on income their main concern was to reduce the incidence of fraud, which in 1948 had resulted in less revenue being collected from this source than in 1947, rather than to increase the rate of taxation.

The complexity of the existing system worked to the advantage of the self-employed and penalized wage-earners. But, since the large numbers of self-employed, who constituted perhaps almost two-thirds of the labour force, tended to vote for the parties of the 'third force', the government was reluctant to lose support in the interests of social justice or price stability. The main thrust of the reforms therefore was to simplify the system. Whereas previously taxes had been collected separately on each different source of income with no coordination at the points of collection, from 1949 onwards it was the income of the individual as a whole, rather than the sources of that income, which were assessed for taxation purposes. The same rules applied to corporation tax which was levied for the first time. And the taxes were to be paid every four months on income earned in that year rather than being paid annually on income earned the previous year.

Even though the reforms were more a matter of presentation than of substance, they still proved to be unacceptable to the agricultural lobby in the National Assembly. As a result in July 1949 the National Assembly decided to revert to the previous system of taxation of agriculture.[58]

Table 4.7 Fiscal receipts 1938–50 (in thousand million 1938 francs)

Receipts	Year					
	1938	1946	1947	1948	1949	1950
Central government taxes						
on income	15.0	13.5	19.2	16.5	19.4	26.0
on wealth	9.2	13.7	9.1	4.8	5.7	5.2
on consumption	28.9	33.5	34.7	40.1	45.4	47.3
Local government taxes	13.5	8.5	7.8	8.2	13.0	14.0
Total	66.6	69.2	69.8	69.6	83.5	92.5

Source: 'Etudes et Conjoncture', *Economie Française*, January–February 1951

In fact the way taxes were increased to help finance investment in 1949 was by increasing production tax by 25 per cent and other indirect taxes by 15 per cent. In 1950 production tax was increased by a further 10 per cent and imposed on road transport for the first time, while non-distributed profits were taxed at 10 per cent.

It was estimated that the reforms of December 1948 reduced fraud by 80,000 million francs and raised an extra 40,000 million francs in 1949 and 1950 in the transition to the new system of four-monthly payments. Any further increase in receipts was due to an increase in economic activity.

Table 4.8 shows government revenue from taxation for each fiscal year between liberation and 1952 compared to government expenditure for the same period. To have superimposed the Monnet Plan for modernization on the restoration of war damage without fundamentally altering the taxation system seems in retrospect a surprising and potentially dangerous act. But while in retrospect it is clear that the private capital market would not play the role foreseen, at the time it was less obvious that this would be so. High inflation rates could be seen as the consequence of the occupation and the liberation, of the stresses of a society returning to normal peacetime existence. It was the failure of the Mayer Stabilization Plan in 1948 which showed that these were not the causes of a temporary bout of high inflation. It was then no more than the logic of the situation that the ECA and the French government alike should turn to increased taxation as the way out of the dilemma. Using the counterpart of Marshall Aid to finance investment was little more than a palliative which could not solve the deeper problems in French society.

Income tax as a proportion of total government revenue rose from 15 per cent in 1938 to 28.6 per cent in 1951. This reflected both an increase in economic activity and a more efficient method of collection after 1949. But the increase in economic activity did not lead to the revival of a capital market (see Table 4.9). As the share of public funds in total investment declined after 1949, in line with the reduction in the counterpart of Marshall Aid, it was replaced by a greater reliance on the reinvestment of profits. Clearly the intention of the postwar reformers and planners to mobilize private savings in order to re-create a capital market had not been achieved by 1952. It was to take longer to change the habits of savers. Under the second plan, 1954–57, public financing of investment in industry declined to 1.3 per cent of total industrial investment, although the state continued to furnish about one-quarter of the investment needs of agriculture, as well as of the energy, housing and transport sectors.[59] At the same time the French government finally faced up to the need to implement a more far-reaching reform of the tax system to ensure the continued promotion of investment. Thus the central purpose of the reform of April 1954, under which the production tax was replaced by a new tax on value added, was not to spread the burden of taxation more equitably in the interests of social justice but

Table 4.8 Government revenue and expenditure, 1938–51
(in thousand million francs)

	Year							
	1938	*1945*	*1946*	*1947*	*1948*	*1949*	*1950*	*1951*
Revenue								
Income tax	9.24	55.7	65.6	153.7	256.4	352.9	551.3	619.0
Income from property	5.80	5.2	10.1	16.3	21.6	20.7	28.7	23.0
Illicit profits	–	5.6	12.1	9.7	7.0	4.6	3.5	4.0
Transfer duties	2.16	6.7	10.0	10.5	13.3	17.2	21.6	22.9
Death duties[1]	–	–	9.8	12.8	15.0	21.4	23.5	24.0
Other duties	1.9	3.9	10.9	16.5	20.6	41.7	45.6	39.1
Stock exchange operations	0.21	0.3	1.0	2.1	2.7	1.6	1.6	1.6
Stamp duty	2.51	3.1	4.5	6.9	11.8	16.4	14.3	18.4
National solidarity tax	–	–	48.9	41.3	17.0	8.8	3.1	1.0
Customs duties	8.82	3.8	18.1	36.8	54.0	101.9	150.3	178.0
Indirect taxes	6.25	10.8	16.4	24.6	41.5	53.7	48.2	45.5
Production tax	9.85	43.5	111.1	171.5	299.3	485.4	588.5	723.0
Transaction tax[2]	–	22.6	42.1	58.1	96.3	141.4	156.9	173.0
Monopoly taxes	0.17	0.4	1.0	1.0	1.8	2.4	1.2	1.4
Taxes on public property and industries	0.89	9.2	11.5	9.2	13.4	14.1	19.2	23.5
Others	6.76	47.4	58.0	59.9	89.2	102.0	174.1	147.0
Fiscal Receipts of the Caisse autonome d'amortissement	6.51	20.1	30.9	55.4	89.6	101.0	120.7	116.9
Total	61.12	238.2	462.0	695.0	1,050.4	1,487.4	1,952.3	2,161.2
Expenditure								
Normal current expenditure	64.9	296	345	444	681	842	1,114	1,297
Reconstruction and equipment of civil services	3.4	14	43	70	98	150	121	140
Military expenditure	29.1	175	171	231	332	377	463	857
War damage and construction	–	35	83	92	200	246	285	312
Economic and social investment	1.6	3	39	77	280	432	426	303
Total	99.0	523	681	914	1,591	2,047	2,409	2,909
Revenue	61.12	238.2	462.0	695.0	1,050.4	1,487.4	1,952.3	2,161.2
Revenue as a % of expenditure	61.7	45.5	67.8	76.0	66.0	72.7	81.0	74.3
American aid:								
Grants	–	–	–	–	140	263	169	149
Loans	–	–	–	–	9	37	–	4
Revenue including US aid as a % of expenditure	61.7	45.5	67.8	76.0	75.4	87.3	88.0	79.6

Source: Ministère des Finances, *Statistiques et études financières, supplément statistique*, Nos 11–12, 1951

Notes: [1] Death duties had been paid into the Caisse Autonome D'amortissement in 1938 and 1946, and into the general budget thereafter.

[2] The Transactions tax which was introduced in April 1939 was known as the Armaments tax until June 1940.

Table 4.9 Subscriptions to public loans and private stocks and shares
(in million francs)

Sector	Year					
	1945	1946	1947	1948	1949	1950
Public and Semi-public	11,352	34,034	21,832	146,088	123,084	34,459
Private	26,476	47,529	42,204	50,934	54,733	49,740
Total	37,828	81,563	64,036	197,062	177,817	124,199

Source: La France Economique de 1948 à 1950 (Paris, 1951), p. 217

rather to end the discriminatory treatment of investment under the production tax. Investment goods were no longer to be taxed at the point of acquisition as well as in the final sale of a product but were to be bought tax free under the new value added system. In this way the fiscal system was to become the main instrument of French-style modernization. The underlying logic was, according to Maurice Lauré, the tax inspector credited with instigating the reform, that investment would promote improvements in productivity. As a result tax receipts would rise faster than national income,

Table 4.10 Sources of investment in metropolitan France, 1947–52
(thousand million francs)

Source	Year					
	1947	1948	1949	1950	1951	1952
Public funds						
Credits and subsidies	78.3	85.8	106	95.2	120.2	140
CAREC: cash payments	104.3	162.1	246	241.0	247.9	246
loans	–	–	21.2	15.0	13.6	10
F.M.E.	–	149.9	221.9	260.0	196	207
Special treasury accounts	53.5	101.1	109.4	109.3	97.4	123
Total	236.1	489.9	709.5	720.5	675.1	742
Other sources						
Resources of specialized financial organizations	20	33	41.9	67.6	94	118
Medium-term bank credit	60.8	34.5	53.1	23.0	48.0	146
Shares	27.0	24.0	39.6	37.4	46.1	57
Stocks	36.9	20.5	9.9	32.9	43.1	37
Self-financing	55.8	230.0	246.5	335.4	726.9	720
Treasury lags	–	–	7.9	−16.6	16.8	–
Total	436.6	841.9	1,108.7	1,200.2	1,650.0	1,820

Source: Ministère des Finances, Statistiques et études financières, supplément, finances françaises, no. 17, 1953

thereby enabling the government to reduce the tax burden. The model was the United States where income inequality was even greater than in France.[60]

Thus the reform fitted with the strategy adopted by postwar governments of financing investment through one-off exceptional taxes, loans, inflation and ultimately the counterpart of American aid rather than through a more far-reaching reform of the tax system, designed to increase the fiscal burden.

Table 4.11 Sources of investment finance, 1947–52 (% of total)

Source	Year					
	1947	1948	1949	1950	1951	1952
Public funds	54.0	58.0	64.0	60.0	41.0	41.0
Specialist financial institutions	4.6	3.9	3.8	5.6	5.7	6.5
Medium-term bank credit	13.9	2.4	4.8	1.9	2.9	8.0
Shares	6.2	2.9	3.6	3.1	2.8	3.1
Stocks	8.5	2.4	0.9	2.7	2.6	2.0
Self-financing	12.8	27.3	22.2	27.9	44.1	40.0

Source: Adapted from Ministère des Finances, Statistiques et études Financières, no. 17, 1953

NOTES

1 Georges Pilliet, op. cit., p. 376.
2 United Nations, Economic Survey of Europe in 1950 (Geneva, 1951), p. 148.
3 Commissariat Général au Plan, Rapport sur la réalisation du plan de modernisation et d'équipement de l'Union Française (Paris, 1953); Ministère des Finances, Statistiques et études financières, supplément, finances françaises, no. 17, 1953.
4 Jean-Pierre Patat and Michel Lutfalla, A Monetary History of France in the Twentieth Century (London, 1990), pp. 97–102.
5 A.N. F[60] 909, report, 3 March 1944.
6 A.N. F[60] 911, report from Mendès-France, Commissioner for Finance, 26 February 1944.
7 Min. Fin. B19951, note, 29 January 1946.
8 Min. Fin. B19951, 'Effects of War and Occupation on French Public Finance', 1 November 1945.
9 Patat and Lutfalla, op. cit., p. 113.
10 Min. Fin. B19951, note, 29 January 1946.
11 Maurice Larkin, France since the Popular Front. Government and People 1936–1986 (Oxford, 1988), p. 59.
12 Claire Andrieu, 'La nationalisation du crédit', in Claire Andrieu, Antoine Prost and Lucette Le Van-Lemesle, Les Nationalisations de la Libération. De l'utopie au compromis (Actes du colloque organisé par le CRHMSS – Paris I en mai 1984) (Paris, 1987).
13 Hans Aufricht and Jane Evensen (eds), Central Banking Legislation. Volume II. Europe (IMF, Washington, DC, 1967).

14 C. Andrieu, 'La Nationalisation', op. cit.
15 Jean Bouvier, 'The French Banks, Inflation and the Economic Crisis, 1919–1939', *Journal of European Economic History*, special issue, 13(2), Fall 1984, pp. 29–80.
16 Jean-Pierre Patat and Michel Lutfalla, op. cit., p. 124.
17 J.C.S. Wilson, *French Banking Structure and Credit Policy* (London, 1957), p. 379.
18 Min. Fin. 5A 29, note, 7 April 1946.
19 J. Bouvier, op. cit.
20 P. Caubone, 'Medium-term Lending by the French Deposit Banks and Banques d'Affaires' in *Banca Nazionale del Lavoro Quarterly Review*, vol. 31, December 1954.
21 Dominique Borne and Jacques Bouillon, 'Réflexions de Paul Ramadier, décembre 1947', *Revue d'Histoire Moderne et Contemporaine*, vol. xxxv, July–September 1988.
22 CNC, *Rapport annuel* (Paris, 1946).
23 N.A.U.S. 851.51/8–746, Caffery to Secretary of State, 7 August 1946.
24 Min. Fin. B19951, Trésorerie 1947, 'Notes et études'.
25 Ministère des Finances, *Inventaire de la situation financière 1913–1946* (Paris, 1946).
26 F.J.M. AMF 5/3/2–30, notes from R. Nathan, 1946.
27 James Stuart Olson, *Herbert Hoover and the Reconstruction Finance Corporation 1931–1933* (Ames, 1977).
28 F. Bloch-Lainé and J. Bouvier, *La France restaurée 1944–1954. Dialogue sur le choix d'une modernisation* (Paris, 1986).
29 This fund had been set up by Poincaré in 1926 to help stabilize the franc.
30 Min. Fin. B33213, 'Projets de Caisse autonome de reconstruction et d'équipement', notes, Monnet, 1947–48.
31 Min. Fin. B33213, note from Vincent, 20 May 1947.
32 F.J.M. AMF 11/2/10, 'Notes sur la création d'une ou plusieures caisses de financement', Delouvrier, 16 June 1947.
33 F.J.M. AMF 11/2/2, Monnet to Schuman, 21 May 1947.
34 Min. Fin. B33213, letter from General Secretary of the CNC to Bloch-Lainé, 10 June 1947. See also B16020, note from Grimanelli, 18 February 1948.
35 B.D.F. Déliberations du Conseil Général, no. 138, 1947.
36 F.J.M. AMF 14/1/9, 'Note sur la présentation à la conférence de Paris d'une demande de crédits de stabilisation', 13 August 1947 and 80AJ 266, note, 16 August 1947 and 8 September 1947.
37 Committee of European Economic Cooperation, *General Report*, July/September 1947.
38 A.N. 80AJ 266, 'Note sur les modifications à apporter au régime des changes', R. Auboin, 29 October 1947.
39 M. Volle, *Pour Une Histoire de la statistique* (Paris, 1977).
40 R.F. Kuisel, *Capitalism and the State in Modern France* (Cambridge, 1981), p. 238.
41 Min. Fin. B19951, report by R. Rosa and A. Hirschman, November 1948; F. Caron, 'Le Plan Mayer: Un Retour aux réalitiés', Fondation Nationale des sciences politiques, *La France en voie de modernisation 1944–1952* (unpublished proceedings of conference, Paris, 1981).
42 W. Baum, *The French Economy and the State* (Princeton, 1958), p. 65.
43 Min. Fin. B33213, Monnet to Mayer, 13 January 1948 and Mayer's reply, 15 January 1948.
44 G. Bossuat, op. cit., p. 117.
45 Min. Fin. B33459 2 January 1948, note for Caffery.
46 N.A.U.S. 850, Box 1570, White to State Department, 22 January 1948.

47 Min. Fin. B18220, memo from US secretary to the Treasury, 17 February 1949.
48 Min. Fin. B33510, Bruce to Queuille, 3 December 1948.
49 Min. Fin. B42268, first meeting of the Investment Commission, 21 June 1948.
50 B.D.F. 'Délibérations du Conseil Général', September 1948, no. 139, Reynaud to Monick, 4 September 1948.
51 Min. Fin. B16022, 'Notes sur le condition des prêts du F.M.E.', undated.
52 Min. Fin. B19951, 'Some recent developments in French finance and credit policy', November 1948 and N.A.U.S. RG286, Box 161, 53A.441, 'New Credit Policy in France'.
53 Min. Fin. B16020, note from Grimanelli, 26 October 1948.
54 A.N. 80AJ 267, note from Commissariat Général au Plan, 26 August 1948.
55 Ministère des Finances, *Statistiques et études financières, supplément statistique*, nos. 11–12, 1951.
56 Min. Fin. B33507, 'Discussions within the Investment Commission', November–December 1948.
57 N.A.U.S. RG286, memo from Bruce, December 1948.
58 L. Trotabas, 'La Législation fiscale de 1948 à 1950', in *La France Économique de 1948 à 1950* (Paris, 1950), pp. 99–109.
59 CGP, *Rapport annuel sur l'exécution du plan de modernisation et d'équipement*, tome I, (Métropol, 1958).
60 Min. Fin. IA 394, 'French Tax Mission to the United States', statement by M. Lauré, 22 November 1950.

5

FRANCE AND THE
RECONSTRUCTION OF
WESTERN EUROPE

The initial interest of the French government in Marshall Aid was to secure the dollars to finance imports for the entire duration of the Monnet Plan. It showed as little enthusiasm for the American condition that European governments should cooperate with each other in presenting a common aid programme as the British government displayed. Jean Monnet declined to become head of the Committee for European Economic Cooperation (CEEC), which was formed in Paris in July 1947 to work out Europe's dollar requirements, on the grounds that this would conflict with his main task of defending French interests within the European Recovery Programme. However, the French position was to change quite dramatically in August 1947 as it came to terms with two major shocks. The first was the severe dollar payments crisis which erupted in August, causing the government to suspend all imports, apart from food and fuel, from the Dollar Area in the second half of 1947 and threatening the implementation of the Monnet Plan. The second, which also undermined the Monnet Plan, consisted of the trade and production figures which the Bizonal authorities submitted to the CEEC in August 1947 covering the four years of the Marshall Plan.

Since exports of coke from the Ruhr were scheduled to be lower in 1948 than in 1947 Monnet pointed out that this would enable German steel production to rise while curbing any increase in French or other European steel production. The Monnet Plan's target of 12 million tons of steel by 1951 would have to be reduced by 2 or 3 million tons, thereby increasing French import needs. The Bizonal plans for coal were based on an output in 1951 some 13 per cent less than in 1938, whereas all the other CEEC countries planned to increase their coal production by on average 11–12 per cent. In spite of the unreliability of food imports from the Eastern Zone and eastern Europe, agricultural production in the Bizone was to be 12 per cent lower in 1951 than in 1935–38. And whereas Germany had run a surplus on shipping in the interwar period, by 1951 this was to become a deficit of 285 million dollars.[1]

For the French the two most pressing issues in August 1947 were that Congress would approve the Marshall Plan and that the Bizonal economy would not be reconstructed before, and at the expense of, the French economy. The failure of the experiment to restore the convertibility of sterling raised the possibility that Congress might once again prefer to offer a loan on a bilateral basis to Britain rather than one to Europe and particularly if the European countries showed no willingness to cooperate with each other.

The change in Britain's financial position together with its involvement in revising the plans for the Bizone ended the French government's feeling of common purpose with the British government. The retention of the principle on which the CEEC had been formed, namely that national governments would continue to exert full control over their economies rather than cede any power to a European body, now carried the risks for France that it would have no means of influencing policy in the Bizone and that the American Congress would reject the Marshall Plan.

THE FRENCH CUSTOMS UNION PROPOSALS

It was primarily to ensure that Marshall Aid would be approved by the American Congress and that France would have some influence over the allocation of it to the Bizone that Hervé Alphand, the head of the French delegation to the CEEC, issued an invitation on 15 August 1947 to any CEEC country which wanted to form a customs union with France.[2] It was not so much the idea of a customs union which was surprising, since such an idea had been under discussion in France from 1943 at least, and with the Benelux countries since 1944, but rather the timing of the announcement given that Italy had made a similar proposal one month earlier which France along with the rest of the CEEC had ignored. But as the earlier discussions had revealed, France was essentially interested in forming a customs union with the Benelux countries and had no serious interest in forming one with Italy on its own. Some of the reasons why the discussions with the Benelux countries in 1944 and 1945 had led to an agreement to provide mutual assistance during the period of reconstruction rather than to the more permanent arrangement of a customs union were the reservations, particularly of the Dutch, about French policy towards Germany.[3] Not only had Germany been an important supplier but it was an important market for the Netherlands. French ambitions which were subsequently enshrined in the Monnet Plan to replace Germany as the major industrial supplier on the European continent ignored this other aspect of Germany's position.

Rather than reject the French proposal of August 1947 outright Britain proposed that the CEEC should set up a study group in Brussels away from American influence in Paris which would investigate the implications of a customs union for the economies of the countries concerned.[4] At the same time the British government, under instructions from the foreign secretary,

Ernest Bevin, set up its own study group to explore the implications of the proposal for Britain. But however enthusiastic Bevin himself may have been about the idea, the rest of the government was sceptical. No mention of a customs union or of European cooperation was made in the report drafted by the British at the end of August 1947 on behalf of the CEEC setting out Europe's dollar needs. As Monnet quite accurately predicted the report and the dollar bill were rejected by the Americans, and sent back to Paris.

In the revised version, written with American help and designed to win congressional approval, a number of changes of significance to the French were made. Thus, specific reference was made to the study group which had been set up to assess the feasibility of a customs union. Specific reference was also made to the need to ensure that German economic recovery would not undermine the economic and security interests of its neighbours. And the Bizonal programme was altered with both coal and agricultural production levels higher than initially proposed.[5]

Meanwhile on 13 September 1947 the French and Italian governments proceeded to set up a study group to investigate the feasibility of forming a customs union between the two countries. Three months later, as the American Congress was debating Marshall Aid, it produced a report broadly endorsing the idea. In no area did it consider there to be major obstacles to forming a customs union. Even in agriculture, which was broadly similar in both countries in terms of the structure of output and level of development, some room for trade was identified, particularly if Italy could produce surpluses of rice and France surpluses of wheat. It was only in wine, fruit and vegetables where some problems were envisaged. Although both countries were mainly dependent on extra-European suppliers for industrial raw materials, there were some raw materials which would benefit from the formation of a customs union such as iron ore, cast iron, steel, phosphates and potassium in France and hemp, silk, sulphur and pyrites in Italy. Furthermore, it was argued, if a customs union encouraged technical cooperation then industries in both countries stood to benefit. But it was in terms of labour and capital that the complementary nature of the two economies was judged to be most apparent and where the greatest gain could be made from a customs union. Italy clearly had a labour surplus and France was judged often to have a capital surplus.[6]

Strengthened by the conclusions of this report, the French tried in January 1948 to interest the Benelux countries once again in joining what had now become a joint Franco-Italian initiative. Although the two governments had agreed that a customs union by stages was possible it was suggested that a committee involving Benelux should explore, without prejudice, the difficulties and advantages of a larger customs union involving the five countries. At a joint Belgian–Dutch meeting to consider the invitation, the Dutch pointed to the need to include the United Kingdom as the other important market for Dutch exports, next to Germany. The formal reply endorsed the French logic that a larger customs union was in the economic interests of Europe but at the same time observed that the possibility of an even larger union than the French were proposing was already being discussed by the study group within the CEEC. If that failed then the Benelux governments would have no objections to helping to realize a more limited regional one.[7]

Meanwhile, the French and Italian governments had decided to press on with their joint venture and created a new mixed commission to define a programme for implementing the customs union. It completed its report almost a year later. Central to its conclusions was the finding that a full tariff union could be formed within twelve months and that a full economic union was feasible five years after that. Although both governments signed a treaty on 25 March 1949 which committed them to achieving the first objective, when it was submitted by the French government to the Conseil Economique for an opinion, it was rejected. Apart from a minority of Catholics few in France supported it. Both sides of industry were opposed to it: workers out of a fear that unemployed and poorly paid Italians would either take their jobs or force down their wages, and industrialists who feared that, without tariff protection, they would be unable to compete with Italian industry. Among the industrialists, the giant textile firm of Boussac which was responsible for one-fifth of French cotton output led the opposition, soon to be joined by the French car and chemical firms.[8] The government responded to this pressure and did not even submit the treaty to parliament for ratification. The Italian government, which had been waiting to see the reaction to the treaty in France, now followed suit and postponed taking any further action.

The other customs union study group which met in Brussels between 11 November 1947 and the end of December 1948 was equally inconclusive. There was considerable opposition mainly from the British and Benelux countries to the pragmatic approach preferred by the French. Ostensibly this opposition stemmed from an uneasiness that the French method did not conform to the definition of a customs union as set out in the draft charter for an International Trade Organization, but it was also due to deep divisions over the removal of protection from key industrial and agricultural products. The French argued, as they were to do at the Havana Conference which met to agree the terms of the International Trade Organization, that the narrow definition of a customs union contained in article 42 of the draft charter was so rigid that it would prevent the formation of a customs union. What was needed, they said, was more flexibility to enable member governments to retain some form of protection if it was necessary for balance of payments reasons, to ensure the survival of strategic industries and agriculture or to maintain trading links with colonies. The French idea was that a certain number of countries should declare their intention of forming a customs union. They would then decide which goods would be traded freely within the union and which would continue to be protected.

The two products over which there was the greatest disagreement were steel and cereals. Britain and the Benelux countries were in favour of free competition in steel within the union, Italy wanted tariff protection and France wanted to re-create the European steel cartel of the interwar period. When it came to cereals France, Italy and the Benelux were in favour of free trade within the customs union and a common external tariff whereas Britain, Greece and Sweden wanted to be able to import cereals from outside the customs union duty free.[9]

During the course of 1948 it became apparent that Switzerland, Ireland, Portugal and Greece had no interest in a customs union, Britain and the Scandinavian countries were interested in exploring all forms of economic cooperation but did not envisage an early decision being taken on any particular one, France was anxious to begin with a partial customs union applied to a limited number of products while the Benelux countries wanted an immediate decision in favour of a complete customs union. Both Italy and the Bizone were interested in either the French or the Benelux approach.[10] It was certain that a customs union would not be formed in time to influence the size or distribution of Marshall Aid.

MARSHALL AID: THE PROBLEM OF DISTRIBUTION

When Congress approved Truman's request for dollar aid for Europe it did so on condition that such aid would be for the purpose of covering Europe's deficits with the Dollar Area and not deficits arising from intra-European trade.[11] The European Cooperation Administration (ECA) then entrusted the task of distributing aid in the first year of the programme to the Organization for European Economic Cooperation (OEEC) which succeeded the CEEC in March 1948. What became immediately clear to the OEEC, however, was that financing intra-European trade was as much a problem as financing Europe's trade with the Dollar Area. The French payments position was particularly serious.

In the autumn of 1947 the French had signed a multilateral payments agreement with the Benelux countries and Italy in the hope that this would boost their trade and alleviate the worst effects of the immediate dollar shortage. Britain, in the aftermath of the dramatic failure of the experiment to restore the convertibility of sterling, refused to participate in the arrangement because the size of its deficit with Belgium could have resulted in an outflow of gold under the terms of the arrangement. Without British participation the clearing arrangements of the group failed to stimulate trade by more than about 2 per cent.[12]

The next step taken by the French to tackle their dollar shortage was to devalue the franc in January 1948 and set up a system of multiple exchange rates for the dollar. Since, by definition, they broke the sterling–dollar cross rates the result, as intended, was that imports were diverted from the Dollar Area to the Sterling Area while exports to the Dollar Area, many of which the British suspected were re-exports from Britain, increased. By March 1948 the French deficit in sterling was so great that the French warned that unless Britain granted a credit in sterling they would have to suspend their imports from the Sterling Area as they had done from the Dollar Area in August 1947.

While the British government was strongly opposed to France's differential exchange rate system it feared the political consequences arising from a disruption to trade at a time when both governments were cooperating to set up the defence arrangements of the Brussels Treaty Organization. In the circumstances it agreed to provide France with sufficient sterling to cover its deficit until the arrival of dollars under the European Recovery Programme.[13] But, of course, as long as the aid to France was calculated on the basis of the French deficit with the Dollar Area it would not solve the French or anyone else's deficit in sterling or in any other European currency. The solution proposed by a committee set up by the OEEC to deal with this problem was to use the counterpart from dollar aid to finance intra-European deficits.[14] This would have conflicted with the use already ear-marked by the French for their counterpart although this was not the reason for its rejection. Rather it was the American announcement that aid to Belgium would take the form of loans rather than grants which made the proposal less attractive to European creditors.[15]

By June 1948 the ECA had agreed that dollar aid could be used to finance intra-European trade provided that such trade was not conducted on a bilateral basis. But since Britain was still resolutely opposed to the use of sterling in any multilateral settlement the problem remained. The group of financial experts to whom the OEEC once again entrusted the problem of aid allocation first tried to establish what common ground existed among the European governments. From this it emerged that they wanted to substitute European production for that of the United States as far as was possible, to raise food consumption above the 1947 level, to give priority to importing the raw materials necessary for the production of basic industries and to substitute exports from the Bizone for exports from the United States. On the basis of these common objectives the experts concluded that the Bizone, Belgium and Britain were to be the main creditors in Europe and France among the main debtors. Dollar aid would then be given to the debtors partly in the form of drawing rights on creditors to finance deficits in Europe.[16]

When the financial experts' report was published eleven of the OEEC countries, including France, accepted it provided that an intra-European payments system was set up immediately. Britain refused to accept the payments system proposed, while the Bizone objected to its role as a net exporter in intra-European trade, accusing France of deliberately reducing its aid allocation.[17] Rather than expose these divisions and have the ECA allocate the aid, which the French feared would not be to their advantage, it was decided that the exercise would be repeated by a larger committee. But this committee also recommended that the Bizone should be a net creditor in intra-European trade and once again the Bizone objected.

At a meeting on 6 September 1948 Britain, France, Belgium and the Netherlands agreed to increase their exports to the Bizone by 75 million dollars as a final compromise solution. France proposed to export one million tons of iron ore as well as 400,000 tons of steel and 1,000 tons of cast iron to the Bizone, albeit somewhat reluctantly, since the Quai d'Orsay felt that France was already being penalized by being denied the reparations to which it considered itself to be entitled, as well as losing its case for control of the Ruhr, and for a limitation of German war industries. And the problem was a financial as well as a moral one since, if the Americans succeeded in reversing the Bizonal position from that of a net creditor in Europe to that of a net debtor, it would, in the French view, make the operation of an intra-European payments system much less effective.

The French were torn between wanting to impose a harsh policy on Germany and wanting the OEEC to retain some control over the distribution

Table 5.1 Aid requests and aid recommendations for 1948/49 and 1949/50 (million dollars)

Country	Country-aid requests		OEEC-aid recommendations		ECA-revised aid figures		Aid allotments	
	1948–49	1949–50	1948–49	1949–50	1948–49	1949–50	1948–49	1949–50
Austria	339.3	217.0	217.0	174.1	215.2	197.0	231.6	166.4
Bel–Lux	358.2	250.0	250.0	312.5	247.9	200.0	206.7	221.7
Denmark	149.9	110.0	110.0	91.0	109.1	109.0	103.0	87.0
France	1,114.9	890.0	989.0	704.0	980.9	875.0	1,084.9	691.2
Germany:								
Bizone	446.0	372.4	414.0	⎰348.2	410.6	404.0	388.1	⎰281.8
French Zone	100.0	100.0	100.0	⎱	99.2	115.0	94.4	⎱
Greece	211.0	198.1	146.0	163.5	144.8	170.0	177.5	156.3
Iceland	11.0	10.0	11.0	7.3	5.2	7.0	8.3	21.9
Ireland	111.0	75.4	79.0	47.0	78.3	64.0	88.3	44.9
Italy	799.5	610.1	601.0	407.0	555.5	555.0	585.9	391.0
Netherlands	657.0	507.0	496.0	309.2	469.6	355.0	473.9	301.6
Norway	104.0	131.8	84.0	94.0	83.3	105.0	82.8	90.0
Portugal	–	100.6	–	33.0	–	10.0	–	48.0
Sweden	109.0	70.7	47.0	48.0	46.6	54.0	40.4	15.3
Trieste	22.0	12.8	18.0	14.0	17.8	12.0	13.8	13.6
Turkey	85.3	94.2	50.0	61.7	39.7	30.0	46.0	59.0
UK	1,271.0	940.0	1,263.0	962.0	1,239.0	940.0	1,316.0	921.0
Commodity reserve					13.5		11.4	
Total	5,889.1	4,690.1	4,875.0	3,776.5	4,756.2	4,202.0	4,953.0	3,510.7

Source: Wexler, op. cit., pp. 62 and 67

of aid even if that meant making further sacrifices in terms of their own dollar allocation. In the end it was decided that, were the ECA to take over the task of allocating aid as it was threatening to do, France would receive even less aid and it was on this basis that it accepted a reduction in its allocation of direct and indirect aid. This enabled the Bizone's contribution to European drawing rights to be cut from 138 million dollars to 10 million dollars.[18]

As it turned out, though, the Bizone did not need the drawing rights for which the Americans had fought so hard, and French predictions were borne out as German exports expanded rapidly. Instead of needing drawing rights from Britain, the Bizone had a trade surplus which cost Britain about 20 million dollars in gold. The Bizone did, however, need to use its drawing rights against Belgium. France used 187.3 million dollars of its drawing rights on Britain and most of its drawing rights with everyone else except Norway.[19]

Table 5.2 Bilateral drawing rights (in million dollars)

| Country | Granted by France | | Received by France | |
	1948/49	1949/50*	1948/49	1949/50*
Austria	2.0	4.1	–	–
Belgium	–	–	40.0	22.0
Denmark	2.7	6.0	–	–
Germany	–	–	53.7	45.0
Greece	5.0	7.5	–	–
Italy	–	–	11.0	8.3
Netherlands	–	–	–	–
Norway	–	5.1	5.0	–
Portugal	–	3.1	–	–
Sweden	–	–	–	–
Turkey	–	3.5	–	–
UK	–	–	200.0	93.0
Total	9.7	29.3	309.7	168.2

Source: BIS, 19th and 20th Annual Reports
Note: * position as at end of March 1950.

THE LONG-TERM PROGRAMME

Given the difficulties involved in allocating the first year's appropriation of dollar aid, and the lack of progress made in the customs union study group, the French proposed that each country should draw up a four-year plan which could then be coordinated into a single European plan to provide the basis for subsequent aid allocations. The plan was to indicate in broad terms how each economy was going to achieve external equilibrium by 1952 without the need for further dollar aid. The balance of payments in 1952 would indicate the nature and direction of trade in that year, including the

Table 5.3 Drawing rights actually used 1948/49 and 1949/50 (million dollars)

Country	1948/49 (9 mths to June 1949)			1949/50 (9 mths to March 1950)		
	granted (−)	received (+)	net balance	granted (−)	received (+)	net balance
Austria	1	64	+63	1	75	+74
Belgium	216	9	−207	186	0	−186
Denmark	3	11	+8	3	16	+14
France	9	289	+280	34	42	+8
Germany	96	46	−50	87	60	−27
Greece	0	76	+76	0	84	+84
Italy	38	0	−38	28	0	−28
Netherlands	11	83	+72	9	89	+80
Norway	4	47	+43	4	71	+67
Portugal	0	0	0	0	5	+4
Sweden	30	8	−22	47	0	−47
Turkey	20	14	−6	12	24	+12
UK	248	30	−218	107	52	−55
Total	−676	+677	±542	−518	+518	±343

Source: BIS, *20th Annual Report*, p. 235

trade of overseas territories. The deadline proposed for submitting these plans was 15 November 1948.[20] In the French case the Plan was to be a modified version of the Monnet plan extended from 1950 to 1952 to bring it into line with the European Recovery Programme.

As in the first version of the Monnet Plan, those drafting the revised plan intended to reduce the deficit in external payments by 1952 through an expansion of domestic output and a reduction in the value of trade relative to output compared with prewar. The target for exports was 70 per cent and for imports 68 per cent of their 1928 volume. In most respects the production targets of the original Monnet Plan were revised upwards to take account of the two-year extension to the plan, although these were not the only differences between the two plans (see Table 5.4). The number of basic sectors was expanded to include motor fuel and the whole of the agricultural sector rather than simply agricultural machinery. Although the target for tractor production was revised downwards agricultural output and exports were to be higher than originally planned.

It was expected that the French Union would still have a deficit with the Dollar Area by 1952–53 in spite of reduced imports. Those imports which could not be compressed were oil, cotton, machinery and spare parts and copper. Exports were predicted to be lower than in 1928, leaving a deficit of about 140 million dollars.

The assumption was that, as the French overseas territories became more developed, they would be able to increase their exports to the Dollar Area and so cover this deficit. In the meantime the French planners were

Table 5.4 Difference between original Monnet Plan (1946) and revised plan (1949)

Sector	Actual Production				Plan (1946)	Plan (1949)
	1929	1938	1946	1948	1950	1952
Energy						
Coal (million tons)	55.0	47.6	49.3	49.0	65.0	60.0[1]
Electricity (thousand million KWH)	14.4	20.8	23.0	27.6	37.0	43.0
Motor fuel (million tons)	0	7.0	2.8	13.0	–	18.7
Industry						
Steel (million tons)	9.7	6.2	4.4	7.2	11.0	12.5
Cement (million tons)	6.2	3.6	3.4	5.8	13.5	8.0[2]
Agriculture						
Tractors (thousands)	1.0	1.7	1.9	12.4	50.0	40.0
Wheat (million quintals)	1.0	81.5	64.0	12.4	81.0	95.0
Meat (thousand tons)	1.0	1,700.0[3]	1,250.0	12.4	1,680.0	2,200.0

Source: Commissariat Général au Plan, *Premier plan de modernisation*, op. cit., and Premier Plan, *Réalisations 1947–49 et Objectifs 1950–52*

Notes: [1] The target for French coal production was reduced because of the incorporation of the Saar into the French customs territory.

[2] The objective for cement was reduced because of the slowness of reconstruction.

[3] Average 1934–38.

counting on surpluses earned in South America and the Far East to cover it, provided that a system of multilateral payments was operating by 1952 to enable them to switch balances from one currency into another. The surplus in the Far East was to come from Indochina's usual surplus with China and Japan, while that with South America was to come mainly from exporting metals and machinery to meet the needs arising from the structural changes taking place in the South American economies.

A balance was to be achieved in payments between the Franc Area and the Sterling Area by increasing exports to the non-participating countries of the Sterling Area so that the resultant deficit would be small enough to be covered by a surplus with Britain. It was hoped that France could help meet the demand in industrializing countries such as India and those of the Middle East for iron and steel, chemical and industrial products, and replace its declining textile exports to Britain with basic agricultural and steel products.[21]

The revised plan was not greeted with the same unanimous approval in France which the first version of the Monnet Plan had enjoyed. Both the payments crisis of 1947 and the high rate of inflation had alerted the Planning Council to the weaknesses of the method of implementation of the plan. In a debate on the revised version which the Planning Council conducted early in October 1948 the plan to increase industrial production by 40 per cent was judged to be incompatible with a reduction of imports, and in particular of imports of investment goods, at a time when the dismantling of industrial plant in Germany was ending. Given that the entire plan for reducing the dollar deficit was seen to depend on a reorientation of trade away from the Dollar Area to the Sterling Area the planners were criticized for not paying sufficient attention to the availability of raw materials in the Sterling Area and the ability of France to pay for them.[22]

And indeed when the British government published its own four-year plan in December 1948 these criticisms were seen to be fully justified. Britain planned to have a balance of payments surplus by 1952–53 which was ear-marked for investment in the Sterling Area. It was assumed that Britain would continue to have a deficit with the Dollar Area which was to be covered by the British dominions running a surplus with the Dollar Area. This meant that sterling could become convertible, provided that the imperial preference system was retained, and that Britain transformed its traditional deficit with western Europe into a surplus.[23] Since the nineteenth century France and much of western Europe had relied on Britain's open-door policy to enable them to earn a surplus on trade with Britain which was then used to finance imports from the rest of the world.

Before the depression of 1929–32 the structure of French trade had been based on France running a trade surplus with Britain, of which silk cloth was the largest item of export, and a surplus with Germany and the Belgium–Luxembourg customs union, of which steel and engineering goods were the largest export items. Altogether these three markets absorbed over 41 per cent of French exports while supplying only 27 per cent of French imports. The resultant surplus then helped to finance French imports from the rest of the world.

The first blow to this trading structure came when the German economy moved into recession. French exports to Germany fell by 70 per cent in value between 1929 and 1932. Then when Britain devalued sterling in 1931 and imposed a general tariff French exports to that market also plummeted. Between 1929 and 1933 the value of French exports to Britain fell by 78 per cent compared with a 63 per cent fall in total exports (see Table 5.5). Although France retaliated by imposing quantitative restrictions on trade in 1931, and was the first country to do so, the fall in imports did not match the contraction in exports. In the case of trade with Britain French dependence on British coal, which accounted for 40 per cent of French imports in 1933, explained the trade deficit. Between 1931 and 1936 successive French governments tried to solve the problem of the external deficit by deflating domestic demand and prices and by diverting exports to the colonies.

But given the damaging effects of this strategy on the French economy in the 1930s it was not one which the postwar planners wanted to continue. However, their freedom of manoeuvre in this respect was constrained by Britain's commercial policies. The implications of the British long-term programme for France, as indeed for much of western Europe, were that

113

Table 5.5 Main French exports in 1929 and 1933 (in thousand francs)

Product	Total 1929	Total 1933	Belgium–Lux 1929	Belgium–Lux 1933	Italy 1929	Italy 1933	Netherlands 1929	Netherlands 1933	Poland 1929	Poland 1933	Switzerland 1929	Switzerland 1933	Germany 1929	Germany 1933	UK 1929	UK 1933	US 1929	US 1933
Silk cloth	3,031,831	724,909	177,758	166,962	63,887	24,479	76,630	43,588	19,106	4,058	227,217	30,948	137,495	18,795	1,152,477	259,818	297,681	62,711
Cotton cloth	2,712,854	965,984	522,854	95,716	199,830	72,125	39,841	7,997	23,254	3,265	127,489	16,788	119,600	7,144	187,283	17,114	185,588	102,352
Iron and Steel	2,660,578	1,302,528	441,859	92,256	113,279	31,317	32,796	46,251	29,870	8,845	194,293	128,989	680,435	399,649	300,587	79,401	30,184	6,513
Machines	2,192,561	856,575	248,332	34,429	35,441	8,829	34,732	13,745	1,640	–	111,402	36,480	127,501	36,037	117,296	28,380	20,278	7,105
Woollen cloth	2,014,905	347,149	732,632	201,763	159,125	30,132	73,871	21,838	161,063	29,480	152,409	43,622	93,430	17,548	520,949	29,133	129,668	28,136
Wool	2,031,859	809,676	267,358	53,332	47,518	13,676	20,640	8,495	5,802	2,799	131,799	34,926	330,623	212,612	257,314	145,677	29,015	5,257
Metal tools	1,850,273	786,810	53,170	–	33,158	–	33,440	29,690	862	–	85,123	33,708	224,493	66,070	84,550	11,522	72,476	4,868
Clothes	1,844,165	–	577,193	287,693	81,170	27,179	62,220	–	5,708	8,660	61,282	–	30,897	–	788,589	–	339,914	–
Chemicals	1,651,320	1,761,375	193,842	61,222	60,604	4,792	93,664	75,443	34,786	4,062	101,504	67,434	234,802	150,148	102,266	55,374	70,385	31,509
Cars	1,608,592	688,606	352,359	125,716	4,773	924	38,455	29,336	5,180	4,005	90,606	39,934	65,405	16,618	106,411	37,465	10,409	899
Woollen thread	1,257,200	384,500	203,357	55,350	16,409	2,252	69,011	61,781	12,795	2,075	42,829	23,712	281,874	31,948	319,849	10,740	3,976	1,768
Wine	1,176,582	476,705	300,739	64,966	32,409	13,826	51,898	12,321	2,663	2,993	72,662	52,240	107,987	9,632	230,089	90,812	–	–
Skins and leather	927,033	291,556	85,883	22,027	9,335	4,753	42,196	20,655	1,730	–	11,182	4,838	205,949	68,656	53,038	16,369	224,110	73,125
Glass, pottery	891,961	280,924	77,673	–	49,792	–	7,360	9,181	12,769	–	33,716	17,681	83,918	26,046	62,168	15,072	64,660	10,870
Finished leather	882,166	–	–	–	–	–	21,319	–	–	–	59,508	–	172,315	–	207,860	–	84,240	–
Paper	866,324	480,315	102,217	71,341	19,008	10,070	23,788	7,985	838	815	47,323	28,808	23,086	5,973	102,887	30,562	145,725	91,687
Perfume	860,954	285,823	46,911	17,521	31,284	6,835	21,481	12,231	7,163	3,713	21,434	9,654	29,564	4,130	108,612	14,352	86,690	17,193
Total	50,139,151	18,443,154	7,224,545	2,140,124	2,209,193	492,472	1,256,866	644,009	468,712	172,714	3,382,500	1,330,225	4,743,585	1,702,551	7,572,712	1,676,747	3,334,636	868,047

Source: Commerce extérieur de la France

if they could no longer run a surplus with Britain in order to finance a deficit with the Sterling Area they would have to import more from the Dollar Area or else reduce their levels of imports and thus of production.

To avoid either of these options the French proposed that trade between the OEEC and the Sterling Area should be increased and organized on the basis of long-term purchasing contracts. The OEEC countries would import raw materials at guaranteed prices in return for guaranteed exports of European products. The European exports, which would include non-essentials, would be organized collectively, on a non-competitive basis with joint publicity and common selling agencies. At the same time European governments would pass financial and commercial legislation aimed at abolishing competition in production and exports among the countries of the OEEC, as well as stimulating intra-European trade by improving the payments arrangements. A large internal market would encourage economies of scale and stable prices and reduce the risks of an excessive dependence on exports. This would take place within the framework of a customs union which could coexist with the British Commonwealth, unless the British chose to fuse the two. Trade between the OEEC and the Dollar Area would be organized on a similar basis.[24]

If the British refused to be drawn into any such arrangement the French were prepared to set up a working party to coordinate the investment programmes of the other major industrial economies in the OEEC, namely Benelux, Italy and the Bizone, with that of France. The overall investment plan which would then emerge could be compared with the other plans – those of Britain and the Scandinavian countries – in order to produce a completely coherent picture from the OEEC. Industrialists would be associated with the process since otherwise those countries, such as Belgium and Italy, with relatively liberal economic systems, would be unable to participate effectively. Pierre Baraduc, head of the European Cooperation Section of the Quai d'Orsay, freely admitted that the scheme was similar to prewar cartel arrangements which the United States would find unacceptable, but he could see no alternative.[25]

The alternative proposed by Britain, which was then drafted into the OEEC's report to the ECA, was that Europe's dollar deficit could best be eliminated if OEEC countries adopted Britain's austerity programme and reduced domestic demand and imports. Only in this way would the external deficit of OEEC countries, which was estimated at 3,000 million dollars by 1952, be eliminated.[26] However, due to objections from France, Italy and the Benelux countries to this recommendation, the report was redrafted between 17 and 23 December 1948. The revised report stressed that any reduction in imports would not lead to balance of payments equilibrium but to a new disequilibrium since potential exports would have to be retained to satisfy domestic demand and partly because unit

115

costs would rise if production was cut back on account of the reduction in raw material imports.

Whereas the first draft of the report analysed exports first and then imports, those drafting the second version preferred to start off by analysing import needs in order to show the demand within Europe for raw materials in the Sterling Area. Thus, instead of treating the latter as a given, it was hoped to stimulate production and exports from these countries to Europe. The report also stressed that exports could be expanded if European countries cooperated more in terms of specialization. The French argued that one basic difference between the British approach and that of France, Belgium and Italy was that Britain saw price as the only factor determining demand, and therefore exports, whereas the others considered that demand could be created, and particularly demand in the Sterling Area.[27]

But when these differences were exposed rather than resolved in the 'Interim Report' presented by the OEEC to the United States the Americans' irritation was considerable. At a meeting held in Washington in January 1949 to discuss the report, Snyder, secretary to the Treasury, made it clear that the Americans had wanted the OEEC Council to instruct member governments on the location of industry, on what should be produced and on how it should be produced. At the very least he argued that European governments should agree to coordinate output in coal, iron, steel and perhaps textiles and discuss cooperation on all new investment.[28]

Reluctantly the British agreed to hold talks with the French planners to see whether a greater degree of cooperation was possible. In preparing for the talks the French government argued that it was necessary for the British and French experts to discuss their respective production programmes in very specific terms to see how they could be coordinated, and to extend this exercise to the plans for their overseas territories. The purpose, it claimed, was to rationalize production in order to reduce costs and thereby boost exports to third markets, particularly the United States. Other ways of reducing costs, such as by reducing wages, were ruled out by the French government on social and political grounds, while devaluation was seen as a temporary solution which had the disadvantage of reducing income from tourism.

If Britain did not cooperate with western Europe the French government felt that British exports, dispersed as they were over many lines of production, would be unable to achieve American levels of productivity, while at the same time western Europe would close its doors to them. But if Britain did cooperate this would mean that it would have to run a payments deficit with western Europe for a period of time to help western Europe cover its deficit with the rest of the Sterling Area. Eventually they would reach equilibrium.

And it was on this point that Britain remained intransigent. Britain was not prepared to lift the controls over the domestic economy to enable

European producers to export to Britain to earn enough sterling to pay for imports from the Sterling Area. As long as Britain retained its controls, the government felt that it could solve its payments problems by 1952. As Stafford Cripps, the chancellor of the exchequer, explained, Britain's over-riding aim was to become independent of the United States. This was not possible without being independent of it financially and it was for this reason that Britain intended to increase its trading links with the Sterling Area. In return for investment in the Sterling Area those countries would then be in a position to cover Britain's dollar deficit by increasing their exports to the Dollar Area. While Cripps was sympathetic to the French payments position, and assured the French planners that Britain would import French wheat and meat if surpluses actually existed by 1952, little the French said would change Britain's international payments strategy.[29]

The failure of the talks with Britain did not deter the French from trying to implement their scheme to coordinate investment programmes by another route. The scheme was motivated by two main concerns. One was to lower French prices in the event of a recession, the early signs of which were evident in both the American and French economies, while the other was to promote cooperation among European producers in order to make their exports more competitive with those of the United States. While the French planners felt that the range of controls available to the state could be used to shield the French economy from a recession originating outside France, such as that of 1929–32, there was no such confidence that the state could deal with a crisis which originated inside the French economy. Indeed Pierre Uri remained unconvinced that a Keynesian policy based on stimulating domestic demand would reverse a recession in France. A more likely consequence, he argued, was that the domestic price level would rise causing exports to decline. In the absence of official reserves such a reduction in exports would necessitate a cut in imports which would lead to a decline in industrial output.[30] Part of the attraction of cooperating with Europe was, if not to prevent such a crisis of overproduction from occurring in the first place, at least to reduce its impact on the French economy. This was to be achieved by cutting or 'rationalizing' industrial production and prices throughout the OEEC. But, of course, if this was to be done, and both the Quai d'Orsay and the ECA argued that it should, then the criteria on which it would be based had to be agreed. For Bissell, the assistant deputy administrator of the ECA, the cost of production was the only consideration,[31] whereas for the Quai d'Orsay other factors, such as the balance of payments position, the social structure and the need to maintain full employment and national security, had to be taken into account when judging the relative desirability of different investment projects.[32]

The British Foreign Office treated the French enthusiasm for the coordination of investment with the utmost suspicion. What it disguised, the Foreign Office felt, was a recognition that the French had overcommitted themselves in terms of investment and rather than admit this, wanted the OEEC to reduce their investment programme as part of a larger exercise in Europe. In Britain's view much the best way to deal with investment was by liberalizing trade in Europe and allowing the market to operate freely.[33] However, opinion was very divided over how best to do this. The ECA considered payments difficulties to be the main barrier impeding a higher level of intra-European trade[34] and advocated that in 1949–50 drawing rights should be made multilateral and to some extent convertible into dollars.

The implications of the ECA's proposal for France, a net debtor in the OEEC, were that it would be able to import from the cheapest market in Europe and the United States, and to that extent it supported the proposals. It saw a danger though in that creditors might reduce their imports from debtor countries as a way of putting pressure on debtors to continue importing from them. But if this could be avoided then France was in favour of the proposal. It was Britain which opposed it as resolutely as it had opposed all measures to allow sterling to be used in multilateral payments schemes which held the risk of a loss of gold or dollars. If any concessions had to be made in return for Marshall Aid then Cripps preferred to make commercial rather than financial ones.[35]

At the same time many Americans argued that an essential prerequisite for the liberalization of trade was an adjustment of European exchange rates.[36] While some currencies, such as the French franc and the Italian lira, had been devalued against the dollar, most of the others had followed Britain and refused to devalue. This in the American view was one of the factors which was distorting intra-European trade. But both the French and the British took the view that it was more important to remove some of the quantitative restrictions on trade so that the relative competitiveness of European producers could be judged before adjusting exchange rates or exposing European producers ·to competition with the United States through a degree of convertibility of European currencies. Where they differed was over the method of reducing these quantitative restrictions. The British method seemed simple and straightforward. On the basis of bilateral negotiations each government would reduce an agreed proportion of its 1948 private trade according to a set timetable. But this, the French argued, would not actually lead to any greater competition in Europe since it was most unlikely that governments would remove restrictions on the same goods. Their preferred method was for each of the participating countries in the OEEC to agree on a list of products over which it was willing to abolish trade restrictions apart from tariffs.[37] This would mean in effect that the OEEC was moving towards setting up a customs union by stages, which was what the French had been advocating for some time. But the British continued to carry more weight in the OEEC than France and it was their method which was adopted.

While the method of liberalizing trade in the OEEC was being debated the French were also involved in discussions with Italy and Belgium–Luxembourg aimed at integrating their economies to a greater extent. Drawing lessons from the opposition to the proposed customs union with Italy the proposed scheme, first known as Fritalux, after the names of the countries involved, aimed to remove quantitative restrictions on the movement of capital and labour within the group, and on trade insofar as it was considered possible given the specific sectoral interests of the member countries. To minimize the inevitable dislocation in the domestic economies, it was agreed that it should be the exchange rates which would adjust rather than domestic prices and employment. This of course breached a fundamental principle of the Bretton Woods system and for that reason the group was surprised that the proposal was viewed favourably by the ECA. But as Averell Harriman, the Special Ambassador to the ECA, explained, many within the ECA were looking for an alternative means of promoting the integration of the economies of the OEEC in view of the failure to achieve it through supranational planning or a customs union. The French scheme was criticized because it did not include enough countries. By the summer of 1949 the ECA had decided to reduce the amount of aid available for individual economies and to assign some of it to a special fund designed to promote regional integration schemes.[38] It was not clear whether the French scheme would qualify for a portion of this fund, but nor was it clear whether the British-inspired OEEC programme of trade liberalization would satisfy the Americans either. Was it actually in France's economic interests that Fritalux would be approved and set up? It was not without risk, particularly because of France's multiple exchange rate system.

When the French government had devalued the franc in January 1948 it had set up three different rates for the franc in terms of the dollar: a fixed rate, a floating rate and a rate halfway between the two. All commercial transactions were carried out at the third rate while all financial transactions were carried out at the free rate. This automatically broke the cross rate between all other currencies and the dollar. The effect on French trade with the Sterling Area was the most immediate and serious and led, as we have seen, to Britain granting France a loan. In return the French agreed in October 1948 to modify their exchange rate structure by conducting all commercial transactions with the non-dollar world at the same rate as with the Dollar Area. This concession did not apply to financial transactions.[39] The risk of liberalizing capital movements within the Fritalux group was that it would encourage the export of capital from France to take advantage of the relatively overvalued exchange rate for financial transactions. This problem would not exist if exchange rates within the group were allowed to float but it would reopen the problem of respecting the sterling–dollar cross rate.

Further problems arose when the Dutch were finally told of the scheme in September 1949. Either Britain or West Germany had to be included or the Dutch threatened that it would mean the end of Benelux. Since Britain and West Germany were the two largest markets for Dutch exports in western Europe their exclusion would mean that the Dutch would be in permanent deficit with the rest of the group. If this led to a fall in the Dutch exchange rate and an outflow of capital this would create disorderly cross rates and weaken rather than strengthen the Dutch economy. But to include Britain and the Sterling Area or West Germany, the French feared, would mean that they would be in permanent deficit with the group.

In some respects Britain's decision finally to devalue sterling against the dollar simplified the French position. Although they protested violently when told of the decision it was the size of the devaluation (30 per cent) and the absence of prior consultation which caused their anger rather than the devaluation itself.[40] Indeed, the French adoption of the system of multiple exchange rates in January 1948 had been partly a recognition that sterling was overvalued in relation to the dollar. Before sterling was devalued the sterling–dollar exchange rate was 1:4.03. The franc–dollar rate was stabilizing around 330:1 and the franc–sterling rate was 1096:1 which gave a sterling–dollar cross rate of 1:3.3. The French therefore wanted sterling to be devalued by about 18 per cent so that they would not have to devalue the franc against the dollar. But when sterling was devalued by 30 per cent, had the French respected the new cross rate without devaluing against the dollar, this would effectively have meant that the franc would have been revalued against sterling to a new rate of 924:1.[41] This would have made French exports to the Sterling Area even more expensive and increased France's sterling deficit. As a result the French felt compelled to compromise by adjusting the franc–dollar exchange rate to 350:1 which gave a new franc–sterling rate of 980:1, a revaluation of 11 per cent. This led to a reduction in the price of Sterling Area imports in the second half of 1949 so that the balance of payments between the Franc Area and the Sterling Area was actually in surplus in 1949 and again in 1950.

The devaluation of sterling enabled the French government to unify its exchange rate for both financial and commercial transactions, thereby removing one of the major risks of participating in Fritalux. At the same time the improvement in French trade and payments with the Sterling Area was to make the inclusion of Britain and the Sterling Area in the regional grouping much more attractive. The overriding question now was whether the United States would support it. With the ECA increasingly desperate for any integrative scheme to present to Congress as evidence of the success of the ERP, the head of the ECA, Paul Hoffmann, gave encouragement to smaller regional groups in an address to the OEEC on 31 October 1949.

Table 5.6 Balance of payments between the Franc Area and the Sterling Area on current account (million dollars)

Sector	1945 R	1945 E	1946 R	1946 E	1947 R	1947 E	1948 R	1948 E	1949 R	1949 E	1950 R	1950 E
Trade	5.7	190.7	97.8	370.6	285.7	431.9	264.8	640.2	417.9	495.4	512.1	531.3
Tourism	0.1	5.4	8.7	6.3	24.4	4.2	26.1	4.3	51.0	5.2	50.8	6.3
Transport Sea Other } Insurance	0.1	18.5	4.4	36.2	22.1	54.3	12.1	50.9	14.4	44.5	36.1	52.7
Income from investment	2.2	15.0	60.6	3.8	86.7	7.4	76.7	1.9	45.8	3.1	26.7	4.4
Other services	2.5	5.7	18.1	8.0	38.9	18.3	32.0	23.3	50.6	25.5	23.2	16.2
Government income and expenditure	8.8	39.3	10.8	12.9	13.4	12.5	0.1	5.7	0.1	7.0	0.7	5.8
Settlement of operations during the war	49.9	127.8	24.4	1.2	54.0	56.5	14.7	13.3	18.2	30.4	4.5	28.5
Balance of payments between overseas territories and other countries	29.2	197.5	55.0	121.8	–	13.9	–	28.6	5.2	–	20.1	–
Other items	17.6	17.2	16.4	15.3	11.4	1.8	16.6	1.5	22.3	0.4	14.3	6.1
Cancellations	2.0	1.7	13.2	4.1	8.3	2.0	8.4	3.2	9.6	4.6	1.6	3.9
Total	118.1	618.8	309.4	600.2	544.9	602.8	451.4	773.0	635.2	616.1	690.1	655.3
Balance of payments on current account	−500.7		−290.8		−57.9		−321.6		+19.2		+34.8	

Source: 'Bulletin mensuel de statistique. Supplément', January–March 1953
Note: R = Receipts; E = Expenditure.

Clearly the British proposal for liberalizing intra-European trade, which was adopted by the OEEC, did not meet American requirements for European integration, although Hoffmann did not specify what exactly these requirements were.[42] The British plan set out a timetable for the reduction of quantitative restrictions to trade within the OEEC. The reductions were based on the value of private trade carried out by member countries in 1948 which were subject to quantitative restrictions. By December 1949 the target set was 50 per cent, rising to 60 per cent in October 1950. A target of 75 per cent was set subsequently, to be reached by February 1951.

The Quai d'Orsay, taking Hoffmann's speech as direct support for the regional grouping of France, Belgium, Luxembourg, the Netherlands and Italy, proceeded to draw up a more detailed set of proposals for the operation of the scheme. Significantly, the group was now to be open to any member of the OEEC, including both West Germany and Britain. In their proposals circulated on 14 November 1949 the French recommended that the movement of goods and services should be liberalized as soon as possible and at a faster rate than within the OEEC while allowing for some exceptions. This was seen as a way of reducing prices through specialization. Exchange controls were to be removed more gradually to avoid the adverse effects on employment in certain sectors which might have resulted from their faster removal. Budgetary and credit policies were to be harmonized and all discriminatory practices such as subsidies and double-pricing were to be eliminated. New investment was to be coordinated by governments or, in the case of private investment, by government-sponsored industrial agreements, while an investment bank was to be set up to promote specialization and ease the problems caused by the disappearance of certain industries. If quantitative restrictions on agriculture were to be removed then it too was to have access to similar facilities. Exchange rates between the four currencies were to float and all restrictions on capital movements lifted. The scheme was to be managed by a general council presided over by the ministers of foreign affairs and grouping together a financial committee composed of ministers of finance and governors of national banks as well as an economic committee composed of the relevant economics ministries, the Ministry of Agriculture and in the French case the Commissariat au Plan.[43]

The aspect of the French scheme which attracted the most criticism was its advocacy of floating exchange rates. Predictably the IMF considered that it was national policies which should be adjusted rather than exchange rates if the abolition of exchange controls led to major economic fluctuations. But it conceded that if these fluctuations were greater than could be tolerated politically then the answer was not to let the exchange rate float but to increase the size of the central reserves from which national governments could borrow.[44]

Within one month of the French proposals being circulated Bissell produced a working paper which finally spelt out what the State Department meant by integration. It entailed the institution of a multilateral trade and payments system in Europe in which non-tariff barriers to trade would gradually be reduced under the supervision of the OEEC while all existing payments agreements would be replaced by a single clearing house known as the European Payments Union (EPU).[45] While the smaller regional grouping of Fritalux met these American conditions, because of its size the Americans were not sure whether it would qualify for dollar aid. The position was left deliberately fluid for some time on account of British opposition to American plans for the larger European Payments Union.

The French too were very divided over the EPU, mainly because of its associated rules for liberalizing trade. On one level the dispute was simply over the timing of trade liberalization. Rather than embark on it halfway through the European Recovery Programme, it was argued that France should retain control over its external trade and payments until the Monnet Plan had been fully completed; in other words modernization had to precede liberalization. On another level it was argued, by the Ministry of

Foreign Affairs in particular, that France would have a deficit with the Sterling Area and the German Federal Republic which it would be unable to cover with a surplus from the rest of the OEEC. Therefore, the EPU would not achieve its objectives of leading to the rebuilding of French reserves, the restoration of the convertibility of the franc and the reintegration of the French economy into the international economic system.[46] This reasoning led to the recommendation that France would be better off expanding trading links with complementary economies in eastern Europe and the French overseas territories in the short term at least.[47]

A third argument centred on the nature of the trade liberalization programme and on the inclusion of the German Federal Republic in it. The Directorate of Mechanical and Electrical Industries within the Ministry of Industry objected to the fact that steel had not been placed on the list of products from which quantitative restrictions were to be removed, whereas industries using steel were on the list. Given the lower price of West German steel all users of French steel would be at a comparative disadvantage and yet they were to be exposed to European competition before the steel industry itself.

This, however, was not the only factor identified by the Ministry of Industry as being responsible for West German economic superiority. The inadequacy of Allied military action during the war and their reparations policy after it meant that the German Federal Republic had a production potential in 1950 equal to that of 1938. The stock of machine tools in France, 500,000, was one-third that of the Federal Republic and they were twice as old. Whereas French industry was saddled with debts, the West German monetary reform had amortized those of the Federal Republic. West German industry also benefited from cheaper basic products – the price of coal was 15–20 per cent less and electricity 25–30 per cent less than in France. West German social charges were lower. Vertical concentration in West German industry led to savings in fiscal charges. Overcapacity and surplus labour in West German industry would, it was felt, reduce marginal costs of production, allow increases in productivity and enable West German industry to dump abroad in the future. The conclusion drawn, though, was not that French industry should be protected permanently against West German exports, but that trade liberalization should be gradual and should be accompanied by a harmonization of the two economies and an end to all West German discriminatory practices.[48]

A fourth argument put forward by the Confédération Générale de Travail (CGT), the main communist-dominated trade union, was that exports from the French overseas territories would be exposed to competition on the French market from exports from the overseas territories of other OEEC countries and that this would undermine the cohesion of the French Union. Rather than be forced to liberalize trade and payments with western Europe as a condition for further American aid, the CGT preferred to cut back on imports from the Dollar Area, accept a decline in living standards and forgo American aid.[49]

The main supporter of the EPU was the Ministry of Finance, on the grounds that it would help to restore competition among European producers and close the price and productivity gap with the United States, thereby ending Europe's need for dollar aid. Without making it a precondition for accepting the EPU it continued to argue that competition would only be restored if countries agreed to liberalize trade in the same products.[50] It also considered that the attempts to re-create a trading structure based on the supposed complementarity of industrialized countries and developing ones were completely misguided. Few developing countries wanted it. France had no option but to trade and become competitive with other industrialized economies.

Some of these objections were overcome with Monnet's inspired proposal to remove all barriers to trade in coal, iron and steel between France and the Federal Republic of Germany. Seized on by the Quai d'Orsay as a major foreign policy initiative, the Schuman Plan established France as the leader of western Europe while enabling it to participate in the EPU and its associated trade liberalization programme with greater confidence.

The participation of Britain and the Sterling Area in the EPU, which was secured only through the provision of special dollar aid to Britain, offered France a much better chance of covering its deficits in sterling than through the existing bilateral arrangements. It also offered an alternative means of earning dollars since, under the rules of the EPU, a surplus earned on trade within the Union would be financed partly in gold.[51] But given that in 1949 and 1950 France had a current account surplus with everywhere except the Dollar Area, would full convertibility not have been a more satisfactory arrangement?[52] Such an option was not under serious consideration in France, since as long as the surpluses were based on a high level of trade protection there was no guarantee that they could be maintained if protection was reduced. Indeed, there was every reason to suppose that the surpluses achieved on both trade and current account in 1949 and 1950 were the short-term effects of the revaluation of the franc against sterling. Thus the only way that convertibility could have been sustained would have been through domestic deflation. So while there was no guarantee that convertibility would have led to trade liberalization there was a chance that the liberalization of trade might lead to currency convertibility.

The EPU and its associated rules for liberalizing intra-European trade provided a commercial regime which helped to address the problem of France's sterling deficits. But whether the surpluses earned on trade with western Europe would continue, once barriers to trade had been reduced, and whether those surpluses would earn sufficient gold to cover France's dollar deficit as well, thereby enabling France to participate in the one-world system of Bretton Woods, were questions the answers to which could not be predicted with any degree of certainty. If, as many in France feared, one result of liberalizing trade after so many years of protection was a marked deterioration in the French balance of payments, the pressure on the French government to return to bilateralism would increase. If, on the other hand, France continued to run surpluses on trade with western Europe in the EPU, that would provide little assurance that the French economy could survive if exposed to competition from the United States within the Bretton Woods system, so great was the productivity gap between western Europe and the United States. It was, therefore, in the French government's interests to prolong the EPU for as long as possible and to try to liberalize trade within its framework.

Since the collapse of the international economic system under the strain of the Great Depression of 1929–32 successive French governments had been powerless to reconstruct a system which would meet French economic needs. In a world of protective trade blocs the French empire had cushioned the economy from the worst effects of the contraction of world trade, but was no substitute for the markets in Britain and western Europe. After the war Britain's determination to retain the Imperial Preference system, set up at Ottawa and now bolstered by a panoply of quantitative restrictions on trade, threatened French recovery and plans for expansion. Attempts to set up trade and payments schemes with the smaller countries of western Europe made no sense economically unless they included Britain and the Sterling Area. Ultimately it was the dollar backing for the American-inspired European Payments Union which created a framework within which the French economy could continue to expand. Since the EPU included most of the countries in the Sterling Area as well as in western Europe it offered a means of settling France's deficit in sterling, which in the aftermath of the Korean War was to be almost as large as that with the Dollar Area.

NOTES

1 A.N. 80 AJ 266, 'Relèvement des niveaux de l'industrie allemande', 18 August 1947.
2 A.S. Milward, The Reconstruction, op. cit., p. 239.
3 R.T. Griffiths and F.M.B. Lynch, 'L'Echec de la Petite Europe: Le Conseil Tripartite 1944–1948', Guerres mondiales et conflits contemporains, no. 152, October 1988.
4 A.S. Milward, The Reconstruction, op. cit., p. 240.
5 A.N. 80 AJ 266, Monnet's notes, September 1947; M. Hogan, op. cit., p. 81.
6 A.N. F^{10} 5607, 'Rapport sur un projet d'union douanier franco/italien', 22 December 1947.
7 R.T. Griffiths and F. Lynch, 'L'Echec de la "Petite Europe": les négociations Fritalux/Finebel, 1949–1950', Revue Historique, vol. CCLXXIV/1, 1986.
8 Min. Ind. 830589/11, 'Bilans hebdomadaires, études et documents'; W. Diebold, Trade and Payments in Western Europe 1945–51 (New York, 1952), pp. 354–69;

P. Guillen, 'Le projet d'union économique entre la France, l'Italie et le Benelux', in R. Poidevin (ed.), *L'Histoire des débuts de la construction européenne, mars 1948–mai 1950* (Brussels, 1986).

9 PRO, T 236/268, various reports of meetings of the European Customs Union Study Group, in 1947 and 1948.

10 PRO, T 236/781, UK Study Group on Customs Unions, 1 November 1948.

11 I. Wexler, *The Marshall Plan Revisited. The European Recovery Program in Economic Perspective* (Westport, 1983), p. 128.

12 W. Diebold jr, op. cit., p. 25.

13 PRO, T 236/1884, meeting on 13 April 1948.

14 MAE DE-CE 1945–1960, 'Plan Marshall', 318, memo, 16 July 1948.

15 I. Wexler, op. cit., p. 128.

16 MAE DE-CE, 1945–1960, 'Plan Marshall', 319, Memo, 18 August 1948.

17 ibid.

18 MAE DE-CE 1945–1960, 'Plan Marshall', 319, Memos 6, 8, 15, 16 September 1948.

19 W. Diebold jr., op. cit., p. 48.

20 MAE DE-CE 1945–1960, 'Plan Marshall', 318, memo of the French delegation, 3 July 1948.

21 OEEC, *Interim Report on the European Recovery Programme, volume II* (Paris, December 1948).

22 Min. Fin. 5A 75, Fonds Cusin, 6 October 1948.

23 OEEC, *Interim Report*, op. cit.

24 A.N. F^{60ter}357, note, 15 January 1949.

25 PRO, T 232/162, Hall-Patch to Berthoud, 7 December 1948.

26 MAE DE-CE 1945–1960, 'Plan Marshall', 319, note, 18 December 1948.

27 MAE DE-CE 1945–1960, 'Plan Marshall', 319, note, 31 December 1948.

28 PRO, T 232/162, note of discussions in Washington, 18 January 1949.

29 A.N. F^{60ter}357, report of conversation with Cripps, 15 January 1949; A.N. F^{60ter}476, Monnet to Petsche, 25 February 1949; A.N. F^{60ter}412, report of meeting in Foreign Office, 11 February 1949.

30 A.N. 80 AJ 13, P. Uri, 'Memorandum sur les conditions du maintien de l'activité économique', 20 June 1949.

31 PRO, T 232/163, meeting in Paris between Bissell, Geiger, Marjolin and Lintott, 13 April 1969.

32 PRO, T 232/163, note from OEEC to Foreign Office, 1 June 1949.

33 PRO, T 232/163, note from Foreign Office to OEEC, 14 May 1949.

34 PRO, T 229/156, note from Rickett, 27 April 1949.

35 A.N. F^{60ter}383, note from the Direction des relations économiques extérieures (DREE), 30 May 1949.

36 A.N. F^{60ter}384, memo, 30 May 1949.

37 A.N. F^{60ter}383, 'Note sur la libération du commerce intra-européen', 20 June 1949.

38 In October 1949 the ECA fixed the sum at 150 million dollars.

39 PRO, T 236/2777, Bank of England report, 31 August 1950.

40 A.N. F^{60ter}469, conversation between Petsche, Snyder and Mac Chesney Martin, 6 July 1949.

41 PRO, T 236/2777, Bank of England report, 31 August 1950.

42 MAE DE-CE 1945–1960, 'Plan Marshall', 351, note, 3 November 1949.

43 A.N. F^{60ter}469, report from Ministère des Affaires Étrangères, 14 November 1949.

44 R. Griffiths and F. Lynch, 'L' Echec de la "Petite Europe": les négociacions Fritalux/Finebel, 1949–1950', *Revue Historique*, vol. CCLXXIV/1, 198.

45 MAE DE-CE 1945–1960, 'Plan Marshall', 351, note, 9 December 1949.
46 MAE DE-CE, 1945–1960, 'Plan Marshall', 351, meeting of Conseil Economique, 26 January 1950.
47 ibid.
48 Min. Ind. 830587 Ind 11, report by Bellier, January 1950.
49 MAE DE-CE, 1945–1960, 'Plan Marshall', 351, meeting of Conseil Economique, 26 January 1950.
50 A.N. F$^{60\text{ter}}$474, Schweitzer to Filippi, 12 May 1950.
51 Creditors received 50 per cent gold and were granted 50 per cent credit in settlement of their surpluses above an initial gold-free tranche established at 20 per cent of their quota. (The quota was fixed at 15 per cent of the basic turnover of a member country in intra-European trade in 1949.) Debtors received credit for the first 20 per cent and then paid gold according to a sliding scale so that overall the credit:gold ratio was 60:40.
52 B. Eichengreen, 'Was the European Payments Union a Mistake? Would a Payments Union for the former Soviet Union be a Mistake as well?', unpublished paper, November 1992.

6

TRADE LIBERALIZATION OR PROTECTION?

The first attempt to liberalize French trade within the OEEC failed. In the face of an acute payments crisis in the EPU the government took the decision in February 1952 to reimpose all the quantitative restrictions on imports which it had removed between 1949 and 1951 and to extend to all markets the export subsidies which had been applied to the North American market in 1949. The payments crisis seemed to vindicate those who had been opposed to trade liberalization at that time, or indeed at any time. Between 1952 and 1957, when the government took the unexpected and highly controversial decision to sign the Treaty of Rome setting up a common market between France, the Federal Republic of Germany, Italy and the Benelux countries, France remained one of the most protected economies in the OEEC. In spite of the protection France and the whole Franc Area had a deficit on current account for much of this period. Until the Geneva Agreement which formally ended French involvement in the war in Indochina in 1954 American aid, both direct and in the form of off-shore purchases, helped France to finance much of this deficit without having recourse to domestic deflation. As a result the economy experienced an unusual period of inflation-free growth between 1953 and 1956. The near cessation of this American aid together with a disastrous harvest in 1956 and an escalation of the conflict in Algeria brought this period of relative stability to an end. In elections in 1956 the centre-right coalition, which had been in power since 1951, was replaced by one dominated by the socialist party. It was this government under Prime Minister Guy Mollet which signed the Treaty of Rome.

To his critics Mollet's decision was a politically motivated one which would have been disastrous for the French economy but for the reforms implemented by the new de Gaulle administration in 1958. These reforms, which were inspired by de Gaulle's financial adviser Jacques Rueff, entailed a devaluation of the franc by 17.5 per cent, the restoration of its convertibility, a reduction in real wages and an end (albeit temporary) to the cross-indexation of agricultural and industrial incomes. These reforms have been seen as a turning point as a result of which the French economy became

128

Table 6.1 The French balance of payments, 1950–56

Sector	1950	1951	1952	1953	1954	1955	1956
				(million dollars)			
Metropolitan France							
Balance on current account	−115	−970	−591	−117	+262	+603	−684
Balance on capital account	+23	−24	+102	−9	−223	−179	−99
Overseas territories							
Balance on current account }	− }	−	−68	−103	−68	−196	−151
Balance on capital account /	−123 /	−88	+42	+43	+57	+47	+44
Overall Balance	−215	−1,082	−515	−186	+29	+174	−891
External Aid							
Direct American aid							
to Metropolitan France	+509	+481	+353	+350	+186	+59	+86
to Indochina	−	−	−	−	−	+134	−
American participation in Indochina	−	−	−	−	+321	+344	+10
Credit from (+) or to (−) EPU	−125	+257	+199	−	−69	−155	+121
Gold and currency movements							
Public gold or currency	−157	+226	−50	−25	−347	−571	+728
Payments agreements	−111	+27	−18	−20	−23	−36	+82
Private currency movements	−48	−31	+41	−51	−95	−50	−146
Foreign accounts held in francs	+145	+16	+57	−85	−28	+35	−1
Others	+2	+108	−57	+26	+26	−34	+11
Total	+215	+1,082	+515	+186	−29	−274	+891

Source: INSEE, Le Mouvement économique en France de 1944 à 1957 (Paris, 1958)

almost the fastest-growing economy in western Europe in the 1960s.[1] Exports surged ahead with an increasing proportion going to the rapidly growing markets of western Europe and away from the sheltered markets of the French Union. While there was some disquiet that, in terms of structure, French exports in 1960 were relatively specialized in agricultural, semi-finished and consumer goods but little specialized in investment goods, this situation was to change as a result of the rapid growth of the French economy in the 1960s.[2]

Mollet's decision marked the culmination of years of debate within the French state over the nature of France's economic problems and how best to continue the process of economic growth and modernization started by Monnet after the Second World War. For some advisers, who tended to be in the Quai d'Orsay, the structural problems within the French economy remained so great that French industry and agriculture would require continued protection and state assistance within the confines of the French Union for years to come. For others the remaining problems, such as the small size of firms and the fragmentation of the domestic market, were caused by protection rather than solved by continued protection. The

Monnet Plan was seen as a unique event, which, through a combination of exceptional circumstances, had been successful in overcoming the major obstacles blocking French economic development. Only exposure to a larger market and a degree of competition would enable growth to continue.

One of the reasons for such fundamentally different interpretations of the state of the French economy in the 1950s was that after almost thirty years of rigorous protection the potential competitiveness of the economy was simply not known. The balance of payments position, which was the indicator used by French planners and international bodies such as the IMF and the OEEC, did not reveal the competitiveness of individual sectors of the economy. The problem was compounded by the fact that in the short period of partial trade liberalization between the autumn of 1949 and February 1952 two separate factors clouded any clear view of the effect of such liberalization. These were the changes in the exchange rate in September 1949 and the Korean War, which began just a few days before the European Payments Union entered into force. How these events were interpreted coloured the debate over the state of the French economy and by extension over the strength of France's position in the world. It was a debate which was in many ways concluded with the ratification of the Treaty of Rome in July 1957. Until then economic liberals argued with protectionists, 'modernizers' with 'Malthusians', imperialists with 'realists', European integrationists with nationalists. Even within these categories there were divisions. Liberals were divided over how best to dismantle protection. Of those in favour of European integration some preferred a sectoral approach building on the success of Monnet and Schuman in the Coal and Steel Community while others advocated a common market. Nor was the debate confined to politicians and political parties outside the communist monolith; it took place within the civil service as well.

That these divisions, of which the rapid turnover of governments was but one indication, did not lead to policy inertia or economic stagnation can be explained partly by the external pressure on France from its partners in the OEEC and the ECSC. This pressure stemmed from a determination to ensure the continuation of a set of arrangements which was proving to be extremely beneficial to individual countries and to western Europe as a whole. In place of the unemployment, misery and mutually destructive protectionist policies of the 1930s, the 1950s were characterized by rapidly increasing employment, rising living standards, increasingly comprehensive social welfare schemes and increased trade. While France had since the war been a confirmed advocate of domestic social and economic reforms it was less persuaded of the importance of increased trade. A guiding principle of the planners – the 'modernizers' – in both Vichy and the Fourth Republic was that France should reduce its dependence on international trade. Only bychanging the structure of the economy by encouraging investment in import-substituting activities could the problem of the external deficit, which

130

Table 6.2 Comparison of forecasts and results of the Second Plan, 1952–57
(indexes of growth)

	Forecast	*Result*
Gross domestic production	124	130
Total consumption	122	133
Gross fixed capital formation	124	147
Exports	121	141
Imports	102	150

Source: Carré, Dubois and Malinvaud, op. cit., p. 463

had bedevilled governments in the 1930s, be solved. But in no sector were the planners' predictions so out of line with economic reality as in that of imports (see Table 6.2). As quantitative restrictions were slowly removed imports from the OEEC expanded. The question was whether this indicated a lack of competitiveness of French industry or an industrial capacity which was inadequate to meet the rapidly growing demand in France.

FRENCH PLANS FOR LIBERALIZING TRADE 1950–51

As early as 1950 the Ministry of Finance had interpreted the state of the French economy as evidence that reconstruction had been successfully completed. The index of industrial production was 23 per cent above that of 1938, although not quite back to the interwar peak, and France had a surplus on current account. The state, as the main financier of the reconstruction and modernization plan, it argued, could now bow out, leaving private capital to take over the financing of most investment. In a scheme drawn up in July 1950 Maurice Petsche, the minister of finance, advocated setting up a European Investment Bank. This bank would then have the responsibility for channelling capital raised on both the American and European markets into modernizing and expanding the successful sectors of the European economy. These sectors would not be selected by the state, as under the Monnet Plan in France, but would emerge as a result of exposure to competition on the European market. One criticism which the French Ministry of Finance had levelled from the outset against the British method of liberalizing trade within the OEEC was that it would not necessarily lead to greater competition in Europe. Since each member government remained entirely free to decide from which products it would remove quantitative restrictions, it would have been as a result of coincidence rather than design if they selected the same products. This led Petsche to propose once again that member governments of the OEEC should draw up common lists of products to be liberalized.

Once again his plan aroused opposition both inside and outside France. Within France there was considerable scepticism that the improvement in the current account position in 1950 was anything more than the short-term effect of the devaluation of the franc against the dollar and its revaluation against sterling in September 1949, which would soon be reversed. Outside France the Petsche Plan had to compete with other schemes designed to promote Europe's competitiveness with the Dollar Area. In the Netherlands the foreign minister, Dirk Stikker, had proposed a plan for liberalizing intra-European trade based on removing tariffs as well as quantitative restrictions from a common list of products agreed by the OEEC. In Italy the preference of the Pella Plan was to retain tariffs and other forms of protection but to liberalize capital movements and set up an investment fund to help dis-advantaged sectors and regions to become more competitive.[3]

However, the continuing improvement of the French payments position in the EPU ensured that the Petsche Plan, or some variant of it which was more acceptable to the OEEC, continued to be discussed within the Ministry of Finance. Unless the French government took some action to increase its imports from other OEEC countries the danger was that it would exhaust its surplus quota in the EPU, thereby entitling other members to suspend their trade liberalization measures *vis-à-vis* France. And as the conduct of the Benelux countries at the GATT negotiations in Torquay showed, unless the French took some action to reduce their tariffs, the low tariff countries might refuse to participate in the reduction of quantitative restrictions in the OEEC.[4] Furthermore, as the preparations for tariff negotiations in Torquay with the Federal Republic, which was participating in GATT for the first time, indicated, French industry was in a very much stronger position than had been thought even a few months earlier.

It was now considered that apart from the lack of competitiveness of French coal and steel, which it was hoped was being taken care of in the ECSC, the rest of German industry was not better placed than French industry. West German wages were higher. Social security payments accounted for 9 per cent of French GNP compared with 9.5 per cent in West Germany. French taxes were the equivalent of 25.7 per cent of GNP compared with 30.3 per cent in the German case. Furthermore, the use of taxes in West Germany was less advantageous to industry than in France. In West Germany 85 per cent of Federal and Länder receipts went on war-related charges and social security with only 11 per cent devoted to productive investment or reconstruction, although the tax rebates for investment and depreciation were very high in West Germany. In France 37.6 per cent of the revenue from taxation was spent on investment and reconstruction. Because the main source of finance for West German industry had to come from its own resources this meant that its prices tended to be higher than French prices.[5]

The result of such an optimistic assessment was that in December 1950 the French secretary of state for finance, Robert Buron, produced a plan to reduce both tariffs and quantitative restrictions within the OEEC. The plan combined elements of the Petsche, Stikker and Pella plans but went further in the direction of integrating the European economies than any of the others by proposing the creation of a common High Political Authority. This authority was to harmonize fiscal policy while supervising the reduction of tariffs by 10 per cent per year for five years and drawing up common lists for the reduction of quantitative restrictions. A floor was to be set for tariff reductions to enable both the British and French to retain imperial preferences and an investment bank and integration fund were to be set up to direct investment and compensate displaced labour.[6] However, as the Ministry for Overseas France pointed out, the imperial trading arrangements of Britain and France were quite different. Whereas Britain had double-column tariffs which enabled tariffs to be reduced while the margin of imperial preference retained intact, the French had single-column tariffs with many imperial products being imported duty free. The plan therefore undermined French imperial preferences. But the greatest opposition to the plan came from the United States which saw it as a challenge to the fundamental non-discrimination principle of GATT. Although discussions of the plan continued within the OEEC in the first half of 1951 they did so in very different economic conditions.[7]

Initially French industry had been well placed to take advantage of the increase in demand arising from the Korean War. But whereas the United States interpreted the North Korean invasion of South Korea as the prelude to a communist invasion of western Europe and urged European governments to join it in a large rearmament programme, the French government, already heavily committed in Indochina, considered the American response to be grossly exaggerated. French industry, following the lead taken by the government, did not join in the international race to stockpile raw materials but chose instead to meet the demand in other countries. As a result, French exports increased quite dramatically between the second and fourth quarters of 1950, particularly to the German Federal Republic, the United Kingdom and the United States. After that they declined partly as a result of the increase in the price of raw materials, particularly those imported from the sterling area, partly due to the restrictions placed first on German imports, to correct its chronic deficit in the EPU, and then on British and American imports.

From April 1951 the French monthly position in the EPU deteriorated. Legislative elections in July 1951 revealed a marked shift to the right in French politics. The communist party lost 44 per cent of its seats while de Gaulle's new party, the Rassemblement du Peuple Français (RPF), which was standing for the first time, secured 20 per cent of the seats in the National Assembly. The period of optimism and confidence had gone. On 15 September 1951 the interministerial economic committee, meeting for the first time since the elections, approved a plan for tariff reductions drafted by the new minister for foreign trade, Pierre Pflimlin. This plan called for all members of GATT to reduce their tariffs by 30 per cent over three years. These reductions were to be calculated not by individual items but by the weighted average of customs protection for each large sector of the economy. Ostensibly Pflimlin's plan was a response to the American criticisms of the earlier French proposals for tariff reduction in the OEEC but, in view of recent changes in American commercial legislation, it was possible to see it in quite a different light. In June 1951 the United States had passed the Trade Agreements Extension Act under which American trade was to be regulated until June 1953. This was based on the highly protectionist legislation of 1934 and included an escape clause, the 'peril point', which had been dropped in 1949, and the 'Buy American Act' under which no good could be imported into the United States if it was 25 per cent cheaper than an equivalent American good. Thus, while the proposal of December 1950 had raised the hopes of the Benelux countries that a means could be found to reduce the high tariff levels in the OEEC, since Pflimlin's proposal was targeted as much at high American tariffs as at high European ones, it threatened to make tariff reduction in Europe even more difficult to achieve.

The Quai d'Orsay, which had not been consulted beforehand, was critical of Pflimlin's proposal, as were the low tariff countries in the OEEC. The initial reaction was that European industry would not be able to compete with industry in the United States, where productivity levels had expanded further as a result of the Korean War. On reflection, though, Pflimlin's plan was interpreted more as an attempt to scupper all moves to reduce the high tariff levels in Europe while deflecting any criticism for the lack of progress away from France and on to the United States. But however sceptical they were of the French motives in presenting the plan, the Benelux countries did agree to give temporary support to Pflimlin's proposal rather than present one of their own for tariff reduction in western Europe.[8] Their scepticism seemed justified when, the following February, the French government restored all its quantitative restrictions on trade to deal with a crisis in both its external and domestic finances.

THE RETURN TO PROTECTIONISM

Not only was France running a trade deficit with the United States but in February 1952 it had a deficit of 163 million dollars with the EPU of which 100 million dollars had to be settled in gold almost immediately. At that time its official reserves of gold and hard currency amounted to 547 million dollars. This was just 100 million dollars more than at the lowest point of the postwar period in September 1947, when it had prompted emergency assistance from the United States and, on the most conservative estimates, was one-fifth the value of privately owned gold holdings. Following the French government's reimposition of trade restrictions the EPU extended an unconditional loan of 100 million units of account to the government in March 1952. This arose largely because of the United States' determination to thwart the attempts of the Belgian government to extend a bilateral credit to France and thereby reduce its own surplus position in the EPU – a surplus which the Americans claimed stemmed from the low level of Belgium's contribution to NATO.[9]

Alongside this external crisis the government of Edgar Faure faced a budget deficit which it claimed was due to a defence burden which far exceeded its domestic resources, and which was greater than that of its continental European partners (see Table 6.3).

Although President Truman had agreed to a number of measures to help reduce this burden, including the transfer of 100 million dollars from the military aid programme to the economic aid programme, as well as 600 million dollars for the purchase of military bases in France and North Africa and 200 million dollars to buy military goods for the war in Indochina,[10] the government was still left with a budget deficit. In February 1952 it proposed to cover the deficit by raising taxes by 15 per cent, an extremely unpopular measure in the circumstances. The bill was defeated in the National Assembly by the communists and the Gaullists causing the government to resign. The only basis on which Antoine Pinay was subsequently able to form a government was by promising to balance the budget without increasing taxes. Among his advisers Pinay included Pierre Flandin, who as prime

Table 6.3 Comparative burden of defence expenditure
(defence expenditure as a proportion of GNP)

Country	1949	1950	1951	1952	1953	1954
Belgium	2.9	2.8	4.2	6.2	6.8	6.9
Luxembourg	1.1	1.6	1.9	2.9	4.3	5.2
Canada	2.6	3.1	6.6	9.3	10.2	–
Denmark	2.0	1.8	2.2	2.9	4.5	–
France	6.4	6.7	8.6	11.1	12.5	12.7
Greece	7.5	7.5	11.0	8.0	8.5	8.6
Iceland	–	–	–	–	–	–
Italy	4.5	4.8	5.3	5.8	5.6	5.8
Netherlands	4.2	5.1	5.5	6.2	7.6	8.5
Norway	2.8	2.4	3.3	4.5	6.0	6.1
Portugal	3.8	3.6	3.4	3.7	4.7	4.1
Turkey	9.2	7.8	7.4	7.8	–	–
United Kingdom	7.1	7.4	9.1	11.4	12.5	12.2
United States	5.6	5.4	10.8	14.7	15.2	14.1
West Germany[1]	6.5	5.4	6.0	7.4	7.4	9.6

Source: PRO T 237/113
Note: [1] Based on occupation costs 1949–51, on occupation costs plus allowable other defence expenditures 1952–53 and on the German proposal plus allowable other defence expenditures 1954.

minister before the war had carried out similar pledges with disastrous consequences for the economy.[11] With the support also of the Bank of France Pinay argued that this pledge would in itself inspire sufficient confidence in the economy for those hoarding gold to subscribe to a loan. Ignoring advice from the Ministry of Finance Pinay launched the loan on 26 May 1952. It raised about 35 tons of gold out of an estimated 3 to 4 million tons. As a result the government, to keep to its election promise, cut both civil investment and the housing budget in what was the last year of the Monnet Plan. The MRP, which had compromised itself by agreeing to participate in a right-wing government on condition that Robert Schuman should remain as foreign minister, tried unsuccessfully to limit the damage by insisting that the second modernization plan should be implemented at the end of 1952.[12]

What actually happened was that industrial production declined, the trade deficit worsened and the Second Plan was not inaugurated until 1954. Whereas France's cumulative deficit in the EPU had amounted to 200 million dollars at the end of 1951, this had risen to 625 million dollars by the end of 1952 and exceeded its quota by 105 million dollars. Two-thirds of the deficit in 1952 was with the Sterling Area and was, as the French government correctly claimed, due to the trade restrictions reimposed by the British in November 1951. Since it would have been pointless to have devalued the franc in these circumstances, the government tried instead to put pressure on Britain to remove quantitative restrictions on those goods exported by France, as well as placing more armaments orders with French firms, inviting the Commonwealth to discriminate in France's favour and increasing the British tourist allowance. In spite of the British government's decision to relax its import restrictions on textiles, French exports, particularly consumer goods, continued to decline. The result was a reduction in confidence leading to a stagnation in industrial production in

Table 6.4 Indices for industrial production, including building, in 1952

Country	1946=100	1938=100	Best prewar year=100
Netherlands	200	145	130 (1939)
France	171	144	108 (1929)
West Germany	–	125	125 (1938)
Italy	152	146	144 (1929)
Belgium	147	139	95 (1929)
Norway	145	149	139 (1939)
Denmark	144	145	135 (1939)
Canada	138	216	205 (1928)
United Kingdom	137	133	127 (1937)
United States	128	248	181 (1929)
Sweden	121	165	151 (1939)

Source: Commissariat au Plan, Rapport sur la réalisation du plan de modernisation et d'équipement de l'Union française. Année 1952 (Paris, 1953)

the second half of 1952. At the same time public expenditure increased, due to the rise in defence expenditure, causing the budget deficit to grow. With little reason to think that Pinay would be any more successful in 1953 than he had been in 1952 the National Assembly rejected his budget in December 1952, causing him to resign.[13]

In the year which was to mark the completion of the Monnet Plan the index of French industrial production was just 8 per cent above that of the best prewar year, 1929. In comparison with other countries, for which 1952 was also a year of recession, French performance was among the worst. In terms of the rate of completion of those sectors selected as priorities by the planners Table 6.5 below reveals a greater measure of success.

Between February 1952 when France suspended trade liberalization and June 1953 the OEEC was broadly sympathetic to the French payments problem. But given that the rest of the OEEC, excluding Britain, had continued to liberalize trade the governments of the Federal Republic of Germany, Belgium, Sweden and Switzerland in particular were to argue that the French action, by ignoring the OEEC principle of reciprocity, was distorting European trade and arguably making trade liberalization even less possible in the future.[14] In September 1953 the Dutch foreign minister, Jan Willem Beyen, formally revived the earlier efforts to reduce tariffs in Europe.[15] This time, however, he proposed that tariff reductions were to take place within the six ECSC countries, and were to lead to a full customs

Table 6.5 Objectives and results in 'Basic Sectors' of First Modernization and Equipment Plan, 1947–52

Sector	Unit	Actual 1929	Actual 1938	Objective 1952–53	Actual 1952	Degree of completion (%)
Energy						
Coal	million tons	55	47.6	60.0	57.4	96
Electricity	thousand million kwh	15.6	20.8	43.0	40.8	95
Petroleum products	million tons (refined)	0	7.0	18.7	21.5	115
Industrial means of production						
Steel	million tons	9.7	6.2	12.5	10.9	87
Cement	million tons	6.2	3.6	8.5	8.6	101
Agricultural means of production						
Tractors	thousands	1.0	1.7	40.0	25.3	63
Nitrogenous fertilizer	thousand tons	73.0	177.0	300.0	285.0	95

Sources: Commissariat au Plan, Rapport sur la réalisation du plan de modernisation et d'equipement de l'Union française. Année 1952 (Paris, 1953); W. Baum, op. cit., p. 39

union, to complement the European Defence Community, then under negotiation, and to comply with the rules of GATT.

The effect of Beyen's proposal on Britain was immediate. A customs union of the six European countries complicated Britain's plans for taking the OEEC into the one-world system of Bretton Woods in which sterling along with the dollar would finance international trade. By raising the issue of liberalizing trade by reducing tariffs it exposed Britain's determination to retain its system of imperial preferences in defiance of the United States and of GATT. As in 1949, the British government insisted that trade liberalization should take the form of reducing quantitative restrictions. It promptly announced its compliance with the 75 per cent stage of trade liberalization and persuaded the OEEC Council to set a target beyond that of 75 per cent.

France was now caught in the pincers of the Benelux policy to remove tariffs within Europe of the Six and the British policy to accelerate the reduction of quantitative restrictions on trade within the OEEC. France, which was the only country in the OEEC not to have reached the 75 per cent stage, was asked to report to the the OEEC Council before 1 March 1954 on the steps which it was taking to reach it. The application of either policy implied a deterioration of the French external deficit, as the extension of quotas from 8 per cent in October 1953 to 18 per cent in December 1953 confirmed.[16] It was to find out why such a small measure of trade liberalization had produced a 30 per cent increase in imports that the Ministry of Finance decided to set up a special commission of inquiry. The obvious starting point was that French prices were higher than those in other OEEC countries. Had the price disparity been a recent phenomenon, associated with the Korean War perhaps, then the Ministry of Finance felt that devaluation would have been an obvious response. But whereas wholesale prices had increased by more in France between June 1950 and November/December 1953 than in other European countries they had also increased by more between 1928 and November 1953, which suggested more complex causes and remedies.

The inquiry which was undertaken by a commission of 24 people under the direction of Roger Nathan, the director of external relations at the

Table 6.6 Increase in wholesale prices in European countries (percentages)

Country	June 1950 to November/December 1953	1928 to November 1953
France	33.5	100
Great Britain	27.1	77
Germany	25.3	97
Italy	12.1	77.5
Belgium	12.9	113

Source: Ministère des Finances, Rapport général de la commission créée par arrêté du 6 janvier 1954 pour l'étude des disparités entre les prix français et étrangers (Paris, 1954), pp. 7–8

Ministry of Economic Affairs between 1946 and 1948, opened on 6 January 1954. By focusing on those costs that were policy-related it identified two general categories – those which stemmed from the policy of increased protection as practised since 1931, and those related to domestic factors such as wages and taxation. In general the commission noted that it was goods produced from domestic raw materials, or which incorporated a high degree of value added, which had enjoyed the greatest protection since 1931. But it was also true that even when France imported goods the price paid was often higher than the world price, particularly if they were transported in French ships, or came from the French colonies or from countries with which France, for foreign exchange reasons, wanted to trade.

But while it was a straightforward matter to calculate, for example, the extra costs to the textile industry incurred from importing Egyptian rather than American cotton, the Commission found it virtually impossible to calculate the extra costs from wages and taxation. Wage rates were higher in France than in the German Federal Republic, Italy or the Netherlands, but lower than in the United Kingdom, Belgium or Switzerland. In addition, overtime rates started after 40 hours in France, after 44 hours in Britain and after 48 hours elsewhere. Other costs to the employer such as social security payments were also higher in France than elsewhere. Conversely, the total fiscal burden, that is taxation as a proportion of GNP, was lower in France than in Britain or Germany. In 1952 it was 23 per cent in France, 25.5 per cent in the Federal Republic and 29.6 per cent in Britain. But these figures, as the authors of the report pointed out, disguised the real burden of taxation on French industry. Since France was less industrialized than Britain or West Germany, and since it was easier for the government to impose taxes on industry than on agriculture or services, French industry was penalized relative to its competitors. Higher taxes reduced savings, and since savings and investment were considered to be closely linked, they prevented firms from making the investment necessary to reduce costs and prices.

The commission's most important recommendations were based on encouraging the expansion of industrial production through fiscal reform. This involved a shift in taxation from indirect to direct taxes, an increase in the standard rate of direct taxation and a replacement of the tax on production by a tax on value added. It felt that any reduction in social charges would lead to a rise in wages and so called instead for a reduction in overtime rates, for a relaxation of the 40-hour week, and for other countries to join France in implementing the Geneva Convention on equal pay for men and women. Provided that these reforms were implemented, then and only then could trade be liberalized.

However, as Nathan stressed in a covering letter, these recommendations represented a compromise between very different viewpoints within the commission. He himself, along with seven others, wanted to recommend that trade liberalization should not be dependent on the prior implementation of fiscal reforms but should be started immediately. Only in that way, he argued, would the urgency of the situation and the need for reform be apparent. In order to ease the shock for French producers until the reforms were implemented, he suggested that as quantitative restrictions were removed a temporary tax could be applied to imports, the size of which would vary according to the disparity in price and the existing tariff protection.

Another member of the commission distanced himself from those conclusions of the report which stressed that taxes and public expenditure were partly responsible for the difference in price between French goods and foreign goods, on the grounds that exports were exempt from French taxes while imports were subject to them, yet price differences remained. The concern of those who recommended trade liberalization was that it should not lead to unemployment. This meant that the government should promote modernization, particularly in export-orientated sectors, while helping those facing over-production to adjust. But neither these criticisms nor the recommendations arising from them were written into the main report.

One of the problems with the Nathan Commission's policy recommendations was that they hindered rather than helped France meet its obligation to the OEEC's trade liberalization programme. And since January 1954, when the commission had been set up, the consequences to France of non-compliance had become more serious.

Britain's resumption of trade liberalization in the OEEC made the restoration of sterling convertibility much more likely than it had been when sections of the Conservative government had proposed it in 1952.[17] And whereas the French had been secure in the knowledge that the Americans opposed the convertibility of sterling on foreign policy grounds, since it would have led to the break-up of the EPU, this was no longer the case by 1954. Publication of the Randall Report in the United States in January 1954 now implied that there was no contradiction between American support for sterling convertibility and for stabilizing political conditions in western Europe through some form of integration. The problem for France was that the convertibility of sterling in 1954 might have entailed the convertibility of the Deutschmark, leaving France with the choice of retaining a non-convertible currency or being forced into a more competitive multilateral system at a time not of its own choosing.

Indeed, the Quai d'Orsay felt that unless the United States, which had a current account surplus (excluding economic and military aid) with all the main regions of the world, did much more to reduce its tariffs and its protectionism, then a one-world system simply would not work. What was needed was for the United states to invest in the economies of developing countries in order to promote a pattern of triangular trade as in the nineteenth century.[18]

But if the franc did not become convertible and the Deutschmark did, this would divert German exports to convertible currencies thereby undermining trade between France and Germany. Not only would it undermine the operation of the European Coal and Steel Community, with damaging consequences for France's foreign policy, but it would make it harder for France to continue the rapid expansion of the importation of German machinery, machine tools and parts which was stimulating the modernization of the French economy. On the other hand, if the franc did become convertible, then France would have to pay back gold or dollars to the EPU. At the same time French industry would lose most of the protection which it enjoyed in the French overseas territories. Since many of these countries did not have tariffs it was largely through quantitative restrictions and exchange controls that France was able to ensure privileged access for French exports. In 1953 the overseas territories had absorbed 37 per cent of French exports, whereas Europe of the Six had absorbed 19 per cent.

In April 1954 the OEEC Council approved a recommendation that member countries should extend trade liberalization to their overseas territories.[19] If the franc were also to be made convertible this would open up these markets to foreign competitors and at the same time reveal the full extent of French privilege at a particularly sensitive time politically. If France had no option politically but to participate in a general move towards convertibility it had to buy more time to bring its external and internal finances into line and to develop policies to cope with some of the wider commercial implications of convertibility.

The American Treasury's view at this time was that the answer to France's problems was to restore the convertibility of the franc. This, it argued, would provide the external justification for the devaluation which many in France had been advocating for some time to enable it to balance its external payments and liberalize trade. Moreover, the dollar assistance which France was receiving for Indochina would, it considered, ease the move to convertibility.[20] But the Bank of England thought that, if faced with the choice, the French, because of their relatively low dependence on foreign trade, would prefer a return to bilateralism rather than upset vested interests and make the franc convertible.

Pierre Mendès-France, shortly before becoming prime minister, warned against any consideration of restoring the convertibility of the franc at that time in view of France's dependence on American aid to balance its external payments. Indeed, he went even further, arguing that such aid, far from helping the French economy, actually locked it into a cycle of dependence. In his view it diverted essential resources away from economically viable production and exports and enabled France to live beyond its means. The fact that France was able to settle its deficits in the EPU disguised the real situation.[21]

On the eve of the publication of the 'Nathan' report on price levels in France and the OEEC, Bidault, who had replaced the pro-European Schuman as foreign minister, discussed with Faure, the minister of finance, the various options open to the French government to liberalize trade. One course of action was to state quite openly that the French government could do no more than proceed to a symbolic liberalization of about 26 per cent of its level of private trade in 1948. However, it would at the same time continue to modernize the economy according to a plan which would in several years' time enable France to fall into line with the liberalization programme of the OEEC. In the mean time France would allow the other OEEC countries to discriminate against it when applying their own liberalization measures. However, the danger was that such frankness could well have been interpreted as a renunciation of French policy to organize the west European economy and would have been disastrous if most of the OEEC currencies became convertible. Even if, and particularly if, the French parliament rejected further integration of Europe of the Six in the EDC, in Bidault's view France would have to keep open the channel of cooperating with the other fifteen in the OEEC and must not be seen as incapable of implementing even its own propositions. In the event that closer cooperation among the Six was agreed, this would in no way lessen the need for cooperation in the larger framework of the OEEC. The ECSC was dependent on the EPU for its own successful operation. If France caused the break-up of cooperation within the OEEC, Bidault feared that it would lead to open competition among the European countries to win favour with the United States.

To avoid this Bidault wanted the Ministry of Finance to abandon this first solution. Since it was proscribed under GATT rules to increase tariffs, in order to meet OEEC obligations on the reduction of quantitative restrictions, he suggested, as the only possible course of action, that a special tax be applied to imports as quantitative restrictions were removed along the lines envisaged unofficially by Nathan. Bidault also insisted that the French government should implement the Second Plan which had been left in abeyance since 1952, with a view to improving levels of labour productivity and the competitiveness of the economy.[22]

The compromise worked out was that France would agree to participate in the OEEC trade liberalization programme but on condition that it could apply import taxes on a selected range of products. This would enable it to maintain its credibility as a European leader, particularly in view of the threatened convertibility of sterling and the break-up of the EPU, while exposing French industry to a greater degree of European competition, without endangering the balance of payments. The imposition of import taxes had the advantage over a devaluation of the franc in that the taxes were not applied to raw material imports or to imports into the overseas territories. At the same time it was agreed to set up a commission to explore

142

the consequences of forming a customs union with the overseas territories, to prepare for the day when the franc would become convertible. It was also agreed that the Second Plan for economic expansion would be implemented. Even then the Second Plan, when it was published in 1954, retained the concern of the Monnet planners to reduce the French economy's dependence on imports. For a 25 per cent increase in national product forecast over five years there was to be no increase in the volume of imports.

ALTERNATIVES TO GATT

Sterling did not become convertible in the summer of 1954, thereby removing the threat to the EPU for another year. But the British and Americans were now actively preparing for the day when European currencies would become convertible. At meetings of GATT in January 1955 they called for the trade liberalization measures undertaken within the OEEC to be extended to all members of GATT on the grounds that once currencies had become convertible discrimination between different monetary areas would neither be necessary nor possible. At that time the OEEC Council was recommending, under UK pressure, that its own trade liberalization programme should be extended to 90 per cent from 1 April 1955 and include 75 per cent in each of the three categories of trade.

France, which had just managed to reattain the 75 per cent target in the OEEC and then only with the help of special import taxes, was opposed to extending these measures to the rest of GATT. The Federal Republic of Germany, the Benelux countries, Italy and Austria were also opposed to the Anglo-American idea in GATT although not for the same reasons as France. Their fear was that the application of the principle of non-discrimination might lead to a reversal of some of the progress made in liberalizing trade in the OEEC rather than increasing international trade.

Benelux suggested inserting a clause in the revision to GATT which stated that the principle of non-discrimination would not apply to those countries which had achieved a closer integration of their economies and which were in favour of increased multilateral trade. This was withdrawn, however, when the United States reassured them that upholding the principle of non-discrimination would not mean that the degree of trade liberalization within the OEEC would have to be reduced, or, if it was, that it would be compensated for by an increase in world trade. In spite of this France, West Germany, Austria and Italy insisted on some safeguard of the progress achieved in the OEEC and argued that more was to be gained from increasing trade on a regional rather than an international basis.[23]

In terms of the global structure of French trade, exports to the EPU were increasing much faster than those to the Dollar Area, or indeed to the Sterling Area. Within the EPU exports to the five ECSC countries had increased by 42 per cent between 1952 and 1954, while exports to the Federal Republic of Germany had increased by 57 per cent. Even this latter figure disguises the dramatic surge in exports of French manufactured goods to the Federal Republic, which more than doubled over the two years. During the recession in North America in 1953–54 when French exports fell by 14.5 per cent, French exports to the Federal Republic of Germany increased by 25 per cent.[24]

It was partly to safeguard this trade with the Federal Republic, and partly to undo some of the damage caused by the French National Assembly's rejection of the EDC Treaty, that the Mendès-France government signed a bilateral trade agreement with the Federal Republic of Germany and opened negotiations to set up a joint economic committee. It was the French government's intention that this committee, by bringing together industrialists, civil servants and trade unionists, would be instrumental in solving some of the problems facing France. In particular it was hoped that it would encourage German investment in French Africa, promote a standardization of military hardware in both countries, encourage cooperation in the atomic field and organize exports to third countries. But the German government, in insisting that the committee should be composed solely of civil servants from both countries, ensured that it would remain ineffectual.[25] And in any case the committee did not meet for the first time until 11 May 1956, by which time both governments were involved in studying the Spaak Report to set up a common market and atomic energy community in the Europe of the Six.

Beneath the rhetoric of trade liberalization the French government was actually pursuing a strategy based on modernizing the economy within the protected confines of the French Union. But the internal and external pressures to change that strategy were considerable and mounting. Following the French retreat from Indochina the cessation of American aid, upon which that strategy had ultimately depended since the war, was to force the French government finally to face up to these pressures and to change the framework within which the further modernization of the economy was to be pursued.

NOTES

1 C. Sautter, 'France', in A. Boltho (ed.), *The European Economy: Growth and Crisis* (Oxford, 1985).

2 F. Caron, op. cit., p. 326; G. Tardy, 'La France dans l'Europe', in J.-P. Pagé (ed.), *Profil économique de la France au seuil des années 80* (Paris, 1981).

3 A. S. Milward, *The Reconstruction*, op. cit., p. 449; G. Bossaut, op. cit., pp. 729–30.

4 MAE, GATT A.10.13., no. 56, note from Service de Coopération Économique, 11 April 1951.

5 A. N. F[10] 5631, 'Note préparatoire pour les négociations', 16 November 1950.

6 G. Bossaut, op. cit., pp. 731–32.

7 W. Asbeck Brusse, *West European Tariff Plans, 1947–1957. From Study Group to Common Market*, unpublished PhD thesis (EUI Florence, 1991).

8 MAE, A.10.13, GATT 13, note from French ambassador in The Hague, 2 October 1951.

9 B.O.E. OV 45/39, note from J.S. Lithiby, 3 March 1952.

10 F. Lynch, 'The Economic Effects of the Korean War in France 1950–1952', *European University Institute, Working Paper*, no. 86/253, 1986.

11 P. Williams, *French Politicians and Elections 1951–1969* (London, 1970), p. 22. Flandin's greater notoriety, though, came from his telegram to Hitler congratulating him after Munich.

12 B.O.E. OV 45/39, conversation between Lithiby and Gaillard, 21–24 May 1952.

13 PRO T 237/176, report by OEEC, 27 April 1954.

14 MAE DE-CE 1945–60, 353, 'Comité de direction des échanges', 3 April 1954.

15 R.T. Griffiths, 'The Beyen Plan', in R.T. Griffiths (ed.), *The Netherlands and the Integration of Europe, 1945–1957* (Amsterdam, 1990).

16 MAE, DE-CE 1945–60, 353, 'Comité de direction des échanges', 3 April 1954.

17 A. Cairncross, *Years of Recovery* (London, 1985), ch. 9.

18 MAE, DE-CE 1945–60, 354, 'Service de coopération économique', note, 6 June 1955.

19 Min. Fin. 13 AD, note from DREE, 17 May 1954.

20 U.S./T/EUR/3/12/v.2, 'Position of France and Italy in a broad move to convertibility'.

21 B.O.E. OV 45/41, Lithiby to the Governor, 22 September 1955.

22 MAE DE-CE 1945–60, no. 353, report of meeting, 12 March 1954.

23 Min. Fin. 13 AD 76, note from DREE, OEEC Council meetings, 29 January and 3 February 1955.

24 A.S. Milward, *The European Rescue of the Nation-State* (London, 1992), p. 140.

25 MAE, 'Accords Bilatéraux, France: Allemagne', note, 2 April 1955.

7

MODERNIZING FRENCH AGRICULTURE

On the eve of the Second World War over one-third of the French labour force was employed in agriculture and yet France remained a net importer of agricultural products with an export cover of 35.2 per cent.[1] Whether the low productivity of French agricultural labour was a cause or consequence of the restricted size of the industrial sector and of the decline of France as a world power in the nineteenth and twentieth centuries has long been a central issue of debate.[2] Since 1892 when Jules Méline had responded to the threat posed to French producers in both industry and agriculture by increasing tariffs, French agriculture had demanded and received many and varied forms of protection.[3] After the collapse of world food prices in 1929 these had included price supports and quantitative restrictions on imports as well as tariffs. However, to conclude that protectionism itself was responsible for the relative inefficiency of French agriculture would be to ignore the evidence of the period after 1945. Indeed, one of the most marked changes in the economy and society of postwar France has been the number of people leaving the land and the vast improvement in the productivity of those remaining on it. Between 1949 and 1962 the rural labour force declined by about 1.75 million; a fall of 31 per cent. In the 1950s the rate of increase in overall agricultural productivity was greater than that in the rest of the economy whereas the reverse had been true since 1896.[4] What is even more remarkable is that this improvement should have taken place in the context of continued massive state protection for agriculture, little changed since the days of the Méline tariff introduced in 1892. But whereas protection before the Second World War had tended to rigidify the inefficiency of the agricultural sector, after 1945 protection accompanied the modernization of the agricultural sector. How was such change achieved?

Initially the proposals for agricultural reform after the Second World War were based on changing the pattern of land use as well as modernizing the methods of farming, in order to reduce and finally abolish protectionism. The view of Pierre Tanguy-Prigent, the young Breton socialist whom de Gaulle had appointed as minister of agriculture in 1944, was that protectionism had served the interests of French industry and the large specialist agricultural producers, particularly of wheat and sugar, rather than those of the small family-based mixed farmers who ranked among the poorest in French society.

In trying to make the small family farm a viable unit and extend individual ownership of the land, which before the Second World War had amounted to about 60 per cent of the cultivated area,[5] Tanguy-Prigent was following the socialist policy first outlined by Jean Jaurès, the party leader at the turn of the century.[6] But because this policy rejected the nationalization or collectivization of the land it found no support in the Marxist wing of the party. It was also rejected by modernizers, like André Philip, who argued that the primary function of the agricultural sector was to supply labour and capital to promote rapid industrialization.[7] In effect what André Philip was proposing was similar to the policy of those labelled the neo-physiocrats, who were writing in the 1930s. For them the collapse in the price of agricultural products after 1929 was due to agricultural overproduction. Thus their recommendation for reducing production lay in creating a highly mechanized large-scale agricultural sector from which the small inefficient peasants would be driven out.[8] Tanguy-Prigent, however, had the support of the academic agronomists who advised retaining the agricultural population while improving its efficiency through a programme of education, mechanization and farm restructuring. But for such a programme to be successful it required the full backing of the government sustained over a long period of time as well as the cooperation of the rural population itself. Neither of these conditions had been met in the 1930s but initially it seemed as if they would be after the Second World War.

One of Tanguy-Prigent's first actions as minister of agriculture was to abolish the organization set up by the Vichy state to assist it in implementing its agricultural policy. Known as the Corporation Paysanne, it had replaced all the existing agricultural groups, which were divided along religious, political and functional lines. Although many of the leaders of the new organization disliked the term 'corporation' since it implied more intervention by the state than they wanted, they enjoyed the power which it bestowed. The conditions of food scarcity during the occupation called for a high degree of state control over food prices, production and distribution. Although these shortages did not disappear when the occupation ended, there was considerable support for disbanding the Corporation Paysanne. Rather than re-create the prewar fragmented system of agricultural representation Tanguy-Prigent chose instead to replace it with an alternative unitary body known as the Confédération Générale de l'Agriculture (CGA). The only group not represented in the CGA were the non-farming landowners. As a peasant farmer himself, it was this group which Tanguy-Prigent saw as one of the greatest obstacles to his objectives of extending family ownership of farms and improving their productivity. And it was to undermine the power of the non-farming landowners still further that he reformed the tenancy laws.

Under laws passed in 1945 a minimum period of nine years was established for a tenancy and the conditions for renewal, rent charges or the circumstances under which eviction could take place were clearly specified. Where landlords took back land this had to be for the purpose of farming it themselves or for their sons. These changes in the tenancy laws, when combined with the reform of the law of succession passed in 1938, were to favour the poorest in the countryside. Under the changes in the succession law a single heir was enabled for the first time to take over a complete farm unit and to compensate his brothers and sisters for their share, over a five-year period, while taking account of his own work on the land.[9] But more radical measures were needed if the small family farm was to flourish in the postwar period.

Tanguy-Prigent's objective, which Monnet was to incorporate in his modernization plan for the economy, was to make French agriculture self-sufficient rather than remain a net importer as before the war. It was estimated that this would mean increasing output by about 12 per cent. If labour continued to leave the land at the prewar rate it was predicted that the rural workforce would decline by about 12 per cent over the five years of the plan, which, if the output targets were to be reached, would require an increase in individual labour productivity of between 25 and 30 per cent. How such an ambition could be achieved was seen to depend on the state acting with the agricultural sector in order to change the pattern of land use, improve the size and structure of farms, and encourage a greater use of agricultural machinery and fertilizers.[10]

THE MONNET PLAN FOR AGRICULTURE

Under the first version of the Monnet Plan the area of land under wheat was to be reduced by just under 20 per cent in the expectation that, by concentrating production on the land best suited to it, yields would improve by 25 per cent, and output would be slightly higher than over the period 1934–38. As a result France would be less dependent on wheat imports than in the interwar period when between 10 and 15 per cent of wheat consumption had had to be imported.[11] Some of the land not used for wheat was to be used to grow other cereals, thereby reducing the amount of imported fodder and saving on foreign exchange. At the same time the output of fresh fruit and vegetables, of which there was an observable increase in consumption over a long period, was to be encouraged. So too were the numbers of livestock, although more were to be used for dairy production than for meat.

These changes in land use were to be achieved through the selective use of price controls, while the improvements in labour productivity were to be brought about through a programme of investment in farm machinery, fertilizers and education.

148

Table 7.1 Targets for arable production under the Monnet Plan

Crop	Production (1,000 quintals)		Area (1,000 hectares)		Planned increase in yields in 1950 compared with 1934–38
	Actual 1934–38	Target 1950	Actual 1934–38	Target 1950	
Wheat	81,510	82,000	5,225	4,200	+25
Oats	45,600	40,000	3,280	2,250	+26
Other cereals	27,620	38,000	2,046	2,240	+26
Potatoes	158,000	168,500	1,420	1,100	+38
Industrial beetroot	86,940	105,000	315	350[1]	+9
Fodder crops	397,532	466,000	1,334	1,330	+17
Oil seeds	60	800	15	200	–
Dried vegetables	2,550	3,240	–	–	–
Fresh vegetables	30,680	52,000	–	–	–
Wine	62,770	50,000	1,531	1,350	–3
Fodder	471,490	668,300	15,531	17,250	+17
Fruit	8,500	12,000	–	–	–

Source: Commissariat Général au Plan, *Premier rapport*, op. cit.
Note: [1] Target proposed by the Commission de Production Végétale.

Table 7.2 Targets for pastoral production under the Monnet Plan

	Livestock (1,000 head)			Production (1,000 tons; except Milk: million hectolitres)		
	Actual 1934–38	Actual 1946	Target 1950	Actual 1934–38	Actual 1946	Target 1950
Meat						
Cows	8,717	7,000	9,000 ⎫	885	750	865
Other cattle	6,983	7,800	7,500 ⎭			
Sheep	9,760	7,000	7,000	105	50	65
Pigs	7,080	4,852	7,400	670	410	700
Horses	2,770	2,350	2,000	40	40	50
Total				1,700	1,250	1,680
Dairy products						
Milk				146	92	150
Butter				200	110	200
Cheese				250	90	300

Source: Commissariat Général au Plan, *Premier rapport*, op. cit.

The planners estimated that the investment necessary to implement the plan for agriculture would amount to 364,000 million francs. This represented 16 per cent of the total investment which they felt that the economy could sustain over the five years of the plan. Over half was to be spent on mechanizing the sector and for this reason agricultural machinery was selected as one of the priority sectors of the plan. Most of the finance was to come from the agricultural sector itself on the assumption that agriculture had prospered under the occupation and been spared in the 1945 currency exchange. 'Prospered' is perhaps a partisan word since in many cases it is argued that savings represented deferred investment rather than net gain.[12] Whichever view is taken, however, there is clear evidence that the money accumulated in the countryside was considerable. In 1942 the Caisse Nationale de Crédit Agricole was authorized to issue five-year bonds to collect these rural savings. By the end of 1945 it had collected nearly 6,000 million francs, or three times the estimated national income of 1946. However, since the Crédit Agricole was neither nationalized nor placed under the control of the National Credit Council it was effectively under the control of the Treasury. Since it was up to the Treasury to decide how and when these savings were to be used, in the interests of reducing inflation, it authorized their release much more slowly than requested. By the end of 1947 only 25 per cent of the total had been released.[13] And with the very high rates of inflation in the postwar years the value of what remained was effectively decimated. Indeed, this proved to be a rather discreet way of dealing with some of the profits made by French farmers during the occupation. In effect inflation represented the transfer of resources from agriculture to industry and transport via the state planning mechanism.

Table 7.3 Forecast investment in agriculture under the Monnet Plan

	1947–50 (thousand million francs)
Agricultural machinery	192
Land consolidation	8
Land improvement	13
Rural roads	6
Distribution of electricity and gas	55
Supply of drinking water	14
Food-processing equipment	46
Improvement of housing and villages	15
Forestry equipment	15
Total	364
Expenditure	
State	12%
Local authorities	10%
Agricultural sector	68%
Non-agricultural private sector	10%

Source: Commissariat Général au Plan, Premier rapport, op. cit.

MECHANIZATION

The priority attached to mechanizing agriculture was partly due to the depletion of the stock of draught animals as a result of German confiscations during the war, partly a recognition of the backwardness of French farming methods, and partly to compensate for the loss of labour since 1940. On this last point the calculations of the Ministry of Agriculture differed from those of the official census of 1946 in estimating the numbers working in agriculture. Whereas the census figures recorded an increase over prewar the Ministry of Agriculture argued that the actual numbers were 700,000 less but that, since those working in agriculture were entitled to higher food rations, there was an incentive to inflate the numbers.[14]

According to the Ministry of Agriculture if France was to have a level of mechanization equal to that of Britain or Switzerland, where farming conditions were considered to be comparable, it would need a stock of about 400,000 tractors instead of the 35,000 which it had before the war.[15] This figure was then halved by the planners in view of the limitations on French productive capacity and foreign exchange. In 1938 there were more than 700 firms and over 2,000 workshops which together managed to produce just 1,700 tractors of which there were 150 different models.[16] Since French tractors were petrol-driven, farmers preferred to buy imported diesel tractors, mainly from Canada and the United States, since diesel was both cheaper and easier to obtain after the war. This preference for imported tractors was disguised initially because French firms were not allocated sufficient metal to enable them to work at full capacity. In the first four months of the Monnet Plan only 3.7 per cent of the ferrous metal allocation was given to firms making agricultural machinery in spite of the fact that it was classified as a basic sector in the plan. But when the supply of cast iron and steel was taken out of state control in October 1948 and January 1949 respectively, and French tractor production increased, sales as a proportion of output declined. In 1950 fears of fuel rationing in the aftermath of the Korean War reduced the demand for

Table 7.4 Tractor availability in France, 1945–50

Year	French tractors		Imported tractors	Total sales
	Production	Sales		
1945	860	860	6,400	7,260
1946	1,900	1,900	7,600	9,500
1947	4,200	3,000	12,200	15,200
1948	12,300	10,500	15,500	26,000
1949	17,000	13,200	11,300	24,500
1950	15,000	9,000	12,000	21,000

Source: La France économique de 1948 à 1950 (Paris, 1951), p. 355

French tractors still further. Thus by the end of 1950 there were only 120,000 tractors in use compared with the 200,000 planned. Imported tractors failed to make up the deficit.

LAND CONSOLIDATION

Indeed the planners had recognized that due to the fragmentation of French land holdings tractors would be appropriate on only about 30 per cent of the land. Further mechanization was thus dependent on the prior implementation of other aspects of the modernization programme, and particularly of the land consolidation programme.

A fundamental problem seen to be inhibiting any development or improvement in French agriculture was the structure of land-holdings. At liberation it was calculated that over half the total number of farms were under 10 hectares in size, and 27.8 per cent were less than 5 hectares in size. That in itself was not an obstacle to mechanization, since according to a subsequent official estimate the minimum size of plot suitable for mechanized farming was 4 hectares. And in any case these farms of less than 5 hectares covered only 5.2 per cent of the total area under cultivation. The basic problem was that many farms were divided into strips, which were oddly shaped and usually not contiguous. There was also a regional dimension to this problem since most of the small, fragmented farms were in the poorest areas. The task was to reallocate or consolidate land rather than increase the size of the individual farm.

The devastation caused to land in the north of France during World War I had provided an opportunity to effect such a reorganization. Initially, under the Chaveau law of 1918, the initiative was given to the local landowners who shared the cost of any improvements with the state. The following year a special law was passed to cover consolidation in the devastated departments of the Somme, Ardennes, Meurthe and Moselle. But once again the local landowners had control over the operation and could suspend it if problems arose. It was not until 1935 that a commission was set up with legally binding powers to settle disputes. As a result progress was very slow and remained confined to the north of France.[17] By 1941 only 285,000 hectares had been consolidated.

The Vichy government with its greater emphasis on agriculture and under pressure from Germany to improve the efficiency of French agriculture introduced new legislation in 1941 to deal with consolidation. For the first time departmental prefects were given the power to initiate discussions, whether at the instigation of the local landowners or of the Department of Agriculture. This did not, of course, remove any of the problems, the most contentious being that of land valuation, but it did enable an official points system to be set up, and inject new dynamism into the process. In 1943 and 1944 119,657 hectares were consolidated.

After the Second World War the demands for farm restructuring far out-weighed the ability of the government to carry out the necessary evaluations, or indeed to provide the necessary credits, since the state had agreed to give credits of up to 80 per cent of the value of the land. And the value varied enormously, depending on whether the land was to be used for future development, tourism or farming. Land values, which had been falling during the 1930s and had begun to pick up between 1940 and 1944, now began to escalate. To ensure that the smallest farmers benefited in this movement, Tanguy-Prigent recommended that a land office should be set up. Land belonging to the leaders of Vichy's Corporation Paysanne and to the most notorious black marketeers was to be confiscated and placed under the control of the land office. This body would then decide whether to sell it or lease it to peasants or cooperatives in order to improve the viability of their own land.

The land office was opposed by the non-farming landowners whom Tanguy-Prigent had excluded from the CGA. They argued that the land office was evidence that Tanguy-Prigent's ultimate objective was the nationalization of all land. Thus far from winning the support of the mass of small farmers who stood to benefit from the reform, Tanguy-Prigent lost the propaganda battle and the National Assembly rejected the bill in 1946.

Under the Monnet Plan a programme of consolidation involving 10 million hectares of land spread over nine to ten years at an average cost of 1,500 francs per hectare was to be implemented. In the first year of the plan, 1947, 500,000 hectares were to be realigned as compared with 57,822 hectares in 1945 and 117,655 in 1946 rising to one million hectares after that.[18] But as Table 7.5 indicates, the speed of implementation was very much slower than that planned and the average cost per hectare very much greater. This was partly due to a lack of technical expertise in the Ministry of Agriculture. With a long history of non-intervention in agriculture the ministry had only two specialist civil servants in its statistical service.[19] But the delay was also due to the low priority given to it by the state.

Table 7.5 Land realignment

Year	Number of land units	Area (hectares)	Credits (francs)	Average price per hectare (francs)
1943	54	48,352	19,076,699	394.5
1944	82	71,305	33,102,923	464.2
1945	57	57,822	36,940,091	638.9
1946	142	117,655	103,651,084	881.0
1947	372	283,069	485,910,976	1,716.6
1948	518	395,958	1,156,014,323	2,919.5
1949	550	434,047	1,604,433,044	3,696.5
Total	1,775	1,408,208	3,439,129,140	

Source: Comité Interministériel de l'Alimentation de l'Agriculture, Rapport annuel 1949–50

USE OF THE PRICE MECHANISM

The greatest problem in implementing the plan for agriculture, though, was in using the price mechanism to change the pattern of land use. There were two aspects to the problem. One arose from the fact that the Ministry of Agriculture had little control over the prices set by the government and the other was that the experience of controls over food prices and distribution during the occupation had greatly reduced the government's room for manoeuvre in any case. The use of the price mechanism in planning agricultural production was justified by the Commissariat Général au Plan on the grounds that it was inconceivable to apply Soviet-style planning to over 3 million farms in France.[20] But there was a fundamental conflict between the Ministry of Finance's concern to control inflation by depressing food prices, particularly those of wheat and bread, and the need to restore and expand agricultural production.

While this conflict was not as stark as during the occupation when the Nazis had wanted to expand wheat production while keeping its price low, it nonetheless proved equally impossible to resolve. The Nazis' objective had been to expand wheat production in France once it became clear that the Ukraine would not serve as the granary of the new European order. To achieve this by using the price mechanism would have required setting a high price for wheat relative to that of meat and importing cheap fodder.[21] But given the importance of bread in the French diet such a policy would have fuelled inflation, increased opposition to the regime and imposed costs in foreign exchange. Since the policy of the postwar government was to reduce the area under wheat, while keeping its price as low as possible for the consumer, there should not in theory have been the same contradiction between the two objectives as under the occupation. By retaining controls over the price of wheat and removing them for meat, the government sought to encourage meat production relative to that of wheat, while at the same time ending one of the most invidious aspects of Vichy's agricultural policy. The mistake made was to set the price of wheat below what both the Ministry of Agriculture and the Office National Interprofessionnel des Céréales (ONIC) judged necessary to cover the costs of production.[22]

In October 1944 Mendès-France had recommended that the price of wheat should be set at 425 francs per quintal, which was slightly more than twice the 1939 level, whereas retail prices as a whole had risen by 180 per cent. This was then challenged by Tanguy-Prigent on the grounds that it would not even cover the costs of production and would result in a fall in output and a flourishing black market. But when the Ministry of Agriculture recommended a price of 500 francs per quintal this was rejected by both de Gaulle and Bidault on foreign policy grounds. Their assumption was that a price of 500 francs was much higher than the international price at which the Dutch imported their grain, which would make cooperation with Belgium and the Netherlands that much harder to achieve. The price was therefore set at 450 francs per quintal, judged as too low to encourage production by the Ministry of Agriculture.[23] A similar argument arose the following year and once again the recommendations of the Ministry of Agriculture and ONIC were rejected.[24] At the Palais-Royal Conference in July 1946 the General Association of Wheat Producers called for the calculation of the price of wheat to be based on the legal formula used by the Popular Front government in August 1936. This would have increased the price from 700 francs to 1,362 francs. The government finally agreed to a price of 1,112 francs, with a bonus of 10 francs for prompt delivery, although not to the legal adoption of the earlier method of calculation.[25]

THE WHEAT CRISIS

The price of wheat in terms of cost of production was not the only factor which affected its cultivation. The fact that the government gave in to political pressure and removed controls on meat prices greatly distorted the relative prices of wheat and meat. By September 1946 the ratio of beef prices to wheat prices was 13:3 compared with an average in the 1930s of between 6:5 and 7:5.[26] The incentive not to sow wheat or to feed it to animals grew and this was to have disastrous consequences in the winter of 1946/47.

The total area sown in wheat in that winter was 18 per cent less than in 1946 and only 65 per cent of the average of 1934–38. By an unhappy coincidence, the winter of 1946/47 proved to be abnormally severe, with frost destroying much of the wheat underground. As a result, yields per hectare fell by 41 per cent and the overall output of wheat fell by 37.7 per cent. However, if the same area had been sown in 1947 as in 1946, then, even with the lower yield, total wheat output would have been about 22 per cent higher, a difference of 710,000 tons. Instead of that, the government was forced to take a number of steps to mitigate the disaster. As a first

Table 7.6 French wheat output, 1934–48

Year	Area (1,000 hectares)	Yield (quintals per hectare)	Production (1,000 quintals)
1934–38	5,224	15.6	81,432
1944[1]	4,163	15.3	63,594
1945	3,783	11.13	42,093
1946	4,131	16.36	67,590
1947	3,393	9.62	32,660
1948	4,231	18.04	76,336

Source: Ministère de l'Agriculture, *Statistiques agricoles rétrospectifs 1930–57* (Paris, 1958)
Note: [1] Excluding the Moselle, Bas-Rhein and Haut-Rhein.

inducement to wheat growers, it passed a decree in March 1947 finally fixing and guaranteeing the price of wheat to cover costs of production.

The new system of price fixing was based on a calculation of the cost of all the elements of production per hectare divided by the average yield per hectare. The price was then set for a three-year period although provision was made for annual adjustment.[27] At the same time subsidies on bread were removed. In April 1947 and again in August the daily bread ration was cut. When the August reduction took the bread ration to a lower level than that reached in the blackest days of the occupation the government passed a decree, proposed by Tanguy-Prigent, under which farmers were required to sow, during the 1947–48 crop year, at least the same acreage of wheat as the 1937–39 average. Farmers who failed to comply were to be fined 10,000 francs for each hectare not sown. Until that took effect the government had to negotiate with the United States to import wheat under the interim aid programme. It is interesting that the quantity imported with interim aid was equivalent to that lost through the failure to sow wheat on the 1946 area. Responsibility for the crisis was attributed to Tanguy-Prigent, who resigned as a result. The following month, however, the entire government of Ramadier was forced to resign. It was a more right-wing government under Robert Schuman which took over on 22 November 1947. Control over agriculture passed from the socialists to the MRP with Pierre Pflimlin, a Christian Democratic lawyer from Alsace, being appointed minister of agriculture.

The most urgent and immediate task facing the new government was the implementation of a stabilization plan to bring inflation finally under control. For those analysing the problem of inflation in the Commissariat Général au Plan it was seen to stem from a number of different factors which had to be tackled simultaneously. But for Pflimlin there was one cause: the shortage of food.[28] This he claimed had pushed up food prices which then had led to pressure for higher wages. When granted, these had been translated into higher prices for manufactured goods. Because the government had not made agricultural reconstruction its first priority this spiral of inflation had continued and escalated, finally resulting in a foreign exchange crisis in the summer of 1947 and a wave of industrial strikes in protest against the decline in real wages. At a time when the average worker spent about 70 per cent of his wages on food,[29] the price of food played a key role in French economic and political life.

The remedy proposed by Pflimlin was to increase agricultural output by every means available. However, given that his analysis was not wholly accurate, his solution was to cause other problems in the future. The food shortage which had caused the crisis in 1947 was of bread, whereas the output of meat, milk, sugar and barley was higher in 1947 than in 1946. Furthermore, until August 1947 the wholesale price of cereals was below that of manufactured goods. The prices of meat and fats were considerablyhigher. Not only was this situation unacceptable to the large wheatgrowers but so too

Table 7.7 Trade of metropolitan France with the rest of the world
(in million dollars)

	1938	1947	1952–53 (estimate)
Total imports	2,001	2,330	2,117
Agricultural imports	294	419	117
Total exports	1,317	1,144	1,983
Agricultural exports	193	168	430

Source: A.N. 80 AJ 14, Commissariat Général au Plan, 'Note sommaire concernant le plan, 1952', 9 March 1949

was the planners' objective of improving wheat yields so that the protection, which the wheatgrowers had enjoyed since the 1890s, could be removed. Pflimlin was sensitive to these objections, but he faced the problem that if wheatgrowers were guaranteed a price which covered the costs of the least efficient, this would bring more land under cultivation and lead to a surplus on the French market, if the planned improvements in labour productivity were achieved. Determined to make a virtue out of political necessity he then argued that such surpluses could be exported. The dollar saving on wheat imports together with the proceeds from exports would help to solve the structural deficit in the French balance of payments.[30] And not only would it help to solve France's problem but it would help to solve the dollar shortage of OEEC countries.

THE REVISED PLAN FOR AGRICULTURE

To the French government and planners who were wrestling with the question of how to eliminate the dollar deficit by 1952, when the European Recovery Programme would come to an end, Pflimlin's ideas were seized upon enthusiastically. In one stroke they seemed to offer a solution to several intractable problems – that of domestic inflation with its destabilizing political consequences, that of the external deficit (and the dollar deficit in particular) and that of responding to pressure from the ECA to integrate the European economies.

Since the Monnet Plan had to be revised anyway to phase it in with the European Recovery Programme, and with the Americans insisting that European countries should cooperate with each other, Pflimlin's plans for revising the targets for French agriculture suited the planners' needs perfectly. In the revised plan for agriculture, which was presented to the Council of Ministers in July 1948, almost all the original targets for production were increased. This was to be achieved by keeping more people on the land rather than through higher labour productivity.[31] Indeed, investment was to be less than in the original plan. Expressed in 1939 francs the Monnet Plan's target was 57,000 million francs

Table 7.8 Revised long-term plan for agriculture (1948–52)

Crop	Result						Targets			
	1934-38	1945	1946	1947	1948	1949	1950 initial plan	1950 revised plan	1951	1952
Wheat										
Area surface (th. hectares)	5,224	3,783	4,131	3,393	4,231	4,213	4,200	4,400	4,530	4,660
Yield (quintals)	15.6	11.13	16.36	9.62	18.04	18.2	19.5	18.4	19.4	20.1
Production (th. quintals)	81,432	42,093	67,590	32,660	76,336	78,500	82,000	81,000	88,000	95,000
Barley										
Area	742	689	731	958	820	880	1,000	1,040	1,150	1,250
Yield	14.1	9.56	14.53	11.71	15.52	16.1	17.0	16.1	17.1	18.1
Production	10,741	6,591	10,626	11,227	12,731	14,120	17,000	16,800	19,600	22,750
Other cereals (incl. barley)										
Area	5,418	3,865	4,236	4,622	4,421	4,478	4,490	4,520	4,620	4,740
Yield	13.8	9.8	13.69	8.59	13.6	12.5	17	15	15.8	16.9
Production	73,600	37,990	58,010	39,724	60,535	56,000	78,000	68,000	73,400	80,250
Oil yielding plants										
Area	15	137	182	140	168	185	200	210	230	246
Yield	12	5.6	7.5	5.4	9.9	10	12	11.7	13	14
Production	180	777	1,359	768	1,640	1,845	2,400	2,450	3,000	3,450
Temporary grasslands										
Area	577	896	921	980	985	990	900	990	990	1,000
Yield	30.1	13.05	24.31	19.51	30.02	20	38	31.5	33.6	35.8
Production	17,376	11,697	22,398	19,099	29,584	19,800	34,000	31,000	33,000	35,800
Artificial grasslands										
Area	3,027	2,720	2,980	3,004	3,034	3,000	3,000	3,180	3,250	3,300
Yield	35.5	20.9	34.7	32.5	41.6	32	46	40.2	42.4	44.8
Production	107,552	56,867	103,248	97,747	126,335	94,000	138,000	128,000	138,000	148,000

Animal fodder										
Area	709	645	670	673	721	750	750	800	830	860
Yield	32.8	22.05	34.81	26.02	37.69	22	59	43.7	45.8	48.4
Production	23,912	14,217	23,319	17,514	27,167	16,500	44,300	35,000	38,000	41,500
Industrial beetroot										
Area	318	197	250	292	308	400	–	350	380	402
Yield	276	227.07	265.45	201.78	305.46	200	300	285	295	307
Production	87,852	44,699	66,293	58,923	94,250	80,000	–	100,000	112,000	123,500
Permanent grasslands										
Area	11,533	12,355	12,224	12,291	12,302	12,300	11,346	12,190	12,150	12,130
Milk										
Production (m. hectolitres)	146	76	95	100	115	125	150	150	160	170
Meat										
Production (th. tons)	1,700	838	1,250	1,445	1,675	1,850	1,680	1,926	2,052	2,200
Fats										
Production (th. tons)	325	274	302	280	362	400	440	447	498	549
Sugar										
Production (th. tons)	769	294	415	598	864	900	–	1,000	1,200	1,300

Source: Commissariat Général au Plan, *État des opérations du plan de modernisation et d'équipement* (December, 1949)

Table 7.9 Forecast investment in the revised plan for agriculture, 1948–52

Sector	(thousand million francs)
Agricultural mechanization	290
Land consolidation and improvement	28
Rural building	26
Processing machinery	94
Rural public services	48
Others	14
Total	500

Source: OEEC, Interim Report on Long-term Programme (December 1948)

Table 7.10 Forecast sources of investment in agriculture 1948–52

Source	(thousand million francs)	(percentage share)
Self-financing and Caisse Nationale de Crédit Agricole	280	56
Government	30	6
FME	110	22
Related industries	80	16
Total	500	100

Source: OEEC, Interim Report on Long-term Programme (December 1948)

compared with Pflimlin's figure of between 35,000 and 40,000 million francs.[32]

The plan was to export 1.5 million tons of wheat by 1952 and 250,000 tons of meat, as well as cheese and powdered milk. The planners hoped to achieve these exports by negotiating long-term purchasing contracts, similar to the ones which Britain had initiated in 1945 with many of its Commonwealth suppliers. The intention was to export 1 million tons of wheat to Britain, 0.3 million tons to Germany and 0.2 million tons to Italy. By substituting French wheat for American or Canadian wheat in these markets, the planners argued that this would help to reduce the dollar deficit of the OEEC.[33] But these targets aroused considerable scepticism in both France itself and OEEC. The Ministry of Finance questioned the soundness of the export projections when no studies had been undertaken of how French prices compared with international prices.[34] Preliminary discussions with Britain showed the full extent of British doubts that the French could actually reach the production and export targets set by 1952. As if to provide clearer proof of the change in their agricultural policy the French announced, at the inaugural meeting of the International Wheat Agreement (IWA), that they intended to be registered as a wheat exporter, whereas the previous year they had signed an agreement with the United States to import almost 1 million tons of wheat annually over five years.[35]

Table 7.11 Investment in agriculture under the Monnet Plan (1947–52)
(in thousand million current francs)

Sector	1947	1948	1949	1950	1951	1952	Total
Agriculture (including fertilizer and agricultural machinery)	47.0	60.8	93.7	107.7	153.8	168.6	631.6
Other basic sectors	119.9	256.9	341.8	401.9	443.9	496.7	2,079.1
Total	166.9	317.7	435.5	509.6	597.7	665.3	2,710.7

Source: Commissariat Général au Plan, *Rapport sur la réalisation du plan de modernisation et d'équipement de l'Union Francaise* (Paris, 1953)

Table 7.12 Sources of investment in agriculture under the Monnet Plan (1947–52)
(in thousand million 1952 francs)

Source	Total	as % of total
Self-financing	405.3	45.0
FME	188	20.7
Treasury advances	19	2.1
Budget	70	7.7
Bank credit and loans from specialist organizations	226	24.9

Source: Commissariat Général au Plan, *Rapport sur la réalisation du plan de modernisation et d'équipement de l'Union Française* (Paris, 1953)

The scepticism was fully justified. In spite of an investment of 908,380 million francs (1952 value) in agriculture between 1947 and 1952 neither the production nor the export targets set by Pflimlin were met. France remained a net food importer, even though output was in most cases higher than the average for 1934–38.

Productivity levels had improved but this was mainly because people had continued to leave the land at a rate of about 110,000 per annum over the period 1945–49 and 130,000 per annum over the period 1950–54. The question is why the government did not accept this reality, allow the rural exodus to continue, import food and concentrate on expanding industry to absorb the agricultural labour. Exports of manufactured goods would then have paid for imported food. Was the rejection of this option based entirely on the same political factors which had led to the revision of the plan in 1948 or on the shortage of foreign exchange and the trade deficit or on a different set of political factors?

THE SECOND PLAN FOR AGRICULTURE

When the second plan for agriculture was being drafted in 1952–53 the decision was taken to set an output target 20 per cent above the 1952 level.

At a time when peasant farmers were rioting in protest at the collapse of meat prices, once the postwar period of meat shortages had come to an end, and at a time when wheat exports had to be subsidized at a rate of 15 dollars per ton, this seemed a perverse decision to take.[36] Yet the expansion was justified by the planners on the grounds that, of the three possible policy options for agriculture, expansion was the only one which would stimulate the development of the whole economy. Of the other two options, one was to increase labour productivity but without increasing production simply by ending protection and forcing people off the land. This option was ruled out on the grounds that the industrial sector was not large enough to absorb the labour transfers, and that it would aggravate France's balance of payments problems by increasing food imports. The other option was for the state to continue protecting agriculture but not take any part in restructuring or modernizing it. This would result in a widening gap between living conditions in industry and agriculture and an acceleration of the rural exodus with the youngest and most able leaving first. For a government committed to guaranteeing a minimum wage and to achieving greater equality in income between agriculture and industry such a policy was politically unacceptable. The planners, however, argued that it was also unacceptable in economic terms on the grounds that over 5 million people working in agriculture constituted a market which was actually more important for French manufacturing industry than the export market. The challenge was to improve labour productivity in agriculture to raise incomes and at the same time reduce food prices for the French consumer. This meant overcoming the fear of French peasants that the investment necessary for such productivity improvements would lead to overproduction and a collapse in prices. Back in 1947 the planners had offered no solution to the problem of food surpluses;[37] now they argued that exports were the answer, and that until such productivity improvements had been achieved the state would have to subsidize both investment in agriculture and exports, and even import food if necessary in order to secure export markets.

Calculations of how much should be produced and exported depended on the predicted elasticity of demand for food in France as national income per capita increased, as the population increased, and as prices rose, as well as changes in the composition of consumption in both France and the rest of western Europe. Those drafting the second plan based their calculations on an income elasticity of demand of 0.3, assuming stable food prices . To cater for changes in consumption, and to reduce the need to import, the plan called for an increase in the production of milk, sugar, wheat, meat, fats and fruit and a decline in the production of alcohol, dried vegetables and tubers. The combined effect of an increase in national income of 25 per cent, predicted under the second plan, together with a degree of import substitution, and a birth rate which had averaged twenty per thousand over the period 1946–54,[38] was expected to lead to an increase in domestic food

Table 7.13 Average wheat, barley and milk yields in Europe, 1925–59

Country	Wheat yields (quintals per hectare)				Barley yields (quintals per hectare)				Milk yields (1,000 litres per cow per year)		
	1925/29	1934/38	1950/52	1955/59	1925/29	1934/38	1950/52	1955/59	1925/29	1934/38	1950/52
Denmark	28	30	36	–	27	30	35	–	3.0	3.2	3.4
Netherlands	30	30	36	38.6	30	28	33	38.5	3.3	3.5	3.8
Belgium	27	27	33	–	28	26	32	–	3.0	3.2	3.6
UK	23	23	27	32.7	21	21	25	30.5	–	2.5	2.8
Germany	20	22	27	–	19	21	26	–	2.2	2.5	2.7
Italy	13	14	16	18.6	11	11	11	12.5	–	1.6	1.8
France	15	16	18	27.8	15	15	16	23.4	1.7	1.9	2.0

Source: U.N. FAO, European Agriculture in 1965, annex 11, p. 19

consumption of 10 per cent. That left 10 per cent of the planned increase to be exported.[39]

At that time the OEEC imported 25 per cent of its total food consumption. The deficit in wheat was 36 per cent, for other cereals 21 per cent, meat 11 per cent, butter 16 per cent, fresh fruit 10 per cent and sugar 45 per cent. Britain and Germany were the largest markets, together accounting for 80 per cent of the deficit. If France was to become a permanent exporter of agricultural products its main competitors in sugar and cereals would be non-European whereas in meat and dairy products they would be European. However, given the low level of overall productivity in French agriculture, due to its relative undermechanization, the low consumption of fertilizer, and the relatively high price of industrial inputs, the planners argued that increases in productivity and in exports would be easier to achieve than in European countries which were more developed technically.

But the Ministry of Agriculture, which was held by conservatives after Pflimlin's departure in 1951, did not believe that export markets could be secured. It considered that after the failure of the attempts to integrate European agriculture in a 'green pool' European countries were becoming more rather than less protectionist. Investment on the scale planned would, it warned, lead to overproduction and falling prices. At a time when France had a chronic trade deficit the consequence of exporting food would be increased imports of manufactured goods and a continued dependence on foreign, mainly American, aid. The budget, which it submitted to the Ministry of Finance in December 1953, reflected this caution. But it was rejected on the grounds that the policy of expansion, put forward by the planners, was the only one which would lead to an improvement in living standards across the whole of agriculture. While one small section of agriculture benefited from the combination of low productivity and high prices it was at the expense of the rest of agriculture and the rest of the French economy. According to the planners, what was needed was to renegotiate France's commercial agreements to ensure that countries imported French food, albeit at world prices, in return for exporting manufactured goods to France.[40]

For such a policy to succeed the state had to be prepared, not only to secure markets and to subsidize French exports if necessary, but to contribute to investment in agriculture on a greater scale than under the first plan. Despite the public rhetoric which had accompanied the revised plan for agriculture under Pflimlin, public investment in agriculture had remained a small proportion of total public investment, averaging a mere 1.8 per cent of the state budget between 1948 and 1953. But in 1954 this changed, with 4.6 per cent of public expenditure being channelled into investment in agriculture. Table 7.14 shows the extent of this public commitment.

Table 7.14 Public investment in agriculture (in million new francs[1])

1938	1947	1950	1953	1956	1959	1962	1965	1968
0.8	25.5	64	20	1,524	1,479	388	1,216	1,411

Source: Ch. André and R. Delorme, *L'Etat et l'économie* (Paris, 1983)
Note: [1] Before 1959 the nominal value is divided by 100 to express it in new francs.

The government also renewed its efforts to secure export markets for the increased agricultural production. In negotiations with the Federal Republic of Germany, which had been the largest single market for French wheat between 1951 and 1954, it tried to reach an agreement in 1955 to export sugar, meat and milk as well as wheat. But, as the Ministry of Agriculture had correctly predicted, the Germans refused to commit themselves to importing French agricultural products in return for their existing industrial exports to France and demanded increased access to the French market instead. This meant that as the French widened their import quotas, as they were under increasing pressure to do from the OEEC, they would have less to offer the Germans in return,[41] and the contribution of agricultural exports to the French balance of payments would be reduced.

The task of modernizing French agriculture proved to be long and slow. Despite increased public investment under the second plan, the gap between the prices of key agricultural products in France and in the most efficient producers in the world actually widened in the 1950s (see Table 7.15).

The task of improving the structure of land holdings, through a programme of state-subsidized consolidation, proceeded much more slowly than had originally been planned. Between 1942 and 1961 only 3.2 million hectares were realigned, although a further 1.9 million were under consideration, compared with the target of 10 million hectares over a ten-year period set under the Monnet Plan. And since consolidation was carried out at the request of those concerned it tended to be the richest areas, particularly in the Paris Basin, which benefited.

In the rest of the country people continued to leave the land to take up employment elsewhere. In spite of the introduction of a guaranteed minimum wage for agricultural workers in 1950, the gap between wages in

Table 7.15 A comparison of prices for selected agricultural
products in 1950 and 1957

Country	Wheat ($ per ton)		Butter ($ per kg)		Eggs (US cents per kg)		Pigs (US cents per kg)	
	1950	1957	1950	1957	1950	1957	1950	1957
France	74	107	1.55	1.53[1]	67.4	87.3[2]	41.2	60.4[3]
Netherlands	–	–	1.10	1.10	59.2	56.6	42.6	45.0
Denmark	–	–	0.83	0.80	43.1	50.7	56.6	56.0
Canada	74	64	–	–	–	–	–	–

Source: OEEC, Fifth Report on Agriculture, 1960
Notes: [1] 1.65 at 1956 exchange rate.
  [2] 94.5 at 1956 exchange rate.
  [3] 65.0 at 1956 exchange rate.

agriculture and industry widened.[42] The first to leave were farm labourers and women. When they were replaced by tractors and other farm machinery the productivity of the labour force which remained improved. Production per man-hour increased at an annual rate of 6.4 per cent in agriculture over the period 1949–69 compared with 5.3 per cent in industry.[43] In 1953 the firms making French tractors were finally able to make tractors light enough to meet the demand of the majority of peasant farmers. This, together with the fuel subsidies, which in that year amounted to almost 20 per cent of all the state transfers to the agricultural sector, greatly increased the number of tractors in use.[44] By 1954 the production of French tractors was 39,800, a staggering increase over the prewar level of 1,700.[45] But such investment was not viable for those with farms of less than 5 hectares. Although the number of these farms declined from 800,500 in 1955 to 548,900 in 1963 that still left France with a large number of backward farms.

For all these reasons agricultural production increased slowly and the surpluses available for export remained small, and in the case of wheat in particular, subject to severe annual fluctuations (see Table 7.16). By the mid-1950s the contradictions in French policy were obvious. French agricultural modernization depended on a policy of industrial and agricultural protection. Food surpluses were to be exported in return for imports of manufactured goods negotiated on a bilateral basis within the OEEC. But under pressure from the OEEC for France to participate in the trade liberalization programme the basis of these bilateral contracts would gradually be eroded as France had less and less to offer in return for agricultural exports. Without guaranteed markets for agricultural exports it was most unlikely that French peasants would take the risk of investing if, as a result, output increased and prices fell. It was equally improbable that the French state would guarantee prices if surpluses remained unsold. What was needed was a multilateral framework in which French agriculture and industry would

Table 7.16 Actual French net agricultural exports, 1948–56 (in thousand tons)

Product	Year								
	1948	1949	1950	1951	1952	1953	1954	1955	1956
Wheat	0	0	457.5	231.7	0	0	973.9	2044.9	0
Wheat flour	0	0	152.5	231.3	195.2	188.1	343.2	490.2	306.2
Sugar (crude)	0	0	0	0	0	0	0	212.1	52.7
Sugar (refined)	31.8	55.9	142.3	217.3	165.3	138.4	175.5	249.0	295.2
Live cattle (000 head)	0	24.6	45.5	0	0	8.3	51.5	123.0	0
Live pigs (000 head)	0	0	49.0	0	0	2.3	0	0	24.9
Beef (fresh, chilled, frozen)	0	0	11.6	1.1	0	3.4	43.9	51.2	0
Pork (fresh, chilled, frozen)	0	2.2	9.4	0	0	0	0	0	0.2
Meat products (prepared)	0.5	1.8	2.4	3.3	3.0	2.9	3.4	2.8	3.6
Butter	0	0	0	0	–	2.2	2.8	11.9	5.5
Cheese	7.0	7.2	0	8.3	1.1	8.2	8.1	10.7	7.9
Condensed milk	0	6.0	10.3	⎰ 12.5	13.7	12.4	13.7	13.6	12.3
Powdered milk	0	0	0	⎱	0.2	0	0.1	0	0

Source: FAO, Yearbook of Food and Agricultural Statistics, Commerce, 1952 vol. VI, 1955 vol. IX, 1957 vol. XI; Annuaire Statistique de la France

continue to be protected against low world prices while benefiting from the incentives to invest and modernize by access to a market larger than the national one.

It was not until 1968 that Pflimlin's target of turning France into a permanent net exporter of agricultural products was finally achieved. Thanks to the common agricultural policy negotiated by de Gaulle the problem of disposing of these surpluses became one for the European Community to address rather than for the French government.

NOTES

1 Daniel Lefeuvre, 'Evolution sectorielle du commerce extérieur français', in Comité pour l'Histoire économique de la France, Le Commerce extérieur français de Méline à nos jours (Paris, 1993).
2 Vernon W. Ruttan, 'Structural Retardation and the Modernization of French Agriculture: A Skeptical View', The Journal of Economic History, vol. xxxviii, no. 3, September 1978.
3 Herman Lebovics, The Alliance of Iron and Wheat in the Third French Republic, 1860–1914 (Baton Rouge, 1988).
4 L.A. Vincent, op. cit.
5 P. Lamartine Yates, Food Production in Western Europe (London, 1940).

6 M. Gervais, M. Jollivet and Y. Tavernier, *Histoire de la France rurale. Vol. 4. La Fin de la France paysanne. De 1914 à nos jours* (Paris, 1977), p. 577.
7 R.F. Kuisel, op. cit., pp. 177–78.
8 G. Wright, *Rural Revolution in France* (Stanford, 1964).
9 ibid.
10 Commissariat Général au Plan, *Premier rapport*, op. cit.
11 J.-C. Toutain, *Histoire quantitative de l'économie française* (Paris, 1961), pp. 246–50.
12 M. Cepède, *Agriculture et alimentation en France durant la seconde guerre mondiale* (Paris, 1967).
13 J.-P. Bompard and G. Postel-Vinay, 'L'Etat-Crédit Agricole. L'Etat et le financement de l'agriculture 1945–1952', in Fondation Nationale des Sciences Politiques, *La France en voie de modernisation 1944–1952* (unpublished proceedings of conference, Paris, December 1981)
14 I. Boussard, 'L'Agriculture française – options et résultats', in Fondation Nationale des Sciences Politiques, *La France en voie de modernisation 1944–1952 (unpublished proceedings of conference, Paris, December 1981).*
15 A.N. F^{10} 5204, 'Ministère de l'Agriculture et du Ravitaillement'.
16 Commissariat Général au Plan, *Premier rapport*, op. cit.
17 E.L. Naylor, *Socio-structural Policy in French Agriculture* (Aberdeen, 1985).
18 Comité Interministériel de l'Alimentation et de l'Agriculture, *Rapport annuel 1949 – 50.*
19 A.N. AJ 80/15, 'Commission de Modernisation de la Production Végétale', annexe I, June 1946.
20 A.N. AJ 80/15, meeting of the Commission de Modernisation de la Production Végétale, 7 June 1946.
21 A.S. Milward, *The New Order and the French Economy* (London, 1970), p. 265.
22 ONIC was the successor to the Office du Blé set up by the Popular Front government in 1936.
23 A.N. F^{60} 897, report of meeting, 2 October 1944.
24 *Revue du Ministère de l'Agriculture*, September 1947.
25 *L'Année politique*, 1946.
26 *Revue du Ministère de l'Agriculture*, September 1947.
27 Comité Interministériel de l'Alimentation et de l'Agriculture, *Rapport sur l'état de l'alimentation et de l'agriculture*, 1955.
28 A.N. F^{60} 904, Report by Pflimlin, 20 January 1948.
29 D. Borne and J. Bouillon, op. cit.
30 *Revue du Ministère de l'Agriculture*, press report, July 1948.
31 R.T. Griffiths and A.S. Milward, 'The European Agricultural Community, 1948–1954', *European University Institute Colloquium Papers*, doc. IUE 6/87 (col. 6).
32 F. Braudel and E. Labrousse, *Histoire économique et sociale de la France. T. IV, vol. II* (Paris, 1980), p. 856.
33 A.N. 80 AJ 14, CGP, 'Agriculture. Contrats d'exportation à long terme', 22 July 1948.
34 Min. Fin. B16021, Grimanelli to the secretary of state for finance, 28 December 1949.
35 INSEE, *Etudes et Conjoncture*, nos. 3–4, 1948.
36 UN Food and Agriculture Organization, *Commodity Policy Studies*, no. 2, April 1953.
37 A.N. 80 AJ 15, Commissariat Général au Plan, 'Commission de Modernisation de la Production Végétale'; R. Dumont, 'Les conditions de réalisation du plan agricole', 7 June 1946.

38 Carré, Dubois and Malinvaud, op. cit., p. 36.
39 A.N. 80 AJ 54, 'Projet de rapport général des Commissions de la Production Agricole et de l'Equipement Rural', 22 September 1953.
40 A.N. 80 AJ 78, 'Note relative au Budget de l'Agriculture pour 1954'.
41 MAE, 'Accords Bilatéraux, France: Allemagne', note, 28 April 1955.
42 OECD, Agricultural Policy Reports, *Low Incomes in Agriculture* (Paris, 1964), p. 184.
43 André and Delorme, op. cit., p. 344.
44 ibid., p. 325.
45 W. Baum, op. cit., p. 297.

8

TOWARDS THE COMMON MARKET

When the Dutch foreign minister Jan Willem Beyen proposed the formation of a common market among the six member states of the ECSC in
April 1955, the French government did not support it. Nor did it support
the alternative proposal, launched on the same day by the Belgian foreign
minister Paul Henri Spaak and favoured by Jean Monnet, which was based
on extending European integration into the fields of energy, transport and
atomic energy. Yet two years later the French government had taken the
momentous and largely irreversible decision to sign the Treaties of Rome
setting up the European Common Market and the European Atomic
Energy Community, Euratom.

The reason which is most frequently put forward for this decision is the
foreign policy imperative of anchoring the Federal Republic of Germany
firmly in the west in a way which would not endanger French security. That
the French economy benefited as a result of participation in the Common
Market is either seen as entirely fortuitous,[1] or as a result of the policies
implemented by the new de Gaulle administration in 1958.

While the idea of setting up a customs union in western Europe had been
under discussion in French circles since the early 1940s, the more direct
origins of the Common Market can be traced to Beyen's first proposal to
the ECSC countries in September 1953. By this time the earlier French
interest in a customs union had turned into firm opposition. When the Six
had met subsequently in Rome and Paris to discuss Beyen's proposal the
Quai d'Orsay had argued, on the one hand, that more time was needed to
observe the effects of the ECSC, and, on the other hand, that it would
overburden the electorate to add a customs union treaty to the European
Defence Community and European Political Union treaties then under
consideration. But having been responsible for the defeat of those treaties
it was difficult for the French to find credible grounds for rejecting the
Dutch proposal when it was made again in the spring of 1955. The French
position was made even weaker by the decision of the American Congress
in 1955 to grant Eisenhower the power to reduce tariffs automatically by
5 per cent each year for three years. While this was half the rate called

for by Pflimlin in 1951 it nevertheless called France's bluff on tariff reductions.

The Quai d'Orsay, which had been opposed to Pflimlin's plan in 1951, was now as resolutely opposed to a customs union of the Six in 1955. On a general level it was sceptical of either the economic or political benefits of a customs union. Rather than promoting greater production it argued that it would encourage monopolies, cartels and price fixing and at the same time increase the gap between rich and poor regions. And far from securing France's place as leader of this customs union it would instead be a vehicle for restoring German political and economic hegemony in Europe.[2]

More specifically it argued that the Benelux countries wanted the common external tariff set at too low a level for France, that even the gradual liberalization of trade would cause insurmountable problems for agriculture while the safeguards needed to cope with the structural changes in industry were not under consideration. Finally, the fear was that it would force France to choose between the French Union and a European union, since the two were judged to be mutually exclusive.[3] On the other hand, if the French wanted to bind the Federal Republic of Germany more closely to western Europe than was the case in the loose arrangements offered by Britain in the Western European Union, then such a negative position was unhelpful. Another possibility was sectoral integration along the lines being proposed by Jean Monnet and his Action Committee for Europe.

Shortly after the rejection of the EDC Treaty by the French National Assembly, Monnet had announced his intention of not seeking renomination as president of the ECSC when his term of office was due to expire in February 1955.[4] At that time Monnet envisaged that the impetus for taking Europe further along the road to political integration could come from atomic energy. In many respects atomic energy was seen to fill the same key economic and military functions as coal and steel had filled in the prenuclear age in Europe. A study commissioned by the OEEC had concluded that the development of nuclear energy could enable Europe to become independent of Middle Eastern oil and American coal, thereby solving its energy and some of its foreign exchange problems.[5] In December 1954 the assembly of the ECSC supported a proposal to extend its own field of competence to cover transport and other forms of energy, including atomic energy. However, because nuclear energy was much more than a substitute for other forms of energy being also the key to superpower status, Monnet insisted that a quite separate community, Euratom, should be set up to deal with it.

As matters stood the French atomic industry was dwarfed by those of the United States and Britain, whereas it had become apparent, when France had tried to collaborate with Norway, the Netherlands and Switzerland, that France dominated the continental European industry. Negotiations with Britain had had to be broken off in February 1955 once the United States had made it clear that it would veto any collaboration on nuclear matters between Britain and France.[6] The suspicion of the French government was that Monnet, in proposing Euratom, was simply bowing to the American wish to control all nuclear developments in Europe and use Euratom to prevent nuclear proliferation. Edgar Faure, like Mendès-France before him and Guy Mollet after him, wanted to retain the option for France of building its own atomic bomb. Although no decision was taken officially in this respect until 1958 all the necessary steps were taken in terms of research funding to make this possible. As long as the French government remained ambivalent about the bomb, it was ambivalent about Euratom.

One consequence for France of rejecting the EDC Treaty was that the Federal Republic of Germany became a member of NATO and although Adenauer unilaterally renounced the manufacture of nuclear weapons, the French had no guarantee that this situation would not change. Mendès-France thought that this self-denying ordinance might last fifteen years.[7] In talks between the French foreign minister Antoine Pinay and Adenauer at the end of April 1955 the latter rejected any form of supranational control over nuclear energy, such as that proposed by Monnet, and argued that the armaments committee of the WEU was the most appropriate forum for nuclear cooperation. On the other hand, Adenauer was in favour of the Common Market, as were the Benelux countries and Italy.[8]

Rather than take an entirely negative position on both proposals for European integration the Quai d'Orsay decided that Euratom was the lesser of the two evils. Provided that it could separate the French military programme from the civilian nuclear energy programme in Euratom the Quai d'Orsay was prepared to support Euratom as a way of blocking progress on the Common Market. On the basis of this strategy, the tactics worked out within the Quai d'Orsay, for which Olivier Wormser, head of the European Cooperation Division, was mainly responsible, were that France should participate fully in all the discussions among the Six but ensure that the link between the Common Market and Euratom was broken. This was to be done by focusing from the beginning on those aspects of the Common Market which were most likely to divide the other five governments, such as the level of the common external tariff, the coordination of investment and the harmonization of social legislation. Having exposed their internal divisions on the Common Market the French would then offer the constructive proposal that the more straightforward Euratom Treaty should be signed first.[9]

Although Pinay himself was much more of an economic liberal than his adviser in the Quai d'Orsay, he nonetheless shared the popular view that much of French industry would not survive in the competitive climate of the Common Market.[10] The fact that Wormser's tactics were not instantly successful when applied by Pinay at the Messina Conference of the Six's foreign ministers in June 1955 was more indicative of the strength of support for a common market among France's partners than of any divisions in the Quai d'Orsay. Pinay was obliged to sign the Messina resolution committing the six governments to a new phase in the construction of Europe based on both a common market and Euratom in order to promote Euratom.

Such opposition to a common market was not shared by the liberals in the French Ministry of Finance. Bernard Clappier, head of the Direction of Foreign Economic Relations in the Ministry of Finance, and later to become governor of the Bank of France, pointed to the improvement in the French payments position in the EPU since 1954 despite an increase in the rate of trade liberalization as evidence that the French economy could survive in a common market. He also cited the experience of the Benelux countries which had achieved a customs union for industrial products without any prior harmonization of economic, social or financial policies even though wages differed by 40 per cent at the outset. Provided that the common external tariff was as high as in the United States and the British Commonwealth, that France could retain temporary safeguards such as the special import taxes and that a special system for agriculture was agreed, he advocated a progressive move to a common market.[11]

It was no accident that the French delegation to the committees set up in Brussels to draft a detailed report on the Messina resolution was left without instructions on the Common Market for almost three months. When they finally came at the end of October 1955 the list of conditions on which the French government's participation in the second and final phase of the Common Market would depend reflected the French government's continued hostility to the idea. The initial stage of tariff reductions was to take four years, after which another agreement would be required to complete the Common Market within ten years. During this first stage the legislation regarding equal pay, the length of the working week and paid holidays, and overtime rates would have to be harmonized in all member countries. From the first reduction in tariffs all discriminatory practices and acts of state intervention, which were not for the purpose of correcting market distortions or price fluctuations, were to be ended. A readaptation and investment fund was to be given sufficient resources to enable it to be effective in the first transitional period. Quantitative restrictions were to be removed according to the procedure used in the OEEC, while the common external tariff was to be calculated according to the weighted average of existing tariffs. Agriculture was to receive separate treatment and the market organized on the basis of a common agricultural policy. And, finally, there were to be a number of safeguard clauses which a member in difficulty could invoke unilaterally.[12]

The question in everyone's mind when the French legislative elections in January 1956 led to a new centre-left government being formed was whether the new government and the new National Assembly would be any more sympathetic to European integration, and the Common Market in particular, than the one which had defeated the EDC treaty. The composition of the third legislature made it seem highly unlikely. The number of communist seats had increased from 100 to 150 while the Poujadist party, which had been formed in 1953 specifically to protest against changes to the tax system, won 42 seats.[13] On the other hand, the number of Gaullist deputies had fallen from 80 to 20. On balance the number of deputies who were strongly opposed to European integration had increased and the 'Republican Front' coalition of socialists and radicals, which governed with a slender majority in the National Assembly, contained a small number of Mendès-France radicals who were also opposed to the Common Market. Thus, even though the rest of the government, led by Mollet, was sympathetic to the Common Market, believing that protectionism itself inhibited the further growth and development of the French economy, it feared a repetition of the EDC fiasco.

Since there seemed to be a majority in favour of Euratom it considered that the momentum generated by the successful ratification of the Euratom Treaty might make it easier to ratify the treaty establishing the Common Market. Thus even though the new government appeared to be continuing the tactics of its predecessor, its overall objectives were quite different. Whereas the Faure government had wanted to sign the Euratom Treaty in order to block the Common Market Treaty the Mollet government hoped that the very success of Euratom would make it easier to ratify the Common Market Treaty subsequently. This change in strategy led to the appointment of Maurice Faure and Robert Marjolin, both strongly in favour of a common market, as advisers to the government.

In bilateral discussions between foreign minister Pineau and his German counterpart von Brentano in mid-February 1956, Pineau tried to persuade the Germans that the Euratom Treaty should be ratified first on the grounds that the Common Market faced so much opposition within France that it could bring down the entire integration process. But the German cabinet, he was told, had recently reaffirmed its commitment to linking the two treaties and had the full agreement of Belgium and the Netherlands.[14]

While not abandoning this strategy the government began to consider alternatives. One option was to canvass support for the Common Market outside the National Assembly by appealing to the economic interests which had most at stake. But no one was in any doubt that this would restrict the government's freedom of manoeuvre rather than enhance it, unless the government had undertaken a study of the opportunities which access to the larger market and to a new source of finance for investment would offer French industry beforehand.[15]

The basis for such a study already existed. In 1955 the Ministry of Finance had commissioned an investigation into the competitive position of a limited number of sectors of French manufacturing industry, in order to determine the size of the import tax which would be needed as quantitative restrictions were removed. The sectors selected were machine tools, agricultural machinery, motor vehicles, cotton, artificial textiles and paper and card. The main European producers of machine tools were the German Federal Republic and the United Kingdom, where production was over three times higher than in France. Other suppliers were Switzerland and Italy, where production was less than in France. They had all removed their quantitative restrictions on imports. Tariff protection on machine tools ranged between 7 and 25 per cent in Italy, but only between 6 and 8 per cent in the Federal Republic, and was fixed at 20 per cent in the United Kingdom, which was similar to France. It was concluded that the main reasons why the French machine tool industry was not competitive in export markets were that social and fiscal charges were higher in France and that the domestic market itself could absorb the increases in production, unlike the situation in the Federal Republic, where surplus capacity existed. And because the market in machine tools was judged to be much less open to new suppliers than the trade in consumer goods the formation of a common market was not considered to be a problem for the French machine tool industry.

Price disparities were also a problem for agricultural machinery. But in this case the reasons were not considered to be the higher wages and social charges in France, but the lack of concentration and specialization in this sector in France and the high cost of investment. If an agreement could be reached whereby the French were to specialize in the production of petrol-driven engines for tractors, leaving diesels for the German Federal Republic, then a common market could, it was argued, be very beneficial.

The motor vehicle industry was heavily protected by tariffs in all the main producing countries. Tariff levels were highest in Italy at 35–45 per cent, but with levels of 30–35 per cent in the Federal Republic and 33.3 per cent in the United Kingdom, the French tariff of 30 per cent compared favourably. Although car production in France had doubled between 1949 and 1954 it was still below the level of the Federal Republic and in both cases output was well below that of Britain. A much higher proportion of production was sold on the domestic market in France than was the case in either Britain or West Germany. (In 1954 the figures were 78.1 per cent, 52.6 per cent and 56.2 per cent respectively.) But since the density of car ownership was considerably greater in both France and Britain, one car for every twelve inhabitants in Britain, and one car for every fourteen in France compared with one for every thirty-four in the Federal Republic, the greatest growth potential was in the West German market. The factors which were seen to undermine the competitiveness of the French car

Table 8.1 Structure of costs in the European car industry

Country	Price of steel products	Weighting of steel price in car retail price before tax	% difference in car price due to steel price	Level of wages including social charges	Weighting of labour costs in car retail price before tax	% difference in car price due to labour costs	Total % difference
France	100	20	–	100	40	–	–
German Federal Republic	100	20	0	75	40	10	10
United Kingdom	80	20	4	93	40	2.8	6.8
Italy	100	20	0	74	46*	6	6

Source: Quai Branly, Interministerial Committee for Questions of European Integration, SGCI 121.9
Note:* Including the obligatory cost of retaining surplus labour.

industry were higher wages and social charges and the fact that French prices incorporated a margin for financing exports which amounted to about 1.5 per cent of the construction price.

On the other hand, prices in both the German Federal Republic and the United Kingdom were said to benefit from greater economies of scale. If French car production could reach the same level, it was argued, savings of 2–4 per cent could be achieved through replicating the same scale economies.

The Ministry of Industry, however, felt that the disadvantages to France of liberalizing trade in cars far outweighed the advantages and argued strongly against it.[16]

The results of the study of the French cotton industry were even more pessimistic. The fact that the French imported Egyptian cotton rather than the cheaper American cotton, as a dollar-saving measure, was one reason for the higher cost of finished cotton goods. Another reason was that, in an industry which employed a high proportion of female labour (more than 50 per cent in France, and 75 per cent in Italy), the differences in wage

Table 8.2 Output and exports of motor vehicles, 1955

Country	Passenger cars	Commercial vehicles, etc.	Total	Exports	Exports as percentage of production
United Kingdom	897,500	339,500	1,237,000	536,300	43
German Federal Republic	692,000	216,400	908,800	409,000	45
France	553,300	171,700	725,000	164,000	22.5
Italy	230,800	38,000	268,300	74,650	28

Source: Quai Branly, Interministerial Committee for Questions of European Integration, SGCI 121.9

legislation affected the final cost. France was one of the few countries to have signed the Geneva Convention on equal pay. This contrasted with Britain where women were paid 34 per cent less than men at that time. Other factors which increased production costs in France relative to its European competitors were fiscal and social payments, the cost of energy and the rate of amortization of investment. But more obvious factors such as the structure of the industry were not in fact seen as significant. In France there were 910 factories of which 407 employed fewer than 50 workers and contributed 7 per cent to GNP. But in no European country was the industry very concentrated. The more serious problem was that the industry faced declining demand and increasing competition from non-European suppliers.

The situation was much the same for artificial fibres. The problems of the textile industry were thus seen to be quite different from those of other industries. However, when the French had argued in the OEEC that they would not be solved simply by liberalizing intra-European trade in textiles, as the British were recommending, they were not supported by the rest of the OEEC.[17] The situation of the paper industry was quite different. Since most of the competition was with Scandinavia it was felt that, given time to reorganize itself into larger production units, the industry would survive in a common market of six.

From the perspective of March 1956 the conclusions drawn from this study were that the problems of forming a common market of the Six were no less than liberalizing trade within the OEEC since imports from the Federal Republic, Benelux and Italy represented 70 per cent of all imports from the OEEC. Unless the formation of a common market was accompanied by a devaluation of the franc, a number of safeguards including the harmonization of social and fiscal legislation would be necessary for most branches of industry. On the other hand, not to join a common market and to retain quantitative restrictions on trade would not ensure that industries would make the changes needed to become more competitive. This was held to be true even for modernized industries for which demand was growing, such as the car industry, the machine tool industry or the electrical construction industry.[18]

Publication of the Spaak report one month later made no provision for the harmonization of legislation or for the adoption of temporary safeguard measures to protect sectors in difficulty. At an interministerial meeting called on 11 May 1956 to discuss the Spaak report, the consensus view was that if market conditions in all member states were not equalized through legislation in the transitional period, France would be unable to proceed automatically to the second stage of the Common Market as the Spaak report recommended.[19] Indeed, the provisions of the Spaak report for achieving a common market inclined the government once again towards pressing for the ratification of the Euratom Treaty first.[20]

The instructions which foreign minister Pineau took to the Venice Conference of Foreign Ministers at the end of May 1956 were that he was to agree to the Spaak report as the basis for the intergovernmental negotiations leading to the two treaties, but with certain reservations. These were that the length of time needed to proceed to the second stage of tariff reductions should not necessarily be four years, as the Spaak report stipulated, but should depend on the progress made in harmonizing legislation. The second condition was that the overseas territories should be included in the Common Market.[21]

One of the most striking features of the Spaak report was the absence of any reference to the overseas territories of three of the participating countries – France, Belgium and the Netherlands. This omission was judged by the French to stem from the wish of all these countries to retain control over their overseas territories in the belief that it would be possible technically to enter into a European common market while at the same time retaining a set of preferential arrangements with their overseas territories.

This belief was based on the assumption that the full integration of the metropolitan economy with that of the overseas territories could be achieved rapidly while the integration of the European economies with each other would take much longer. Once the integration process had been achieved, in both cases, it would be possible to keep each trading area distinct simply by controlling the origin of goods. Although it was felt that the costs, particularly to France, of investment in its overseas territories would probably depress its living standards relative to those of its partners, such disparities could in theory be catered for by adjusting the exchange rate. Thus, on the face of it France had the choice of joining the European Common Market with or without its empire. And judging from the absence of discussion in the Spaak report France would be under no pressure from western Europe to include the empire.

Nonetheless, certain practical problems were envisaged if France joined the Common Market without the empire. One was that it would have to retain tariffs on imports of tropical produce from the Common Market in order to protect the higher-priced exports from the empire on the French market. Another was that the continuing cost to France of investment in the empire would be at the expense of the modernization of the French economy even though certain industries would continue to enjoy preferential access to imperial markets. Whether the empire itself would be content to remain outside a European common market was felt to depend on whether the price advantage which its exports enjoyed on the French market was greater than the price advantage which French exports enjoyed on imperial markets.[22] Whether France would want to join the Common Market with the empire depended on the terms on which they joined, and it was largely to consider those terms that the French set up a special committee chaired by Alexandre Verret.

The first time that French ministers met after the Venice Conference was on 4 September 1956. In the light of the very positive endorsement which the National Assembly had given to the French plans for Euratom in July 1956 (provided that the Euratom Treaty did not hinder the French government's right or ability to build an atom bomb),[23] Maurice Faure warned that France's partners would delay progress on the Euratom Treaty unless the French government took a decision in favour of the Common Market. He offered three possible options to the government. The first which was to accept the Spaak report would undoubtedly be rejected by the French National Assembly. The second was to reiterate the French government's previous position which was that France was not in a position to enter a common market at that time but wished to pursue its European policy by setting up Euratom first. The third option was to modify the Spaak report in a number of respects. To the two modifications which Pineau had already articulated at Venice, namely the harmonization of social legislation and the inclusion of overseas territories, four more could be added. These were that the French government would commit itself only to the first stage of tariff reductions of four years; that it would retain its special import taxes and export subsidies; that it should be allowed to take emergency measures to deal with a balance of payments deficit unilaterally; and that it should postpone the starting date of the Common Market until the problems in North Africa had been resolved satisfactorily. It was this third option which ministers were invited to discuss.

The debate turned less on the conditions of acceptance of the Common Market and more on the costs of non-acceptance. It was clear that if the government did not commit itself to the Common Market it would lose the Euratom Treaty and be driven into isolation in both its economic and foreign policies. While the French government could minimize the risks to the economy of joining the Common Market it was not obvious how it would minimize the risks of not joining. It was a persuasive argument of which only a minority, including the socialist Paul Ramadier and the Gaullist radical Jacques Chaban-Delmas, remained unconvinced. Of the conditions which Maurice Faure proposed, it was recognized that it would be unreasonable for France to insist that its partners changed their social legislation in the first stage of tariff reduction if at the same time France refused to commit itself to the second stage of the Common Market. The view was that France would commit itself to the second stage if the other conditions were met.[24]

Shortly after this meeting Mollet made a trip to London to suggest a fourth possible option to the British prime minister, Anthony Eden. The highly secret nature of his proposal and the absence of any prior discussion in France reveals something of the desperation of Mollet at this time. Referring to the critical period in June 1940 when Churchill had proposed forming a union between Britain and France in order to keep France in the war, Mollet suggested forming an Anglo-French economic union, to keep France out of the Common Market. Among other things this would have entailed pooling the gold and dollar reserves of the entire Sterling and Franc Areas which, Mollet argued, would have helped to solve both Britain's and France's recurrent balance of payments problems, thereby strengthening both countries economically.[25] Although what was under discussion was an economic union, in the days leading up to the invasion of Suez the political effects of such a union on the position and effectiveness of both Britain and France in the world were central issues.

Mollet's proposal was discussed at some length by the British Cabinet but there was never any suggestion that it should be acted upon. The Treasury, while not blind to the high rates of investment and growth which had been taking place in the French economy, thought that it would take a further ten to fifteen years for the structural weaknesses of the French economy to be overcome. An economic union with France would, it warned, simply encourage the backward sectors of the British economy to demand continued protection. Nor would the pooling of the gold and dollar reserves of the two countries' monetary areas be mutually beneficial, it argued. Far from strengthening confidence it would undermine that of the holders of sterling balances while doing little to entice the French private holders of gold and dollars to release them to the government. A further problem identified by the Treasury was the potential commercial conflict between the British and French African colonies, as well as the cost of investment in the French colonies.

Mollet's proposal coincided with discussions within the British Cabinet of their proposal to form a free trade area in the OEEC. Known as 'Plan G',this was to be Britain's response to the Common Market of the Six. Britain's intention was to sign a treaty between the European Free Trade Area and the Common Market which would guarantee free trade between the two areas, as soon as the Common Market was set up. Mollet's proposal raised the possibility that France could form a customs union with Britain within the general framework of Plan G. This would mean that there would be an Anglo-French customs union in a free trade area with a German–Benelux–Italian customs union and perhaps a Scandinavian customs union. The problems in this arrangement were immediately obvious to the Treasury. Not only would it mean altering the European Coal and Steel Community in some way, but for Britain it would raise all the difficulties of imperial preference, and of the inclusion of agriculture (which Plan G expressly avoided).

Predictably the concern of the Foreign Office was that an Anglo-French economic union would interfere with Britain's relations with the United States, the Commonwealth and the rest of Europe, particularly West Germany.[26] What the Cabinet wanted was to pursue Plan G and in that way secure closer economic cooperation between the Common Market, including France, and the rest of the OEEC. The only offer to Mollet was that once these arrangements were in place Britain would consider Mollet's subsequent proposal that France could join the British Commonwealth. Indeed there was some support in Cabinet for extending membership of the Commonwealth to Belgium, Holland and perhaps Norway as well![27]

Soon after Plan G became official British policy it was seized upon by opponents of the Common Market as an alternative to Europe of the Six. One of the most outspoken of the Common Market's critics was the West German economics minister, Ludwig Erhard. On learning from Maurice Faure that the French government remained committed to the harmonization of social legislation in the first stage of the Common Market, Erhard resolved to use that issue to block progress on the Common Market.[28] He insisted on attending the meetings of the six foreign ministers on 20–21 October 1956 at which the main issues under negotiation were the method of moving from the first to the second stage of the Common Market, the nature and duration of export subsidies, the criterion for applying safeguard clauses and the harmonization of social legislation. After lengthy debate over whether one country should have a veto over the transition to the second stage Pineau finally agreed to a compromise arrangement whereby at the end of the first four-year period a unanimous vote in the Council of Ministers would be required in order to move to the second stage. If one country did exercise its veto a further vote would be held after two years for which majority rule would apply. Pineau, however, insisted that this compromise was dependent on social legislation being harmonized during the first stage of tariff reductions. On Erhard's instructions the Germans opposed such harmonization. They had calculated that the institution of a 40-hour working week would increase their wage bill by 5 per cent, and that the Federal government would be unable to impose it. The result, as expected, was that no agreement was reached on either issue.[29]

At this stage the Quai d'Orsay began to reassess its position regarding the harmonization of social legislation. Judging that it might be easier to ratify the Common Market treaty in France if the terms of association with the free trade area could be presented at the same time, and since the British government had made clear its opposition to any enforced harmonization of social legislation within the free trade area, the Quai d'Orsay feared that if France continued to make it a precondition for the Common Market this would complicate the negotiations with the free trade area.[30] Although it had frequently been used as an explanation for the uncompetitiveness of French industry, opinion was in fact very divided on the economic, as opposed to the political, argument.

A number of official studies had been undertaken by national and European bodies, which had produced conflicting results. The High Authority of the European Coal and Steel Community argued that, rather than compare wages and social charges only, all costs to the employer needed to be taken into account. These included family allowances, perks, costs of recruitment and professional training. While social security costs in France were higher than in the other member states, all costs were not. In the car industry social charges were 45 per cent of hourly wages in France, 35 per cent in the German Federal Republic and 25 per cent in Belgium, but the overall costs of labour were 192 francs per hour in France, 185 francs in the Federal Republic and 266 francs in Belgium. The average hourly wage in the steel industry was 284 francs in the Federal Republic, but 262 francs in France. Indeed, the differences in the overall wage cost between regions in the same country was often greater than between countries. In the coal industry for example the differences in the overall wage cost between France and the German Federal Republic was 36 francs per hour while that between Lorraine and the mines in the centre of France was 59 francs and between Lorraine and the Nord/Pas-de-Calais mines 47 francs.[31]

But a study carried out by INSEE in 1955 had concluded that of all the factors entering into the calculation of wage costs, the length of the working week and therefore of overtime pay as well as differences between male and female wage rates were the most important. This made a calculation of average costs fairly irrelevant.[32] However, if officials in the Quai d'Orsay were considering a change in the French negotiating position on social legislation in order to facilitate agreement with Britain and the free trade area, Adenauer was determined that the Common Market treaty should be signed and ratified before the terms of association between the Common Market and the proposed free trade area had been agreed. It was Adenauer, therefore, who insisted on making the compromise regarding the harmonization of social legislation during a secret meeting with Mollet on 6 November 1956. The dramatic events of Suez and Hungary which were unfolding as he travelled to Paris could only have strengthened his resolve. For Mollet, who had to overcome the fears of the sceptics in his own party and in the Radical Party, the advantages of the German concession outweighed the advantages of agreeing the terms of association between the Common Market and the free trade area, particularly since those terms of association could well torpedo the ratification of the Common Market treaty in the Federal Republic.

The details of the agreement on the Common Market which was subsequently approved by the Six were that if at the end of the transitional period French industry felt itself disadvantaged by the overtime rates being applied in other Common Market countries the European Commission would grant safeguards to those industries affected. The French system of import taxes and export subsidies would be examined each year by the European Commission and Council of Ministers and the French government would be obliged to take steps to reduce them. The French would be permitted to continue their practice of applying differential rates to each imported good unless the lack of uniformity was considered prejudicial to its competitors.

And finally the Commission and Council of Ministers could by qualified majority insist that these taxes and subsidies be suspended if the French balance of current payments was in equilibrium for one year and the reserves had reached a sufficient level.[33]

But this agreement was by no means the end of the story. The whole issue of the inclusion of overseas territories, which the French government had not raised until the Venice Conference in May 1956, was to take up much of the negotiators' time between November 1956 and when the treaties were signed in March 1957. Why the overseas territories should have become so important that France threatened in January 1957 not to proceed from the first to the second stage of the Common Market unless satisfactory terms of association were agreed is discussed at length in the next chapter.[34]

Surprisingly, perhaps, the French were much less intransigent over the question of agriculture. That agriculture would remain protected in the Common Market had never been disputed. But while it was agreed that at the end of the first stage of the Common Market a common agricultural policy would be put in place the details of that policy were not debated. All that the French were guaranteed was that in the first stage there would be a continuation of their existing system of long-term export contracts for their food surpluses and on more advantageous terms.[35]

Thus, when Mollet tested the support of the French National Assembly for the treaties in a debate lasting from 15 until 22 January 1957 the government had secured almost all its conditions for the Common Market, although not for Euratom. It had lost the case that a European isotope separation plant would be set up, and it had lost the case that Euratom would exercise a complete monopoly over the supply of nuclear materials. But by couching the debate in terms of French security needs it played on the sense of national vulnerability which recent events had heightened. A clear majority of 124 voted in favour of the treaties in order to avoid isolation in foreign policy and to guarantee France's economic security by tying the Federal Republic to western Europe.[36] The treaties were signed two months later.

At the beginning of April 1957 the government announced a second five-year nuclear programme which was to be entirely independent of Euratom, and in June 1957 the government, now led by Maurice Bourgès-Maunoury, took action to suspend all trade liberalization measures in order to deal with an acute balance of payments crisis. Nonetheless, in July 1957 the Common Market and Euratom treaties were ratified with little further debate in the National Assembly and with an increased majority.

The Mollet government has subsequently been criticized for not taking action earlier to deal with the mounting deficit on current account.[37] Whereas the French current account had actually been in surplus with both the EPU and the Dollar Area in 1954 and 1955 this was reversed in 1956 and deteriorated still further in 1957. However, the government judged, probably correctly, that any measures taken to restrict imports before the treaties had been signed would have complicated the Common Market negotiations. Instead it took measures to encourage investment and production and to extend social welfare provision. The results were an increase in industrial production of 9.3 per cent in 1956 and 8.5 per cent in 1957, an extension of paid holidays to three weeks and a rise in the minimum old-age pension. The deterioration of the current account position was explained by the government more in terms of exogenous shocks than domestic policy. The escalation of the Algerian War, the increase in the price of oil imports after Suez, and an exceptionally bad wheat harvest in 1956 which necessitated importing wheat from the United States all put a strain on France's foreign exchange resources, it argued. This was not an explanation with which the rest of the EPU or indeed the co-signatories of the Treaty of Rome necessarily agreed. While there were some discreet criticisms of the French government's decision to go ahead with building the isotope separation plant to be financed out of its own resources, no one drew the conclusion which the French were secretly expecting, that the deterioration in the external accounts was mainly due to the reduction in American aid. Instead of financing 20 per cent of French imports as in the past, it was now covering 3.5 per cent.[38] In spite of these criticisms the French were granted an aid package from the IMF and the EPU totalling 656 million dollars which made France the largest debtor in the EPU when it was wound up in December 1958.[39]

Thus, the French government's decision to sign the Treaty of Rome was not its preferred foreign policy option. Even though the government justified it to the National Assembly in foreign policy terms, it was the strength of the economic case together with the fact that there was no foreign policy alternative after Britain's rejection of Mollet's proposal, which ensured its success, both economically and politically. The situation was therefore clear to Mollet before the Suez fiasco and his private meeting with Adenauer.[40]

Success for France meant failure for Britain. The consequences for Britain of the government's refusal either to participate in the Common Market negotiations or to explore alternative arrangements with France were to be profound both politically and economically. France had recovered from a protracted economic depression, a major political defeat and, in the throes of losing an empire, was able to take a major foreign policy decision which was to secure its position in Europe for years to come while retaining links with its former empire.

NOTES

1 W.J. Adams, op. cit.
2 MAE DE-CE 1945–1960, A.30–6, 'Marché commun mars–juin 1955', note from Service de Coopération Économique, 20 April 1955.

3 MAE DE–CE 1945–1960, A. 30–6, 'Marché commun mars–juin 1955', note from Service de Cooperation Economique, 14 April 1955.
4 P. Gerbet, 'La Relance européenne jusqu'à la Conférence de Messine', in E. Serra (ed.), *The Relaunching of Europe and the Treaties of Rome* (Brussels, 1989).
5 A.S. Milward, *The European Rescue*, op. cit., p. 205.
6 P. Guillen, 'La France et la négociation des Traités de Rome: l'Euratom', in E. Serra (ed.), op. cit.
7 F. Duchêne, op. cit., p. 265.
8 MAE DE–CE 1945–1960, 'Allemagne', 368, meetings between Pinay and Adenauer, 29–30 April 1955.
9 Quai Branly, Interministerial Committee for Questions of European Integration, SGCI 121.11, report by O. Wormser, 25 May 1955.
10 P. Gerbet, op. cit.
11 Quai Branly, SGCI 121.9, note from Clappier, 21 June 1955.
12 MAE DE–CE 1945–1960, dossier général, January 1956–October 1956, 613, note from Service de Coopération Economique, 7 May 1956.
13 D. MacRae, *Parliament, Parties and Society in France 1946–1958* (New York, 1967), p. 158.
14 MAE DE–CE 1945–1960, 'Allemagne', 368, meeting in Brussels, 11 February 1956.
15 MAE DE-CE 1945–1960, 613, note, 23 February 1956.
16 Min. Ind. IND 771523/47, note from DIME, 30 June 1955.
17 Min. Fin. 13 AD 76, report of meeting of Textile Committee of the OEEC, 8–12 December 1953.
18 MAE DE-CE 1945–1960, A.30–6, 'Marché commun. Dossier général. Jan. 56–Oct. 56', no. 613, report from Service de Coopération Economique, 26 March 1956.
19 MAE DE–CE 1945–1960, A.30–6, 'Marché commun. Dossier général. Jan. 56–Oct. 56', no. 613, report of meeting, 6–11 May 56.
20 P. Guillen, op. cit.
21 Quai Branly, SGCI 121.1, Venice Conference, 29–30 May 1956.
22 Quai Branly, SGCI 121.9, note from J. Gouot, 11 May 1956.
23 W. Kohl, *French Nuclear Diplomacy* (Princeton, 1971), p. 24.
24 Quai Branly, SGCI 122.21, meeting of the Interministerial Committee, 4 September 1956.
25 PRO, CAB 130/120, 'Union with France: Economic Considerations', memorandum by the Treasury, 22 September 1956.
26 PRO CAB 130/120, memorandum by the Foreign Office, 22 September 1956.
27 PRO, CAB 130/120, meeting of ministers held at 10 Downing Street, 1 October 1956.
28 A.S. Milward, *The European Rescue*, op. cit., pp. 213–14.
29 Quai Branly, SGCI 122.13, meeting of foreign ministers, 20–21 October 1956.
30 MAE DE-CE 1945–1960, no. 613, note, 20 October 1956.
31 Quai Branly, SGCI 122.22A, note from the High Authority of the ECSC, 27 June 1956.
32 Quai Branly, SGCI 121.9, 'Direction Générale des prix et des enquêtes économiques', 23 May 1956.
33 Quai Branly, SGCI 122.13, note from Secrétariat, Brussels, 8 November 1956.
34 MAE DE-CE 1945–1960, A. 30–6, 1957, Bousquet to Pineau, 25 January 1957.
35 MAE DE-CE 1945–1960, November 1956–December 1957, no. 614, telegram from Louis Joxe, 2 February 1957.
36 H. Küsters, *Die Gründung der Europäischen Wirtschaftsgemeinschaft* (Baden-Baden, 1982).

37 Patat and Lutfalla, op. cit., p. 158.
38 MAE DE-CE 1945–1960, A. 30–6, 1957, Bousquet to Pineau, 19 June 1957.
39 Min. Fin. 13 AD 68, report from Calvet, December 1958.
40 Christian Pineau and Christiane Rimbaud, *Le Grand Pari. L'aventure du Traité de Rome* (Paris, 1991), pp. 218–22. This asserts that it was Suez which convinced the French government to sign the Treaty of Rome.

9

THE RETREAT FROM EMPIRE

One of the assumptions underlying policy in the Fourth Republic was that the French empire,[1] which had acted as a refuge for the French economy in times of depression,[2] could be developed economically in order to strengthen France's position in the postwar world. When the French government signed the Treaty of Rome setting up the European Economic Community it brought that strategy to a formal end. One of the obvious questions which this raises is whether the strategy was abandoned because it had not worked or because it had worked so successfully that the French economy was strong enough to face competition in the markets of both Europe and the empire.[3]

Until the contraction of international markets in the Great Depression of 1929–32 the main economic value of the French empire in peacetime had been as a source of profit for private French investors. Rates of return there had been much higher than elsewhere except in the early 1930s and late 1950s.[4] Its value in wartime was much greater. However, despite the recognized contribution of the empire to the French effort in the First World War, the attempt by Albert Sarraut, the minister for colonies, in 1921 to implement a public investment plan in the colonies failed on financial grounds.[5] It was not until 1931, after the devaluation of sterling, when the colonial market suddenly became relatively more important to France, that two laws were passed authorizing the government to underwrite loans to start public works programmes in each colony. Then in 1934 the government considered the introduction of a French-style Ottawa Agreement with its colonies but rejected it largely because of the threat which it posed for certain French agricultural interests, in particular wheat, wine and citrus fruits.[6] The preferred alternative was a mixture of protection and prohibition. In some cases the government used import quotas to reduce the external competition for selected colonial exports, particularly of coffee and tropical fruit, on the French market and for French exports of textiles and motor vehicles on the colonial market. In other cases the government chose to restrict the trade in and in some cases the production and transport facilities for colonial products. As a result trade with the colonies fell,

186

Table 9.1 Imports of French overseas territories in 1938 (million francs)

Product	Origin of imports			
	France	Other overseas territories	Rest of the world	Total
Food	1,416.7	588.5	1,482.5	3,487.7
Raw materials				
of agricultural origin	102.2	21.4	199.4	323.0
of non-agricultural origin	878.1	30.5	1,486.0	2,394.6
Manufactured goods	4,022.4	191.9	1,927.9	6,142.2
Others	2,222.1	108.8	1,127.6	3,458.5
Total	8,641.5	941.1	6,223.4	15,806.0

Table 9.2 Exports of French overseas territories in 1938 (million francs)

Product	Destination of Exports			
	France	Other overseas territories	Rest of the world	Total
Food	8,428.3	412.9	1,542.3	10,383.5
Raw materials				
of agricultural origin	884.2	42.2	991.2	1,917.6
of non-agricultural origin	440.5	40.5	628.7	1,109.7
Manufactured goods	30.7	46.4	57.1	134.2
Others	970.5	311.2	1,216.9	2,498.6
Total	10,754.2	853.2	4,436.2	16,043.6

Source: Min. Ind. 830589. 11. DGEN 'Vues sur le commerce extérieur de l'empire en fonction du plan décennal d'équipement', study presented by M. Louis Delanney, March 1944

although due to the much greater reduction in trade with Europe, trade with the colonies, as a proportion of total trade, was actually greater by 1937 than it had been in 1927. However, while France was the largest market for colonial exports it was far from being their main supplier. In 1938 65 per cent of colonial exports consisted of food products, of which 80 per cent went to metropolitan France. On the other hand, one-third of the colonial imports of manufactured goods came from non-French sources. In fact France supplied only half their machines, mechanical engineering goods and cars but two-thirds of their cotton goods.

THE IMPERIAL PLANS OF VICHY AND THE RESISTANCE

It was not until 1940, when possession of the empire was seen as the last remaining symbol of France's former greatness and the one hope that

France could climb out of the abyss to which it had sunk, that attitudes to the empire changed. One of the many lessons of defeat in 1940 was that in times of national emergency neither the manpower nor the strategic location of the empire guaranteed French security.

The divisions in France in 1940 were also reflected in the empire. All of North Africa and West Africa as well as Indochina became loyal to Vichy while the smaller, more remote regions of New Caledonia and French Equatorial Africa supported de Gaulle and the Free French. After the mission organized by de Gaulle with the British to secure control over Dakar and of all French West Africa in September 1940 failed, de Gaulle was excluded from further Allied planning to liberate the French empire.[7]

As Allied victory and the liberal international order which such victory presaged became more certain, Vichy planners turned their attention to the commercial role which the empire would play in that international system. The originality of the Vichy planners' approach to the empire lay in their concern with the balance of payments of the French empire as a whole rather than the trade and payments between France and the empire. According to their calculations, even though the colonies had a surplus on trade with France which was matched by an outflow of private investment in the other direction, both France and the empire had a deficit with the rest of the world. And it was this deficit, with its disastrous consequences in the 1930s, which the Vichy Plan aimed to correct.

A guiding principle of the Vichy planners was that commercial policy in the future would have to be integrated with domestic economic policy in order to implement the national plan. The French colonies, which had been cut off from trade with metropolitan France during the war and given complete autonomy in tariff-making, were to resume trade with metropolitan France but on a different basis. One overarching objective of the national plan was to improve the foreign trade position of the empire as a whole to reduce its vulnerability to depressions originating outside France. The contribution which the empire was to make towards this goal was, first, to substitute French products for those previously imported from the rest of the world. This was to enable the French to expand their production of steel, mechanical engineering goods and motor vehicles in particular. Where France was unable to meet the demand for imports, as in the case of tea in Morocco, it was suggested that indigenous habits and customs should be changed. Second, the empire was to increase its exports of industrial raw materials such as rubber, tungsten, wolfram, iron, natural phosphates and nickel as well as of food and agricultural products to the rest of the world provided that French needs had been met first. In both these ways the empire was to reverse its debtor position with the rest of the world and become a net earner of foreign exchange. A precondition for this was that France would maintain its system of imperial preferences.

The Vichy state's concern to maintain and strengthen the integrity of the French empire after the war was shared by de Gaulle and the CFLN. But in view of the growing strength of nationalist movements in the empire, and the anti-imperialist stance of Roosevelt, it was felt that the allegiance of the empire would have to be secured through a more positive policy than that advocated by the Vichy planners. At a conference held in Brazzaville in January–February 1944 the CFLN pledged that, as the future government of France, it would define a new economic policy for the colonies which would have as its priority an improvement in their living standards. To this end it agreed to implement a more liberal tariff policy which took account of the differences between colonial economies.[8] But at the same time there was an equally strong concern to frustrate Roosevelt's anti-imperialist strategy, based on abolishing the system of imperial trading preferences operated by both France and Britain. Thus, in the summer of 1944 when an American mission, led by Ambassador Culbertson and including representatives from the Department of Commerce, the Foreign Economic Administration and private businessmen, visited North Africa in order to explore ways of restoring private trade and to consider how the area's resources could be exploited for the American market they were frustrated by French officials whom they saw as determined to enforce France's closed-door policy towards its colonies. Trade, they were told, would remain in the hands of the French state, as would any discussions of economic development in the French empire. The Americans were complaining that both they and the British were excluded from importing from North Africa and that the French policy of stockpiling goods, particularly food for metropolitan France after its liberation, was inflationary. The conclusion of the Culbertson mission was that the American government, with the cooperation of the British, would have to save the French from 'their policy of erecting barriers around their poverty'.[9] However, the following year Monnet advised the French government not to discuss ways of associating private American interests in financing colonial projects, on the grounds that he would secure finance for them by negotiating Export–Import Bank loans with the United States.[10] When Monnet was subsequently given responsibility for drawing up a plan for reconstruction and modernization he insisted that it would be a plan for the whole French empire.[11]

POSTWAR PLANNING FOR THE OVERSEAS TERRITORIES

In January 1946 the Ministry for France Overseas stressed to Monnet that the objectives of France's colonial policy should be to develop the productive potential of the overseas territories in order to increase their purchasing power and living standards. This would mean that the system of imperial preferences, which had the effect of increasing the price level in the colonies and thereby making their exports uncompetitive on the international market, would have to be replaced by a system of free trade. This moreover had the advantage of conforming to the American preference.[12] From that point on Monnet and the planning commissariat exerted little influence over the plans for the overseas territories, leaving it to the Ministry for France Overseas to draw them up in association with the local representative assemblies. What emerged as a result was not a five-year but a ten-year plan for their development as well as the creation of a separate fund, the Fonds d'investissement pour le développement économique et social des territoires d'outre-mer (FDES), to provide for its financing. North Africa and Indochina were not included in this ten-year plan. Partly as a result of having been cut off from France during the war, and partly as a result of the pressure from a rapidly expanding population, particularly in Algeria, the three North African territories, Algeria, Morocco and Tunisia, had already initiated large public works programmes of their own in 1945. These remained entirely independent of the Monnet Plan.

The ten-year plan for the overseas territories estimated their investment needs at 285,000 million francs of which 155,000 million were for the first five-year period. Two-thirds of the investment was to come from public funds and one-third from private sources. It was not until 1948, however, that the first report of the plan for the overseas territories, known as the Pleven Report, was published, the delay being explained by the number of French nationals who were sent at considerable expense to these territories to compile the plan.[13] But by that time the entire basis of the Monnet Plan had been altered to take account of the change in American policy and the offer of Marshall Aid.

THE REVISED PLAN FOR THE FRENCH UNION

The revised Monnet Plan which covered the four-year period 1948–52 was for the first time an integrated plan for the French empire and included the plans for North Africa and for the overseas territories. This meant that the planning framework for the overseas territories was reduced from ten years to four years. At that time, only 30 per cent of the public investment planned for 1947 and 1948 had actually been undertaken. The revised plan marked a major change in the French government's aims and objectives for the overseas territories. Instead of trying to increase the living standards of the indigenous populations, made all the more necessary as a result of the rapid increase in population, the objective of the revised four-year plan was to increase their exports to the rest of the world and thereby eliminate the foreign exchange deficit of the Franc Area as a whole. In this respect the revised four-year plan bore a more marked resemblance to the Vichy Plan than to the earlier Monnet Plan. One of the reasons for this change was the recognition that in the IMF the French Union was treated as a single monetary area whereas in the emerging GATT the constituent parts of the French Union were treated as quite separate customs areas. From this it followed that the French government would be best able to exert control over the French Union as a whole by strengthening it as a monetary area. To this end the revised plan proposed that instead of being net drawers on the foreign exchange reserves of France, the rest of the French Union was to earn a foreign exchange surplus by 1952. To achieve this investment was no longer to be directed towards improving the agricultural and transport infrastructure but was to improve the extraction and export of raw materials and food. Indeed, when the Investment Commission was set up in June 1948, in an attempt to bring the financing of investment under control, none of the ministries responsible for North Africa or the overseas territories was included as a permanent member.[14]

By 1952 it was intended that the overseas territories would be supplying metropolitan France with raw materials and food in order to economize on its foreign exchange and would also be increasing its exports to North America, the Far East and western Europe. The aim was for the rest of the French Union to have a balance of payments surplus of 167 million dollars by 1952 which would cover the deficit of metropolitan France. This was to be achieved by compensating for the decline in per capita food production in North Africa by increasing food production in the rest of the overseas territories. There was also to be a programme of industrialization based upon textiles and cement which was intended to reduce import needs. The main exports to metropolitan France were to consist of oils, cotton, sisal, wool, rubber, mineral products and wood while the main exports to the rest of the world were to be food, wine, fruit, rice, vegetables, coal, phosphates, rubber and wood. In return metropolitan France was to export textiles, steel, food, fertilizers, manufactured goods, investment goods and petroleum products to the overseas territories.[15]

One of the questions raised by integrating the plans of the whole French empire into a single four-year plan to fit into the European Recovery Programme was how to allocate the dollar aid received as a result. The dilemma faced by the French government was that whereas, on the one hand, it was felt that the United States would be more sympathetic to the needs of the overseas territories than to those of France itself, on the other hand, it was much easier to identify the sort of large investment projects, which the ECA favoured, in metropolitan France than in the overseas territories. The only solution seemed to be to explain to the United States that France was increasing the dollar allocation to the overseas territories out of the dollar resources of the Franc Area as a whole, while allocating most of the dollar aid received through the European Recovery Programme to metropolitan France.[16]

191

In the first year of Marshall Aid the Import Committee, in conjunction with the Commissariat Général au Plan, had fixed the dollar import needs of the overseas countries, excluding North Africa but including Indochina, at 160 million dollars. In the first four months of ERP this amounted to 52 million dollars, or 13.5 per cent of the total. But in fact the government decided to give the overseas countries only 30 million dollars in the first four months of the ERP programme, of which only 19.4 million dollars was Marshall Aid. Once the costs of coal and other fuel needed for transport were deducted it left 15.9 million dollars in aid. For 1948 as a whole the overseas territories were to get 80 million dollars instead of the 160 million dollars judged to be necessary. The French were worried that both the overseas territories and the United States itself would complain about the small size of the dollar aid to the overseas territories relative to that for metropolitan France. Indeed, their fears were justified when in July 1949 the ECA proposed to set up a special fund to finance investment in the overseas territories, the resources for which were to come out of the general aid allocation to the OEEC. Even though the OEEC was hostile to the idea[17] a fund was set up but the amounts allocated were so small as to make the whole idea and fuss which it created quite exaggerated. In fiscal year 1949–50 France received 4 million dollars and in 1950–51 28 million dollars.[18] After that the fund was wound up. To 30 June 1951 France received 2,278 million dollars of aid within the framework of the European Recovery Programme, out of which all the overseas countries, including those in North Africa, received 232 million dollars.[19]

Under the terms of the bilateral agreement signed by the French and American governments on 28 June 1948 the American government was to retain 5 per cent of the French franc counterpart of Marshall Aid to cover its administrative expenses. This condition was common to all the bilateral agreements between European governments and the United States. In the French case it quickly became apparent that the Americans intended to use the franc counterpart to buy raw materials of a strategic interest in the French empire, such as graphite and mica in Madagascar and cobalt in Morocco. The bilateral agreement was followed in 1949 by a new agreement between the two governments which permitted the United States to give credits in French francs to the producers of raw materials and minerals in the French empire to enable them either to increase output or to prospect in new areas. These loans would then be repaid out of the raw materials produced as a result.[20]

The fear of the Quai d'Orsay was that this new agreement would pave the way for private American investors to take control of the French empire and deprive France of its markets. At the same time it was becoming clear that the scale of investment needed in these economies was beyond the political capacity of the French state to provide, and that private investors were not prepared to fill the gap. Rather than invite the participation of

American capital, the Quai d'Orsay preferred a solution based on the OEEC drawing up and supervising an investment plan for all the overseas territories which would then be for the benefit of all the participating countries.[21] But when the British made clear in their four-year plan, submitted to the OEEC in December 1948, that they envisaged investing in the developing countries of the sterling area the surplus earned on foreign account, this scotched the French idea. Why would the British agree to submit their investment to the scrutiny of the OEEC when they had no need of financial help from the OEEC?

The task of ensuring the financing of French investment in the overseas territories was the responsibility of the Caisse Centrale de la France d'Outre-mer. This was a public body with financial autonomy whose statute dated back to 2 February 1944. It was also responsible for issuing banknotes and for channelling and distributing investment funds. These funds took the form either of loans or grants. Grants which were in effect a public subsidy were placed in the FDES and then distributed by the Caisse Centrale de la France d'Outre-mer. These grants were then given to public, semi-public and private companies involved in implementing the plan, either as direct loans or as part of the capital base for nationalized companies. Whether credits were given in the form of grants by the FDES or loans through the Caisse depended on the nature of the project. The plans for the overseas territories included both general projects, which were common to them all, and specific projects for each territory. The general projects, which mainly involved scientific research, were financed entirely from grants through the FDES. More specific projects, which were entirely economic, were financed 50 per cent by a grant from the FDES and 50 per cent from a loan from the Caisse. The breakdown for social expenditure was 66 per cent grant and 34 per cent loan.

While the contribution to investment in the plan from local resources was negligible in the overseas territories, this was not the case in North Africa. In Algeria, Morocco and Tunisia local resources, either from the budget or from the resources of both public and private companies, amounted to 359,800 million francs between 1947 and 1953 compared with a total of 298,000 million francs from metropolitan France.[22]

Over the period 1947–53 public funds from France invested in the overseas countries amounted to 645,000 million francs. These included credits from the Caisse Central de la France d'Outre-mer, the Treasury, the Budget, the FME and the FDES. They increased steadily over the period, rising from 2.3 per cent of the investment financed out of public funds in the French Union as a whole in 1947 to 17 per cent by 1953. On average French public funds covered 28 per cent of the investment in North Africa, and 76 per cent in other overseas countries. By 1953 public funds from metropolitan France covered half the investment in all overseas countries – 157,000 million francs out of 314,000 million francs.[23]

One of the effects of this investment in the empire was an increase in the demand for imports. Only the system of import quotas and foreign exchange controls, the latter having been imposed on the French franc in 1939 and extended to the currencies of the Franc Area in 1940, ensured that this demand would not produce an even greater external deficit than in the 1930s. What it did produce, though, was a large deficit in trade with metropolitan France which it was believed was financed by the outflow of capital from France, even though no records were kept of the flows of private capital in either direction between France and the empire. As we have seen, one of the purposes of investment under the four-year plan was to reverse the empire's deficit on trade with both metropolitan France and the rest of the world by 1952. But in 1949 under pressure from the United States the British initiated a programme of trade liberalization within the OEEC, which had it been extended to the overseas dependencies of member states would have changed the basis on which the French imperial strategy rested.

As the Quai d'Orsay saw it there were several aspects to the question of including the empire in the trade liberalization programme. One was whether French producers would be able to withstand competition from OEEC countries on the French market, but also in the markets of the empire. Another was whether empire producers would be able to withstand competition on the French as well as on their own markets. Many overseas countries were already complaining about the competition which they faced on the French market from other OEEC countries, which was undermining their plans to increase production. In particular, North African exporters of wine, oil and citrus fruit were complaining about the imports allowed in under the very restrictive bilateral agreements which France had signed with Portugal, Italy, Greece and Turkey and opposed any liberalization of trade with the OEEC. North African countries claimed that it was impossible to reduce their prices on account of their social policy and minimum wages, in themselves a function of the high prices of investment and consumer goods imported from France. On the other hand, it was clear that if all quantitative restrictions on trade with the OEEC and its overseas territories were removed, the French empire would be able to import from Europe and the sterling area more cheaply. This, however, would have had a disastrous impact on many French producers and particularly on producers of cotton and woollen goods. It would also have left firms producing agricultural machinery, which under the expansion targets set by the Monnet Plan were to export 30 per cent of their output to North Africa, with surplus capacity.[24] For these reasons a more gradual programme of trade liberalization was adopted. Although the French government informed the OEEC on 6 February 1950 that it intended to extend to the overseas territories all the measures of trade liberalization which were applicable to metropolitan France,[25] in fact the French technical ministries were so opposed to such a measure that very little trade with the overseas territories was actually liberalized. This made it difficult for the French government to put pressure on other OEEC countries to reduce their import restrictions on goods from the French overseas territories. The only way that France could promote colonial exports was through bilateral negotiations.[26]

As a result the measures of trade liberalization undertaken by metropolitan France between 1949 and February 1952 were extended to some overseas territories and not to others. Exactly the same degree of trade liberalization was applied to New Caledonia, Oceania and St Pierre and Miquelon. West Africa participated in the more restricted list which was equivalent to 25 per cent of its 1948 private trade with the OEEC, while French Equatorial Africa, Togo and Cameroon, which did not have tariffs because of their international commitments, did not benefit from this trade liberalization. Nor did Madagascar, where tariffs had been suspended since the war. On the other hand, when metropolitan France reimposed all its quantitative restrictions in February 1952 this decision was not extended to the overseas territories.[27]

A NEW COMMERCIAL REGIME FOR THE EMPIRE

By 1952 it was clear that the economic and commercial policies pursued within the French empire since the war, and certainly since 1948, had not achieved their objectives. The policy of preferential trading and subsidized investment had not turned the empire into a net contributor of foreign exchange. On the contrary the empire's deficit on current account with the rest of the world, while declining, was still higher than in the interwar period (see Table 9.3). While there were some variations between countries and from year to year the trend was for the overseas countries to run a large trade deficit in dollars and other currencies but a surplus in sterling.

Table 9.3 Balance of payments of the French Union, 1927–51
(annual average in million dollars)

	1927–31	1932–35	1936–38	1945–48	1949–51
Metropolitan France					
Balance of trade	−0.45	−0.44	−0.43	−1.32	−0.44
Balance of invisibles	+0.69	+0.32	+0.36	−0.16	−0.10
Balance of empire on current account	−0.05	−0.05	−0.07	−0.26	−0.13
Total balance of Franc Zone on current account	+0.19	−0.17	−0.14	−1.74	−0.67

Source: INSEE, 'La Balance des payements de La Zone Franc', *Bulletin Mensuel de Statistique. Supplément*, January–March 1953

Furthermore, unlike the situation in metropolitan France where private investors were taking over the financing of much investment as public investment supplemented by the counterpart of Marshall Aid declined, this was not the case in the French empire.

While metropolitan assistance to the overseas territories under the first plan was 55 per cent subsidy and 45 per cent loans from the FME through the intermediary of the Caisse Centrale de la France d'Outre-mer, 100 per cent of the metropolitan contribution to the development plans of North Africa took the form of loans from the FME. Largely for political reasons the first plan put more emphasis on social rather than economic investment in North Africa, which meant that these economies were not growing fast enough to finance the increased demands on the general budget arising from the better provision of social amenities. Given that most of the resources of the FME came from the counterpart of Marshall Aid, as this ended the metropolitan budget had to assume all the costs. For these two reasons the financing of the second plan for North Africa threatened to be contentious. Either investment would have to be cut or the contribution from metropolitan France would have to be increased.

Furthermore, because the metropolitan contribution took the form of loans rather than grants, albeit at interest rates lower than those prevailing in the market, France did not gain the benefit of any political capital.[28] When the FME was replaced by the Fonds d'expansion économique (FEE) the French government lost all control over the uses made of it by the North African governments. The loans simply became part of the local budget.[29]

In April 1954 the OEEC, largely at Britain's insistence, agreed to extend its trade liberalization to member countries' overseas territories. For France, which as we saw in Chapter 6 was already under considerable pressure to catch up with the progress made by the rest of the OEEC in liberalizing trade, this meant increased competition on both the home market and those of France overseas. But while it was clear that as quantitative restrictions were removed, exports to France from the overseas territories would still enjoy a margin of preference due to French tariffs, the same would not hold true for French exports to the overseas territories, since many of them did not have tariffs with the rest of the world.[30] This was a major difference between the French and British empires. For France the system of import quotas and exchange controls was a far more effective form of preference on colonial markets than tariffs. In the case of Morocco, for example, which under international law was prevented from giving French exports preferential tariffs, the proportion of French goods in its total imports had still increased, from 33 per cent in 1938 to 59 per cent in 1952. Other territories which had not reimposed tariffs since their suspension during the war had also increased their imports from France.

TARIFF REGIMES IN THE FRENCH UNION

French tariffs which had been agreed at Geneva in 1947 at a level based on the average of the tariffs in the last three prewar years[31] applied to metropolitan France, the Saar, Monaco, Corsica and Algeria, as well as French Guyana, Guadeloup, Martinique and Réunion, which had become departments of France on 1 January 1948. The tariff regime in those territories which came under the control of the Ministry for France Overseas dated back to 1928. However, the Vichy government, without abrogating the 1928 law, passed three others which gave the overseas territories the power to suspend or abolish tariffs without seeking the agreement of the French government. Although the tariff question had been debated on many occasions since the war neither the 1928 law nor the Vichy laws had been changed or replaced.

The 1928 law divided the overseas territories into two groups. The first, which was composed of Madagascar and the Comores, was assimilated to metropolitan France in so far as it shared its tariffs (apart from a number of exceptions). Since 1943, when the tariff had been suspended, all goods from these territories had been imported duty free into France.

The second group was subdivided into two categories. The first category, which included French West Africa, Oceania, New Caledonia, and St Pierre and Miquelon, had operated a preferential regime. This meant that all goods from metropolitan France were imported duty free while a tariff was imposed on imports from the rest of the world. In return, most of the exports from these territories were admitted free of duty into metropolitan France. The second category, which operated a non-preferential regime, included Togo and Cameroon, French Equatorial Africa, French territory in India, the French coast of Somalia and the New Hebrides. In most cases no tariffs were applied.

The rest of the French empire which did not come under the authority of the French Ministry for France Overseas had different tariff regimes. The three states of Indochina, Cambodia, Laos and Vietnam had formed a customs union after gaining tariff autonomy on 15 October 1940. With some exceptions on either side no tariff preferences were given on trade with metropolitan France. Tunisia, which juridically had tariff autonomy, operated a 'customs union' with metropolitan France with respect to a certain number of animal, vegetable and mineral products, as well as some textiles. Wine was an exception since Tunisian wine exports were restricted in France. Although, under the act of Algesiras, Morocco was prevented from setting up a preferential regime, its exports up to certain limits were imported free of duty into metropolitan France.

After the Second World War the Ministry for France Overseas had wanted to revoke the imperial preference system set up on 13 April 1928 and allow the overseas territories to trade freely with the rest of the world.

But, as we have seen, from 1947 onwards in view of the critical foreign exchange position the government, under pressure from the Ministry of National Economy, had placed a higher priority on protecting the current account position of the French empire as a whole than on promoting the interests of the overseas territories themselves. This meant substituting French goods in these markets for goods which could be imported more cheaply from the rest of the world. It was agreed, however, that the margin of preference for French exporters should be as low as possible.[32]

Although the United States had made clear in its *Proposals for Expansion of World Trade and Employment* that preferential trading areas which were not full customs unions would not be acceptable in the postwar liberal international order, it had had to relax its position in the face of British and French opposition in the Geneva negotiations in 1947. It was clear that the need to secure the cooperation of Britain and France in stabilizing political conditions in western Europe was the paramount concern of the United States at that time.[33] But by 1954 the need to stabilize political conditions in the French Union was becoming the paramount concern of the French government. Since it was felt that the system of imperial preferences was itself a source of discontent, the government set about reforming the tariff laws of the French Union. The 1954 law abolished all tariffs on trade between metropolitan France and the overseas territories and between the territories themselves, while giving the local assemblies the power to fix their external tariffs unless opposed by the French Council of Ministers. Algeria and the overseas departments continued to share the metropolitan tariff. Tunisia was to form a formal customs union with France in 1955. Indochina had different tariff arrangements with each of the members of the French Union. Morocco, as a result of its international statute, applied a uniform tariff of 12.5 per cent on all imports while its exports enjoyed certain preferences in the French market. Togo and Cameroon offered no preference to exports from the rest of the French Union on account of international treaties even though their exports were admitted free of duty into the markets of the French Union. Whether the new tariff regime was to be a step towards turning the French Union into a full customs union or whether some other system of holding the French Union together was preferable now had to be debated.

THE FUTURE OF THE FRENCH UNION?

On 10 May 1954, just three days after France's defeat at Dien Bien Phu, which was to mark the end of French involvement in the war in Indochina, the government set up a study group to investigate the future economic structure of the French Union. Under the direction of General Corniglion-Molinier, a minister of state, it met for the first time on 15 October 1954. The main question which the study group had to address was on what basis the disparate structure of the French Union could be held together in the international economy for the benefit of all the constituent parts.[34] Quite apart from the pressure from the OEEC for the existing system to be changed, it was coming under attack both in France itself and in the rest of the French Union. France overseas blamed its relative underdevelopment on having to import investment goods and other manufactures from metropolitan France which, apart from steel, were at prices higher than world prices. The French taxpayer complained about having to cover both the external and the domestic budget deficits of the empire, while French agriculture complained about the increasing competition from colonial exports on the domestic market.

There was plenty of evidence to support each case. A study, quoted by the Ministry for France Overseas, calculated that in 1953 the overseas territories had paid 1,320 million francs above world prices for flour, 1,870 million francs for cars and lorries and 16,090 million francs for investment goods. In the case of Algeria, which was by far the largest single market in the Franc Area for goods from metropolitan France, the price difference was considerable. In 1954 Algeria imported 21 per cent of all French car exports. Belgium–Luxembourg, the second largest market, was far behind, taking 12 per cent. Furthermore, the unit value to Belgium–Luxembourg was much lower, 42 million francs compared with 53 million francs to Algeria. Similarly, Algeria was the single largest market for metallurgical goods, taking 16 per cent of all exports. The average unit price was 19 million francs, compared, for example, with an average unit price of 7 million francs for exports in the same category to Brazil. Whereas metropolitan goods sold in the French Union at a price level on average 19.7 per cent higher than the world prices of similar goods, goods from the rest of the French Union sold in France itself at a price level only 9.5 per cent above that of world prices. Thus French industry benefited to the extent that the profits made on exporting to the French Union at much higher prices than to the rest of the world could be used to subsidize French exports to third markets. But whether the French economy benefited as a result was not so clear.

As the Commissariat Général au Plan pointed out, France had basically three choices. One was to participate in the international economic system under the leadership of the United States, Britain and Canada. This would mean that the French Union might have to conform more closely to the rules of GATT and become a full customs union. The second option was to participate fully in the trade liberalization programme of the OEEC. However, since the OEEC was committed to the abolition of all regional discriminatory practices this option could only have been a temporary one. The third option was to form some sort of common market in western Europe along the lines of the European Coal and Steel Community. Each option carried separate risks. Given the very high degree of dependence of the empire countries on trade with France, rather than

Table 9.4 Geographical distribution of trade within the French Union in 1955
(thousand million francs)

Origin of imports	Algeria	Tunisia	Morocco	D.O.M.[1]	T.O.M.[2]
France	200	47	79	{38.0	166
Rest of Franc Area	16	4	10		25
Europe of the Six (excluding France)	6	3	22	1.2	24
Other foreign countries	22	9	53	4.8	50
Total	244	63	164	44.0	265
France as a % of total	82	75	48	–	63

Source: Quai Branly, SGCI 122.21, report from Verret Committee, 5 October 1956
Notes: [1] Départements d'Outre-mer; [2] Territoires d'Outre-mer.

with each other, the further expansion of trade resulting from the formation of a customs union in order to conform to GATT rules was not considered to be healthy or desirable.

Nor would turning the French Union into a customs union solve the problem of mobilizing capital for investment in the French empire. In the six years between 1949 and 1955 France had invested 1,340,000 million francs from public funds in the empire compared with 100,000 million francs from private investors over the eight-year period 1947 to 1955. Only about 14,000 million francs of this private investment was foreign investment. And for 1954 it was calculated that the outflow of private capital from the three North African countries was actually greater than the inflow from France. A further objection to the formation of a customs union was that it would divide the French Union internally since those territories governed by international treaty would be unable to participate.

The greatest criticism of the report of the subcommittee which had been set up to explore the consequences of forming an imperial customs union came from agricultural interests. They argued, as they had in the 1930s, that such a move would benefit French industry at the expense of agriculture. Given that agricultural production was expanding in both France and the empire as a result of technical progress as well as government policy, agriculture would become more dependent on exports to third countries and thus more dependent on lowering its prices. Rather than form a customs union, a more rational solution, they argued, was to make agricultural production in the empire complementary to, rather than competitive with, that of metropolitan France. They also wanted agricultural exports to be given more help than in the past through commercial treaties based on importing industrial goods in return for agricultural exports.[35]

Although in January 1955 the option of forming a common market in western Europe was no longer under discussion after the French rejection of the EDC Treaty, the study group saw this as no more than a temporary setback. Indeed it recognized correctly that what would have to be explored were the implications of a common market in Europe for the French Union. It was largely due to the conclusions of the special subcommittee set up to study this issue that the French government decided in May 1956 to announce the participation of the empire in the European Common Market.

From the standpoint of January 1955 it was felt that to integrate the French Union into a west European common market would benefit western Europe since it would bring to it a larger market, sources of supply and opportunities for investment. It was also expected to benefit the empire in so far as it led to a reduction in the price of its imports, to an expansion of its exports, provided that these exports were competitive, and to an increase in investment. Whether such investment would promote an increase in living standards depended on whether it was designed to promote indigenous industry or simply to extract raw materials in the traditional colonial practice.

But for France itself the dangers of such a fusion were considerable. First, French industry stood to lose the facility of using profits made on highly priced exports to the French empire to subsidize exports to the rest of the world. And second, since those territories with an international statute would be excluded on juridical grounds, the formation of a European common market would lead to the disintegration of the French empire. On the other hand, it was clear that France could not provide on its own the investment necessary to promote the industrialization of the French empire, the inadequacy of which in itself was a powerful force for its disintegration.

The position of the French empire had been studied when the European Coal and Steel Community was being set up and the conclusion reached at that time was that the treaty applied only to European countries. Given the demand for iron ore in the Korean rearmament boom the three North African countries had in any case preferred to remain outside what they saw as a commercially restrictive community. Although the Italian government had campaigned throughout the negotiations leading to the Coal and Steel Community treaty for the inclusion of Algeria, with its rich deposits of iron ore, the French government had not agreed to the Italian demands on both juridical and practical grounds. The reasons given were that since international agreements prevented either Morocco or Tunisia from joining, in view of their contiguous borders with Algeria, it would have been problematic to have included Algeria.[36]

But quite unlike the negotiations leading to the Treaty of Paris, setting up the ECSC, those which started at Messina in June 1955 and led to the publication of the Spaak report in May 1956 ignored the overseas countries

Table 9.5 Estimated annual investment in the French Union from external sources, 1955–61 (thousand million francs)

Country	Investment
Algeria	136
Morocco ⎱ Tunisia ⎰	90
Overseas departments	15
Overseas territories	125
Total	366

Source: Quai Branly, SGCI 122.22A, Note, 20 July 1956

completely. Were France to join the Common Market with the empire it was calculated that it would be relinquishing some if not all of the profits from a market whose worth was estimated at 500,000 million francs per year. On that basis it was proposed that its European partners should contribute to the military, administrative and economic costs of these territories according to their GNP, as well as reimbursing France some of the investment in infrastructure which it had made beforehand.[37] For GNP per capita to be increased by 4 per cent per annum throughout the French empire it was calculated that external investment would have to be of the order of 366,000 million francs per annum over the period 1956–61. This figure took no account of the cost to France of carrying out its political responsibilities, which in 1954 had totalled 161,000 million francs.[38]

It was this calculation which explained the sudden announcement at the meeting of foreign ministers of the Six held in Venice at the end of May 1956 that the French wanted to discuss the inclusion of the French empire in the Common Market. This announcement was followed by the creation of a special committee in France to assess the full implication of bringing the empire into the European Common Market.

The Verret Committee, as it became known, recognized that while some French producers, particularly those of cotton textiles, sugar, milk and some branches of the mechanical engineering industry, would suffer as a result of the loss of their monopoly position, the cost to the French economy of not associating the French empire with the Common Market would be very much greater. The political and demographic pressure throughout the countries of the French empire meant that France would have to devote an even greater amount of public funds towards financing their development programmes. According to one estimate, based on the conclusions of the Maspétiol report which looked at the financial relations between metropolitan France and Algeria,[39] the French contribution would have to be doubled if living standards were to rise at a politically acceptable rate.[40]

One perceived advantage of associating the French empire with the Common Market was that if costs were to be equalized this should include the cost to France of investment in the French Union. Another advantage was that it would help to correct the empire's deficit on current account. Since the other five Common Market countries were exporting more to the French empire than they imported from it, it was hoped that under the terms of the empire's association the Common Market countries would have to increase their imports from, as well as their capital exports to, the French empire.[41]

However, the initial reactions of the other five governments to the French proposals when they were finally made were not encouraging. Not only did they not want colonial responsibilities on political grounds, but given their ideological preference for limiting the role of the state in the economy they did not support the French argument that public investment in the French empire would have to be increased. And from an economic standpoint they feared that, were they to contribute to such investment, it would be at the expense of living standards in their own countries.[42]

In the light of this reaction the French government tried to strengthen its position by holding talks with Belgium, the other main colonial power. A meeting was arranged between Gaston Defferre, the minister for France overseas, and Alain Savary, the secretary of state for Tunisian and Moroccan affairs, with Belgian ministers on 27 September 1956. This produced a broad measure of agreement despite the great dissimilarities in their imperial positions and responsibilities. One of the greatest differences perhaps was that whereas French investment in its empire came largely from public funds, in Belgium's case it was essentially private. In the joint report, which was produced from the meeting, it was proposed that all the overseas countries should participate in the Common Market through the form of association rather than integration. This would allow for the different political and juridical positions among the countries concerned, and enable certain preferential trading arrangements to be retained for economic reasons. Exports from the overseas countries were to be accepted on the same terms and conditions as goods originating in the Common Market, thereby giving them preference over exports from third countries. Similarly, exports from the Common Market were to enjoy the same preference as exports from France and Belgium in their empires. The Common Market countries were to contribute to the investment needs of the overseas countries even when such investment was not immediately profitable. Where the Belgians disagreed with the French was over the French stipulation that such investment needs should be determined locally rather than at source. They remained neutral, though, over the question of whether the overseas countries should be allowed to impose special import taxes.[43]

The reaction of French ministers to the Franco-Belgian report was mixed. At a meeting in the Hotel Matignon on 9 October 1956 the minister of finance, Paul Ramadier, argued that trade within the French empire was possible only within a closed system and that to open it to the Common

Market countries would entail the loss of about 100,000 jobs in France, mainly within the textile industry. If the government chose to take such a risk, he warned that it would necessitate the devaluation of currencies throughout the Franc Area. Either this would encourage those countries to leave the Franc Area or force France to devalue the French franc. It was an argument which Mollet rejected completely. With the force of the entire postwar experience behind him Mollet insisted that the closed trading system of the French empire was not viable and had to be changed, and that it would not solve the problem of the overvalued franc for France to join the Common Market on its own as Ramadier's argument implied.

The other contentious issue raised by the report was whether the French empire should be consulted about the proposed arrangements. Félix Houphouët-Boigny, the leader of the Ivory Coast who had been invited to the interministerial meeting as head of the Rassemblement Démocratique Africain, argued that overseas France was not opposed to joining the Common Market as associates or even as members as long as it would get guaranteed markets for its agricultural and industrial exports. Since this had been the basis on which Deferre had helped to draft the report it was the lack of consultation or provision for representation of the local assemblies in the European institutions which worried some ministers.[44]

When the Franco-Belgian report was published on 15 November 1956 the reaction once again was quite hostile. The Dutch were the most critical, arguing that investment in the overseas countries should be financed privately rather than from public funds as the report proposed. They also objected to the lack of reciprocity in the trading arrangements such that the overseas countries would have free access to the Common Market while being allowed to impose duties on imports from the Common Market. When the Dutch also objected to the public funds from the Common Market helping to promote the development of the south of Italy it inclined the Italian government to support the Franco-Belgian proposal.[45]

The Germans were more concerned about the lack of distinction between economic and social investment. This prompted them to come up with their own 'Marshall Plan' based on providing German capital to promote the economic development of the French empire. This the French rejected not only because it was politically unacceptable for Germany to be in effect subsidizing the French empire but because they interpreted the proposal as a means for the Federal Republic to avoid importing 'inferior' goods, particularly coffee, cocoa and bananas from the French empire.[46]

What seems to have been important in finally producing an agreement was the intervention of Houphouët-Boigny. In an address to all the heads of delegation he impressed on them the danger for Franco-Belgian Africa of British policy in its African colonies. By granting them independence without at the same time making any provision for investing in their social and economic development the British were effectively sowing the seeds of communism in Africa, he claimed. On the other hand, western Europe had an opportunity to offer Africa a more positive future by offering it secure markets and investment.[47] However, the Common Market countries were prepared only to offer such security for a five-year period initially, with no guarantee that a second convention regarding trade and investment would be concluded at the end of that period. This was a risk which Mollet encouraged the French government to take. A more important question was the size of the contribution which the Common Market countries would make to investment. The Quai d'Orsay recommended an annual figure of 35,000 million francs whereas the Ministry for France Overseas thought that the French should insist on 50,000 million francs given that their own contribution was of the order of 200,000 million francs. It was judged, however, that Mollet would be unable to secure even 35,000 million francs from the other governments and that to get that amount he would have to stress political rather than economic factors. A further problem was that the convention did not extend to Morocco and Tunisia, which had formally been declared independent on 2 March 1956 and 20 March 1956 respectively, but it was hoped that they would be invited to form an association with the Common Market.[48]

When the six prime ministers had a private meeting at the Hotel Matignon in Paris on 19 February 1957 a number of decisions were finally taken about the terms of association of the overseas countries. It was agreed that a convention for five years would be concluded which stipulated the contributions of the Six to the social and economic investment in the overseas countries, as well as the terms on which they would trade. Over this five-year period investment would total 200,000 million francs of which France and the Federal Republic would contribute 34 per cent each, Belgium and the Netherlands 12 per cent each, Italy 7 per cent, and Luxembourg less than 1 per cent. This investment would be on a gradually rising scale. Of the total investment the French overseas territories[49] were to receive 180,000 million francs, the Belgian empire 10,500 million francs, the Dutch empire 12,250 million francs and the Italian empire 1,750 million francs. This meant that the other five countries were contributing on average just over 20,000 million francs annually to the French empire – a figure which was significantly less than the French had hoped.

As far as trade was concerned it was agreed that the same rules would apply for tariff reduction and for reducing quantitative restrictions between the Common Market countries and the overseas countries as between the Common Market countries themselves. However, in the French overseas territories the tariff reductions would apply only to the difference between the tariffs on imports from France and the tariffs on imports from the other five.[50] These arrangements did not prevent or even forestall the break-up of the French Union as a political entity or reconcile the French government to the loss. A few months after the entry into force of the Common Market

Guinea secured its political independence from France. It was followed in rapid succession by eleven others and finally, after a long and costly war, by Algeria – the most important by far of French possessions.

Even after independence these countries continued to trade with France and to link their currency to the French franc. Their importance to the French economy, though, declined dramatically. Whereas in 1953 37 per cent of French exports had gone to the Franc Area compared with 19 per cent to Europe of the Six, by 1962 these figures had been reversed. It is clear that the formation of the Common Market in western Europe was not a cause of the decline in trade with the empire but a recognition of the growing importance of western European markets to the French economy. The early postwar hopes that the non-metropolitan Franc Area would generate a surplus in trade with the rest of the world proved illusory. At no time in the period 1952–58 did these countries generate a trade surplus with the rest of the world. Indeed, most of their deficit arose from trade with the Dollar Area. They did manage a small surplus on trade with the EPU in 1952 and 1954 and with the Sterling Area until 1955. After 1955 they had a deficit with all the monetary areas. Thus, while the commercial strategy pursued by the French government since the Second World War did not prove to be viable in the long term, French economic and commercial strategy was responsible for overcoming French producers' resistance to increasing output and capacity in both industry and agriculture. Once that resistance had been overcome and exports were produced all that was required was a change in commercial strategy to stimulate further production and exports.

APPENDIX 1: DATES OF INDEPENDENCE FROM FRANCE

20 July 1954	Indochina
2 March 1956	Morocco
20 March 1956	Tunisia
28 September 1958	Guinea
1 January 1960	Cameroon
27 April 1960	Togo
20 June 1960	Mali
26 June 1960	Madagascar
1 August 1960	Upper Volta
7 August 1960	Ivory Coast
11 August 1960	Chad
13 August 1960	Central African Republic
15 August 1960	Congo
17 August 1960	Gabon
28 November 1960	Mauritania
1 July 1962	Algeria

Source: P. Arnaud-Ameller, *La France à l'Epreuve de la Concurrence Internationale, 1951–1966* (Paris 1970), p. 56

APPENDIX 2: TRANSFERS OF PUBLIC FUNDS FROM METROPOLITAN FRANCE TO THE REST OF THE FRENCH EMPIRE (THOUSAND MILLION FRANCS)

Country	1952	1953	1954	1955	1956
Morocco	49.8	46.2	61.3	76.6	105.5
Tunisia	29.8	27.0	32.3	45.2	56.4
Algeria	89.4	82.8	90.5	133.6	271.0
Total North Africa	169.0	156.0	184.1	255.4	432.9
Togo	51.8	41.3	37.6	54.9	57.9
Cameroon	30.5	21.9	25.0	24.7	33.6
Madagascar, Comores	18.1	18.0	15.6	22.2	21.5
Total	100.4	81.2	78.2	101.8	113.0
New Caledonia Pacific territories } St Pierre and Miquelon	2.6	3.2	2.0	2.4	1.9
Overseas departments	10.5	11.5	10.2	13.1	16.2
Indochina	217.1	172.6	193.2	80.6	
Overall total	499.6	424.5	467.7	453.3	564.0

Source: Ministère des Finances, Statistiques et Etudes Financières, Supplément no. 108, December 1957, p. 1446

NOTES

1 The term 'empire' was replaced in the 1946 constitution by that of 'union' to signify the intended replacement of the former imperial relationship with that of an association.
2 Jacques Marseille, *Empire colonial et capitalisme français. Histoire d'un divorce* (Paris, 1984).
3 D.K. Fieldhouse, 'The Economics of the French Empire', *Journal of African History*, vol. 27, 1986.
4 J. Marseille, op. cit.
5 V. Thompson and R. Adloff, 'French Economic Policy in Tropical Africa' in L.H. Gann and P. Duignan (eds), *Colonialism in Africa 1870–1960. Volume 4. The Economics of Colonialism* (Cambridge, 1975).
6 S. Moos, 'The Foreign Trade of West-European Countries', *Bulletin of the Oxford Institute of Statistics*, Vol. 7, nos 1 and 3, 1945.
7 R. Betts, *France and Decolonisation 1900–1960* (London, 1991), pp. 49–52.
8 Conseil économique, Etudes et Travaux, no. 12, 1950, 'Définition d'une politique économique, sociale et monétaire d'ensemble des pays de l'Union française', annexe III, Paul Bernard.
9 N.A.U.S., Foreign Post Records R.G. 84, 690, note, 11 September 1944, and 851.50/8–3144, Culbertson to Hawkins, 31 August 1944.
10 N.A.U.S., 851.50/9–745, Hannigan to Labouisse, 7 September 1945.
11 N.A.U.S., 851.50/10–345, Little to McVey, 3 October 1945.

12 MAE, GATT, A.10.13, 3, Ministry for Overseas Territories, note, 22 October 1946.

13 Min. Fin. B 33533, Commissariat Général au Plan, 'Bilan du premier plan de développement économique et social des territoires d'outre-mer présenté à la commission d'étude et de coordination du Plan de Modernisation et d'Equipement des territoires d'outre-mer', by M. Huet.

14 At that time the Ministry for France Overseas had responsibility for Black Africa; the Ministry of the Interior had responsibility for overseas departments and Algeria; and the Ministry of Foreign Affairs had responsibility for territories with an international statute: Morocco, Tunisia, Togo, Cameroon and French Equatorial Africa.

15 A.N. F^{60ter} 477, Ministry for France Overseas to Ministry of Finance, November 1948.

16 MAE DE-CE, 1945–1960, 386, note from the Caisse Centrale de la France d'Outre-mer, 18 May 1948.

17 MAE DE-CE 1945–1960, 386, note from Service de Coopération Economique, 13 July 1949.

18 MAE DE-CE, 1945–1960, 387, note from Service de Coopération Economique, 21 July 1952.

19 MAE DE-CE 1945–1960, 387, Service de Coopération Economique, note, 21 July 1952.

20 MAE DE-CE 1945–1960, 387, 21 July 1952, Note: 'Aide américaine aux TOM'.

21 A.N. F^{60ter} 409, memo from Quai d'Orsay, 19 November 1949.

22 Min. Fin. B 24947, documentation on investment in North Africa.

23 MAE DE-CE 1945–1960, 387, 9 March 1954, note from Service de Coopération Economique.

24 MAE DE-CE 1945–1960, 351, note from Service de Coopération Economique, 16 July 1949.

25 MAE DE-CE, 1945–1960, 352, note from DREE, 20 October 1950.

26 MAE DE-CE, 1945–1960, 352, note for M. de Courcel, 3 December 1951.

27 MAE DE-CE 1945–1960, 353, note from Ministère de la France d'Outre-mer, 23 October 1954.

28 Min. Fin. B 24947, 'Relations de trésorerie', 'Note au sujet du financement des dépenses d'équipement en Afrique du Nord', 22 October 1952.

29 Min. Fin. B 24929, Fangeat to Bissonnet, 17 November 1954.

30 A.N. 80 AJ 71, document from Ministère des Affaires Etrangères, undated.

31 Technically the agreement reached between France and the United States in May 1946 was that France would convert its prewar tariffs from specific duties into ad valorem duties without increasing the effective degree of protection. However, because of the increase in French prices between 1936 and 1938 the degree of protection offered in 1938 by the tariffs which had been revised by the Blum government in 1936 was much less than in 1936. It was for this reason that the French were allowed to base their postwar tariff rates on the average of the last three prewar years rather than those of 1938 (MAE, GATT, A.10.13, 4, note, 15 October 1947).

32 Conseil Economique, 'Etudes et travaux', no. 12, 'Définition d'une politique économique sociale et monétaire d'ensemble des pays de l'union française', 1950.

33 MAE, GATT, A.10.13, 4, note from Baraduc, 3 October 1947.

34 A.N. 80 AJ 72, meeting held on 14 March 1955.

35 A.N. 80 AJ 71, report from M. Moussa, 25 October 1955.

36 A.N. 80 AJ 274, Hirsch to Gaston Deferre, 10 November 1953.

37 Quai Branly, SGCI 121.9, note from Beaurepaire, 11 May 1956.

38 Quai Branly, SGCI 122.22A, note, 20 July 1956.

39 'Rapport du Groupe d'études des relations financières entre la Métropole et l'Algérie', June 1955.

40 Quai Branly, SGCI 122.21, report from Verret Committee, 5 October 1956.

41 ibid.

42 Quai Branly, SGCI 122.21, 'Participation au marché commun des pays et territoires non européennes de la Zone Franc'.

43 Quai Branly, SGCI 122.21, report of meeting of 27 September 1956.

44 Quai Branly, SGCI 122.21, interministerial meeting, 9 October 1956.

45 MAE, Marché Commun, A.30.6, Bousquet to Pineau, 22 November 1956.

46 MAE DE-CE 1945–1960, A.30.6., Bousquet to Pineau, note, 18 February 1957.

47 MAE DE-CE 1945–1960, A.30.6, 1957, Bousquet to Pineau, 24 January 1957.

48 Min. Fin. B 24930, note, 'Association des Pays d'Outre-mer au marché commun', 12 February 1957.

49 This excluded those territories not under the control of the Ministry for France Overseas .

50 MAE, DE-CE 1945–1960, A.30.6, 1957, Bousquet to Pineau, 21 February 1957.

CONCLUSION

After a period of vigorous recovery from the Second World War the French economy settled down to a steady growth of GDP averaging 4.2 per cent per annum over the period 1951–58. Yet when General de Gaulle returned to power in 1958, after twelve years in opposition, the structure of the economy had changed little in the interval. People had left the land in their tens of thousands but they tended to find employment in the expanding service sector, and particularly in government employment, rather than in industry. Indeed, one of the chief characteristics of the Fourth Republic was seen to be its incapacity for change, its *immobilisme*.

Writing in 1958 about the impact of the state on the French economy the American economist Warren Baum concluded that 'not much progress has been made in the postwar period towards the achievement of the main objectives of state intervention'.[1] He explained this in terms of the pursuit of such apparently conflicting policies and objectives as economic growth with the preservation of the status quo, the promotion of investment with inflation, and external equilibrium with an over-valued exchange rate.

The perspective from which Baum viewed the French economy and from which he judged state actions was that of a static, equilibrium model. It has been the argument of this book that this is the wrong perspective from which to view the Fourth Republic. As a medium-sized power which had suffered the humiliation of defeat in 1940 France was determined to find a role in the world which would guarantee French security and arrest France's seemingly inexorable decline to the status of that once great imperial power, Spain.[2]

If 1940 clearly marked the nadir for France it came at the end of a decade of economic stagnation provoked by the collapse of the international economy in 1929. Thus not only did French policy-makers have to deal with the legacy of a prolonged period of economic stagnation but they had to address its causes as well. To the extent that those causes lay outside France, in the operation of the international economy, any solution had to focus on the relationship between France and the international economy. But even if the depression originated outside France there were a number of factors, specifically French, which explained why the French economy failed to participate in the general recovery from it after 1932. While the most proximate reason lay in the retention of an overvalued currency, other underlying factors often referred to as 'blockages' explained why French monetary policy was so unsuccessful. These included a large and relatively unproductive agricultural sector, a small, uncompetitive industrial sector, a preference among savers to hoard gold rather than invest their savings productively, and an empire which was economically undeveloped.

My concern has been to demonstrate that by 1958, when the Treaty of Rome setting up the European Economic Community entered into force, many of these blockages had either been overcome or were being addressed within the new structures of the European Economic Community. Thus the period 1944–58 marked in France a transition from a highly protected and controlled imperial economy, which was dependent on the United States for national security and financial assistance, towards a more independent state which was linked to neighbouring states at similar levels of economic development in a set of legally binding arrangements under the Treaty of Rome. Of course the period marked a transition for other European countries, too, including Britain, although this is rarely the perspective from which national economic experience is viewed.

In the case of France the existing literature focuses either on the point of departure in explaining how indicative planning worked, or on the destination by examining the impact of the Common Market on the French economy. The gap between the two has been filled by theories of integration which purport to explain the transition in terms of a movement towards political unity in Europe beginning with the Treaty of Paris in 1952 and as yet unended. The evidence presented in this book does not substantiate these theories. Indeed, what is striking is that there were a number of different destinations envisaged between the end of the war and 1957 when the decision was finally taken to form a common market in 'Europe of the Six'. What they all had in common was a growing recognition that modernization necessitated an extension of state activity beyond the national frontier – that growth would come from the dialectical relationship between the national economy and the international economy.

But because of differences between the political parties, both in the government and in the National Assembly, and within the administration, too, there was no agreement over how to deal with this relationship. Initially it was ignored in favour of trying to reform the relationship between the state and the national economy.

The image of a strong, centralized state intervening in the economy according to a set of rational policy choices, was far from the reality. Traditionally, policy-making had been fragmented with individual ministries responding to sectional interests without regard for the impact of their policies on the economy as a whole. As a result decisions tended to be made on crude financial criteria giving the Treasury unrivalled power within the machinery of state. It was to challenge this power that the Popular Front government created a new Ministry for the National Economy which was to define and defend the interests of the economy as a whole. Although its record did not match expectations, this institutional arrangement was revived by de Gaulle in his first provisional government after liberation. Once again it was not a success. The problem was not, as is most commonly thought, that although the Ministry of National Economy under Mendès-France was given responsibility for drawing up a national plan, ultimately power remained with the Ministry of Finance which rejected Mendès-France's monetary policy, upon which the success of the plan was seen to depend. While this was a problem for Mendès-France himself, even when the Ministry of National Economy was fused with the Ministry of Finance, problems with economic policy-making and planning remained. Essentially these problems stemmed from the separation of all external economic issues from economic policy-making and planning. The ministry was conceived of as a ministry for the national economy narrowly defined, and excluded from policy-making towards the colonies, or towards other countries. Foreign policy remained the preserve of the Ministry of Foreign Affairs, housed in the Quai d'Orsay in Paris, which for most of the Fourth Republic was under the control of the MRP.

The significance of the small planning group set up under Jean Monnet in January 1946 was that it was free from these inflexible administrative arrangements and could view French economic interests from a perspective which was wider than the narrowly national one. When Jean Monnet argued at the end of the war that France faced a choice between modernization and decadence, and on that basis drew up a plan for modernizing the economy, it was a plan primarily to prepare the French economy for participation in the open multilateral system envisaged by the United States. After fifteen years in which there had been no net investment in the French economy the plan was designed to improve its competitive position by directing investment into a number of priority sectors and thereby reduce the French economy's need for protection.

This objective was to be achieved by expanding the manufacturing base in order to make the economy less dependent on international trade than in the past. It was also designed, in conjunction with Allied policy towards Germany, to shift the centre of industrial power from Germany to France and thereby contribute to French security. Where the Monnet Plan differed most from the previous plans of both Vichy and Mendès-France was not in terms of objectives but in terms of the means of fulfilling those objectives. Thus the Vichy planners envisaged depressing consumption and living standards for a number of years in order to devote up to 30 per cent of national income to investment. Mendès-France also favoured such austerity provided that the sacrifices were spread equitably throughout French society and that the investment effort was supplemented by reparations from Germany. Monnet's greater appeal lay in his claim that investment and living standards could both be raised provided that the French government negotiated a loan from the United States. His emphasis was on aid from the United States rather than reparations from Germany and on using that aid to raise both demand and supply in the French economy. For Monnet the most important change in the postwar world was the American commitment to end its isolationist policies – policies which, in his view, had been the single, most direct cause of the Great Depression of 1929–32.[3] While this analysis of the causes of the depression has subsequently found favour with economists, at that time it was an original view.[4] American aid, Monnet argued, would help the French government to modernize the economy and dismantle many of the controls over trade which had been adopted in response to that depression.

One problem with this analysis was that it ignored the importance of Britain and British policy to French recovery. It was the British decision in 1931 to devalue sterling and introduce a preferential tariff within the British empire which had provoked a sharp fall in French production and a greater dependence on trade with the French empire. Britain's attempts after the war to tighten its controls and run a payments surplus with France and western Europe to help cover its dollar deficit added a sterling shortage to France's dollar shortage without offering any means of covering them. Any attempts to close the dollar gap by stimulating intra-European trade, such as the French proposal to set up a multilateral payments system with Italy and the Benelux countries, known as Finebel, could not solve the French sterling problem.

Of course British policy both in 1931 and after the Second World War was itself a response to American policy. After 1945 the combined effect of American aid and commercial policy was wholly inadequate to finance a multilateral international order of the kind which had operated under British leadership at the end of the nineteenth century. Whereas Britain had enabled the international system to function by exporting capital and at the same time running a trade deficit through its open-door policy, the United States operated a trade surplus after the war and devoted a smaller proportion of its GNP to capital exports than Britain had done.[5]

But if the British policy based on the strict control of external trade and payments thwarted French recovery plans the change in British policy in 1950 was equally unhelpful. The commitment of British governments from 1950 onwards to the rapid restoration of a one-world multilateral system threatened to force the French economy back into the restricted commercial framework of the empire. Despite three devaluations of the franc and a period of floating between 1945 and 1950, the French economy was not in a position to compete freely in the international economy except at the risk of undermining the social reforms made since liberation and abandoning the objective of economic growth. Even participation in the European Payments Union was considered by some sections of the French administration to be too risky. However, the overriding advantage of the EPU to France was that it brought the Sterling Area into the same trade and payments framework as western Europe. The problem was Britain's determination to make the EPU no more than a short-term transition to a one-world multilateral system.

Of greater importance to France than the apparent change in American commercial policy identified by Monnet was the change in American foreign policy. The American commitment to the promotion of European integration which found its first expression in the Marshall Plan was to prove far more durable than its earlier hopes of setting up a liberal multilateral order in the postwar world. Indeed, in 1950 the American Congress rejected the International Trade Organization which was to have been the commercial counterpart of the international monetary system agreed at Bretton Woods. But if European integration assumed a greater importance in American strategic planning after 1947, the particular forms which it was to take owed much to the French. And whereas the Cold War was central to the American interest in European integration it was a factor, but not a necessary one, influencing France. Of much greater importance was the need to find a framework within which the 'blockages' to French economic development and thus to its security could be removed. The recognition that this framework could not be that of the French Union operating within the international system, as chosen by the Monnet planners, developed out of a protracted debate in France itself.

The decisions to sign the Treaties of Paris and Rome were not taken primarily for the foreign policy reason of containing Germany. The particular forms which integration took were more a response to the problems of French economic development which could not be solved within the purely national framework. Thus the Schuman Plan addressed the problem which a relatively small, protected steel industry was seen to have created for French manufacturing industry and for French security in the interwar period. Building on the investment in the steel industry undertaken within the framework of the Monnet Plan and made possible by Marshall Aid, the Schuman Plan aimed to make the French steel industry compete in western Europe. In return the French steel industry was to be guaranteed access to the coal and coke resources of the Ruhr on equal terms with the West German steel industry. But it was only in coal, iron and steel that barriers to trade were removed and then only within a small geographical area.

Apart from the brief attempt in 1950–51 to remove some of the quantitative restrictions on trade within the OEEC the French economy, outside the ECSC, remained as protected as it had been in the 1930s. Jacques Marseille's argument that the highly protected economy inherited from Méline was largely a myth by 1950 since average tariff rates on manufac-

214

CONCLUSION

tured goods were lower in France than in Britain, the Federal Republic of Germany or Italy ignores the importance of these quantitative restrictions on trade.[6] It was partly because tariff rates in France were in many cases lower than elsewhere and in some parts of the French empire were non-existent that the French government retained its quantitative restrictions on trade for longer than the rest of the OEEC.

Not only was France under strong and growing pressure to reduce these quantitative restrictions on trade within the OEEC from 1954 onwards, but the modernizers in France felt that it was only through exposure to greater competition that continued growth of the economy would be ensured. The exception to this was agriculture. The attempt to restructure French agriculture in order to reduce its need for protection in the postwar world collapsed in the wheat crisis of 1947. From then onwards the logic of the revised plan to modernize agriculture through a policy of expansion meant that not only would agriculture continue to need protection in the domestic market but also in export markets. Once again, as in the case of steel, a solution to the problem of agricultural modernization was not possible within a purely national framework.

Because of the continuing dollar shortage caused partly by American tariffs, European governments retained controls over trade and capital movements with the United States for much longer than had been envisaged under the Bretton Woods Agreement. French attempts to bargain bilaterally with the United States to achieve a reduction in American tariffs and thereby ease its dollar shortage, a shortage made all the more severe by the near cessation of American aid following France's withdrawal from Indochina, also failed. French attempts to negotiate a permanent structure of preferential trade and payments arrangements with Britain and the Sterling Area received no support in London. With continued protection being seen as a barrier to the further modernization of the French economy the solution finally adopted was to expose the French economy to a degree of competition within a common market of the Six in Europe. In doing so the French government also managed to share its problems of modernizing agriculture and its empire with its partners in the Common Market. Thanks to the dynamics of the new relationship between France and western Europe the French economy continued to grow throughout the 1960s and beyond, and France was able to use the Common Market to strengthen its bargaining position with the United States.

NOTES

1 W. Baum, op. cit., p. 347.
2 Robert Frank, *La Hantise du déclin. La France 1920–1960: finances, défense et identité nationale* (Paris, 1994).
3 A.N. F^{60} 918, meeting in the Ministry of National Economy, 24 October 1945.

4 See C. Kindleberger, *The World in Depression 1929–1939* (London, 1973).
5 A.S. Milward, *The Reconstruction*, op. cit., p. 93.
6 J. Marseille, 'Introduction' in Comité pour l'histoire économique et financière de la France, *Le Commerce extérieur français de Méline à nos jours* (Paris, 1993).

BIBLIOGRAPHY

Abramovitz, M., 'Catching Up, Forging Ahead and Falling Behind', *Journal of Economic History*, vol. 46, 1986.

Abramovitz, M., *Thinking about Growth* (Cambridge, 1989).

Adams, W.J., *Restructuring the French Economy. Government and the Rise of Market Competition Since World War II* (Washington, DC, 1989).

André, Ch. and Delorme, R., *L'Etat et l'économie* (Paris, 1983).

Andrieu, C., *Le Programme commun de la Résistance. Les Idées dans la guerre* (Paris, 1984).

Andrieu, C., Prost, A. and Le Van-Lemesle, L., *Les Nationalisations de la Libération. De L'Utopie au compromis* (Paris, 1987).

Arnaud-Ameller, P., *La France à l'epreuve de la concurrence internationale, 1951–1966* (Paris, 1970).

Asbeck Brusse, W., *West European Tariff Plans, 1947–1957. From Study Group to Common Market*, unpublished PhD thesis (EUI Florence, 1991).

Asselain, J.-C., *Histoire économique de la France du XVIIIe siècle à nos jours. Vol. 2. De 1919 à la fin des années 1970 (Paris, 1984).*

Aufricht, H. and Evensen, J. (eds), *Central Banking Legislation. Vol. II. Europe* (IMF, Washington, DC, 1967).

Azéma, J.-P., *De Munich à la Libération 1938–1944* (Paris, 1978).

Azéma, J.-P. and Bédarida, F. (eds), *Les Années noires, Tome 1, De la défaite à Vichy* (Paris, 1993).

Balogh, T., 'French Reconstruction and the Franco-US Loan Agreement', *Bulletin of the Oxford Institute of Statistics*, vol. 8, nos. 8 and 9, 1946.

Bauchet, P., *L'Expérience française de planification* (Paris, 1958).

Baum, W., *The French Economy and the State* (Princeton, 1958).

Betts, R., *France and Decolonisation 1900–1960* (London, 1991).

Bloch-Lainé, F. and Bouvier, J., *La France restaurée 1944–1954. Dialogue sur le choix d'une modernisation* (Paris, 1986).

Bompard, J.-P. and Postel-Vinay, G., 'L'Etat-Crédit Agricole. L'Etat et le financement de l'agriculture 1945–1952', in Fondation Nationale des Sciences Politiques, *La France en voie de modernisation 1944–1952* (unpublished proceedings of conference, Paris, December 1981).

Bonin, H., *Histoire économique de la IVe République* (Paris, 1987).

Borne, D. and Bouillon, J., 'Réflections de Paul Ramadier, December 1947', *Revue d'Histoire Moderne et Contemporaine*, vol. xxxv, July–September 1988.

Bossuat, G., *La France, l'aide américaine et la construction européenne 1944–1954* (Paris, 1992).

FRANCE AND THE INTERNATIONAL ECONOMY

Boussard, I., 'L'Agriculture française – options et résultats', in Fondation Nationale des Sciences Politiques, *La France en voie de modernisation 1944–1952* (Unpublished proceedings of conference, Paris, December 1981).

Bouvier, J., 'The French Banks, Inflation and the Economic Crisis, 1919–1939', *Journal of European Economic History*, special issue, 13(2), Fall 1984.

Bower, T., *The Paperclip Conspiracy: The Battle for the Spoils and Secrets of Nazi Germany* (London, 1987).

Braudel, F. and Labrousse, E., *Histoire économique et sociale de la France. Tome IV, vol. II* (Paris, 1980).

Brown, W.A., Jr. and Opie, K., *American Foreign Assistance* (Washington, DC, 1953).

Buchanan, N. and Lutz, F., *Rebuilding the World Economy* (New York, 1947).

Buchheim, C., *Die Wiedereingliederung Westdeutschlands in die Weltwirtschaft 1945–58* (Munich, 1990).

Burn, D., *The Steel Industry 1939–1959. A Study in Competition and Planning* (Cambridge, 1961).

Bussière, E., 'The Evolution of Structures in the Iron and Steel Industries in France, Belgium and Luxembourg: National and International Aspects, 1900–1939', in E. Abe and Y. Suzuki (eds), *Changing Patterns of International Rivalry. Some Lessons from the Steel Industry* (Tokyo, 1991).

Cairncross, A., *Years of Recovery* (London, 1985).

Caron, F., *An Economic History of Modern France* (London, 1979).

Caron, F., 'Le Plan Mayer: Un Retour aux réalitiés', in Fondation Nationale des sciences Politiques, *La France en voie de modernisation 1944–1952* (unpublished proceedings of conference, Paris, 1981).

Carré, J.-J., Dubois, P. and Malinvaud, E., *French Economic Growth* (Stanford and London, 1976).

Caubone, P., 'Medium-term Lending by the French Deposit Banks and Banques d'Affaires', in *Banca Nazionale del Lavoro Quarterly Review*, vol. 31, December 1954.

Cepède, M., *Agriculture et alimentation en France durant la seconde guerre mondiale* (Paris, 1967).

Chardonnet, J., *La Sidérurgie française. Progrès ou décadence?* (Paris, 1954).

Clayton Garwood, E., *Will Clayton: A Short Biography* (Austin, 1958).

Comité pour l'histoire économique et financière de la France, *Le Commerce extérieur français de Méline à nos jours* (Paris, 1993).

Commissariat Général au Plan, *Estimation du revenu national français* (Paris, 1947).

Commissariat Général au Plan, *Rapport sur la réalisation du plan de modernisation et d'équipement de l'Union française* (Paris, 1953).

Crouzet, François (ed.), *The Economic Development of France since 1870* (Aldershot, 1993).

DePorte, A.W., *De Gaulle's Foreign Policy 1944–1946* (Cambridge, Mass., 1968).

Diebold, W., Jr., *Trade and Payments in Western Europe 1945–51* (New York, 1952).

Dobson, A.P., *The Politics of the Anglo-American Economic Special Relationship 1940–1987* (London, 1988).

Dougherty, J., *The Politics of Wartime Aid* (Westport, 1978).

Duchêne, F., *Jean Monnet. The First Statesman of Interdependence* (New York, 1994).

Eichengreen, B., 'Was the European Payments Union a Mistake? Would a Payments Union for the former Soviet Union be a Mistake as Well?', unpublished paper, November 1992.

Eichengreen, B. and Wyplosz, C., 'The Economic Consequences of the Franc Poincaré', in E. Helpman, A. Razin and E. Sadka (eds), *Economic Effects of the Government Budget* (Cambridge, Mass., 1988).

Ellwood, D., *Rebuilding Europe. Western Europe, America and Postwar Reconstruction* (London, 1992).

Feinstein, C., 'Benefits of Backwardness and Costs of Continuity', in A. Graham with A. Seldon (eds), *Government and Economies in the Postwar World* (London, 1990).

Fieldhouse, D.K., 'The Economics of the French Empire', *Journal of African History*, vol. 27, 1986.

Footit, H. and Simmonds, J., *France 1943–1945* (Leicester, 1988).

Fourastié, J., *Les Trente Glorieuses ou la Révolution Invisible de 1946 à 1975* (Paris, 1979).

Frank, R., *La Hantise du déclin. La France, 1920–1960: finances, défense et identité nationale* (Paris, 1994).

Fridenson, P. and Straus, A. (eds), *Le Capitalisme français. 19ᵉ–20ᵉ sièclè. Blocages et dynamismes d'une croissance* (Paris, 1987).

Gerbet, P., 'La Relance européenne jusqu'à la Conférence de Messine', in E. Serra (ed.), *The Relaunching of Europe and the Treaties of Rome* (Brussels, 1989).

Gerbet, P., *Le Relèvement 1944–1949* (Paris, 1991).

Gervais, M., Jollivet M. and Tavernier, Y., *Histoire de la France rurale. Vol. 4. La Fin de la France paysanne. De 1914 à nos jours* (Paris, 1977).

Ghebali, V.Y., *La France en guerre et les organisations internationales 1939–1945* (Paris, 1969).

Gimbel, J., *The Origins of the Marshall Plan* (Stanford, 1976).

Girault, R. and Frank, R. (eds), *La Puissance française en question 1945–1949* (Paris, 1988).

Griffiths, R.T. (ed.), *The Netherlands and the Integration of Europe, 1945–1957* (Amsterdam, 1990).

Griffiths, R.T. and Lynch, F.M.B., 'L'Échec de la "Petite Europe": les négociations Fritalux/Finebel, 1949–1950', in *Revue Historique*, Vol. CCLXXIV/1, 1986.

Griffiths, R.T. and Lynch, F.M.B., 'L'Échec de la Petite Europe. Le Conseil Tripartite 1944–48', *Guerres mondiales et conflits contemporains*, no. 152, 1988.

Griffiths, R.T. and Milward, A.S., 'The European Agricultural Community, 1948–1954', *European University Institute Colloquium Papers*, doc. IUE 6/87 (col. 6).

Gruson, C., *Origines et espoirs de la planification française* (Paris, 1968).

Guillen, P., 'La France et la négociation des Traités de Rome: l'Euratom', in E. Serra (ed.), *The Relaunching of Europe and the Treaties of Rome* (Brussels, 1989).

Guillen, P., 'Le Projet d'union économique entre la France, l'Italie et le Benelux', in R. Poidevin (ed.), *L'Histoire des débuts de la construction européenne, mars 1948–mai 1950* (Brussels, 1986).

Hackett, J. and Hackett, A.M., *Economic Planning in France* (London, 1963).

Hogan, M.J., *The Marshall Plan. America, Britain and the Reconstruction of Western Europe, 1947–52* (Cambridge, 1987).

INSEE, *Annuaire Statistique. Résumé Rétrospectif* (Paris, 1951).

INSEE, 'La Balance des payements de la zone franc', *Bulletin Mensuel de Statistique. Supplément*, January–March, 1953.

INSEE, *Le Mouvement économique en France de 1944 à 1957* (Paris, 1958).

Jackson, J., *The Politics of Depression in France 1932–1936* (Cambridge, 1985).

Jackson, J., *The Popular Front in France. Defending Democracy 1934–38* (Cambridge, 1988).

Kaplan, J.J. and Schleiminger, G., *The European Payments Union. Financial Diplomacy in the 1950s* (Oxford, 1989).

Kemp, T., *The French Economy 1913–1939. The History of a Decline* (London, 1972).

Kindleberger, C., *The World in Depression 1929–1939* (London, 1973).

Kindleberger, C., *The Marshall Plan Days* (Allen & Unwin, 1987).

Kipping, M., *L'Amélioration de la competitivité de l'industrie française et les origines du Plan Schuman*, unpublished mémoire (Paris, 1992).

Kohl, W., *French Nuclear Diplomacy* (Princeton, 1971).

Kuisel, R.F., *Capitalism and the State in Modern France* (Cambridge, 1981).

Küsters, H., *Die Gründung der Europäischen Wirtschaftsgemeinschaft* (Baden-Baden, 1982).

Lacroix-Riz, A., 'Négociation et signature des accords Blum–Byrnes (octobre 1945–mai 1946) d'après les archives du Ministère des Affaires Etrangères', *Revue d'Histoire Moderne et Contemporaine*, July–September 1984.

Lacroix-Riz, A., *Le Choix de Marianne* (Paris, 1985).

Lamartine Yates, P., *Food Production in Western Europe* (London, 1940).

Landes, D.S., 'French Entrepreneurship and Industrial Growth in the Nineteenth Century', *Journal of Economic History*, IX (1), May 1949.

Landes, D.S., 'Religion and Enterprise: The Case of the French Textile Industry', in E. Carter, R. Foster and J. Moody (eds.), *Enterprise and Entrepreneurs in Nineteenth and Twentieth Century France* (Baltimore, 1976).

Larkin, M., *France since the Popular Front. Government and People 1936–1986* (Oxford, 1988).

Lebovics, H., *The Alliance of Iron and Wheat in the Third French Republic* (Baton Rouge, 1988).

Lefeuvre, D., 'Evolution sectorielle du commerce extérieur français', in Comité pour l'Histoire Économique de la France, *Le commerce extérieur français de Méline à nos jours* (Paris, 1993).

Lévy-Leboyer, M. and Bourguignon, F., *The French Economy in the Nineteenth Century. An Essay in Econometric Analysis* (Cambridge, 1990).

Ludmann-Obier, M.-F., 'Un Aspect de la chasse aux cerveaux: les transferts de techniciens allemands en France: 1945–1949', *Relations internationales*, no. 46, 1986.

Lynch, F., 'The Economic Effects of the Korean War in France 1950–1952', *European University Institute*, no. 86/253, 1986.

MacRae, D., *Parliament, Parties and Society in France 1946–1958* (New York, 1967).

Maddison, A., *Dynamic Forces in Capitalist Development* (Oxford, 1991).

Maier, C.S., *In Search of Stability: Explorations in Historical Political Economy* (Cambridge, 1987).

Maier, C.S., 'The Politics of Productivity: Foundations of American International Economic Policy after World War II', in P. Katzenstein (ed.), *Between Power and Plenty: the Foreign Economic Policies of Advanced Industrial States* (Madison, 1978).

Maier, C.S. and Bischof, G. (eds), *The Marshall Plan and Germany* (New York and Oxford, 1991).

Margairaz, M., *L'Etat, les finances et l'économie. Histoire d'une conversion 1932–1952* (Paris, 1991).

Marseille, J., *Empire colonial et capitalisme français. Histoire d'un divorce* (Paris, 1984).

Massé, P., *Le Plan ou l'anti-hasard* (Paris, 1965).

Mendès-France, P., *Oeuvres complètes. Vol. II. Une Politique de l'économie. 1943–1954* (Paris, 1985).

Milward, A.S., *The New Order and the French Economy* (London, 1970).

Milward, A.S., *The Reconstruction of Western Europe, 1945–1951* (London, 1984).

Milward, A.S., *The European Rescue of the Nation State* (London, 1992).

Ministère des Finances, du Budget et des Affaires Economiques, *Inventaire de la situation financière* (Paris, 1951).

Mioche, P., 'Le Démarrage du Plan Monnet: comment une entreprise conjoncturelle est devenue une institution prestigieuse', *Revue d'histoire moderne et contemporaine*, July–September 1984.

Mioche, P., 'Les Difficultés de la modernisation dans le cas de l'industrie française de la machine-outil, 1941–1953', *European University Institute Working Paper*, no. 85/168, 1985.

Mioche, P., *Le Plan Monnet. Genèse et élaboration 1941–1947* (Paris, 1987).

Mioche, P. and Roux, J., *Henri Malcor, un héritier des maîtres de forges* (Paris, 1988).

Moos, S., 'The Foreign Trade of West-European Countries', *Bulletin of the Oxford Institute of Statistics*, vol. 7, nos 1 and 3, 1945.

Mouré, K., *Managing the Franc Poincaré. Economic Understanding and Political Constraint: French Monetary Policy* (Cambridge, 1991).

Muth, H.P., *French Agriculture and the Political Integration of Western Europe* (Leyden, 1970).

Naylor, E.L., *Socio-structural Policy in French Agriculture* (Aberdeen, 1985).

Nordengren, S., *Economic and Social Targets for Postwar France* (Lund, 1972).

O'Brien, P.K. and Keyder, C., *Economic Growth in Britain and France 1780–1914. Two Paths to the Twentieth Century* (London, 1978).

OECD, Agricultural Policy Reports, *Low Incomes in Agriculture* (Paris, 1964).

OEEC, *Interim Report on the European Recovery Programme, volume II* (Paris, December 1948).

Oliver, R.O., *International Economic Cooperation and the World Bank* (London, 1975).

Olson, J.S., *Herbert Hoover and the Reconstruction Finance Corporation 1931–1933* (Ames, Iowa, 1977).

Patat, J.-P. and Lutfalla, M., *A Monetary History of France in the Twentieth Century* (London, 1990).

Perrot, M., 'Données statistiques sur l'évolution des rémunérations salariales de 1938 à 1963', *Etudes et Conjoncture*, no. 8, August, 1965.

Pilliet, G., *Inventaire économique de la France, 1948* (Paris, 1948).

Pineau, C. and Rimbaud, C., *Le Grand Pari. L'Aventure du Traité de Rome* (Paris, 1991).

Poidevin, R., 'René Mayer et la politique extérieure de la France, 1943–1953', *Revue d'Histoire de la Deuxième Guerre Mondiale*, no. 134, April 1984.

Pressnell, L.S., *External Economic Policy since the War. Volume I. The Post-War Financial Settlement* (London, 1986).

Rioux, J.-P. *The Fourth Republic 1944–1958* (Cambridge, 1987).

Rist, L. and Schwob, P., 'La Balance des paiements', *Revue d'Economie Politique*, vol. I, January–February 1939.

Roehl, R., 'French Industrialization: A Reconsideration', *Explorations in Economic History*, 13(3), July 1976.

Roseman, M., 'Division and Stability: Recent Writing on Post-War German History', *German History*, vol. 11, no. 3, 1993.

Rousso, H., 'L'Economie: pénurie et modernisation', in J.-P. Azéma and F. Bédarida (eds), *Les Années noires*, (Paris, 1993).

Rousso, H. and Bauchet, P., *La Planification en crises (1965–1985)* (Paris, 1987).

Ruttan, V.W., 'Structural Retardation and the Modernization of French Agriculture: A Skeptical View', *The Journal of Economic History*, vol. xxxviii, no. 3, September 1978.

Sautter, C., 'France', in A. Boltho (ed.), *The European Economy: Growth and Crisis* (Oxford, 1985).

Sauvy, Alfred, *Histoire économique de la France entre les deux guerres* (Paris, 1965).

Shennan, A., *Rethinking France: Plans for Renewal 1940–1946* (Oxford, 1989).

Shonfield, A., *Modern Capitalism: The Changing Balance of Public and Private Power* (London, 1965).

Stokes, R., *Divide and Prosper. The Heirs of I.G. Farben under Allied Authority 1945–1951* (London, 1988).

Tardy, G., 'La France dans l'Europe', in J.-P. Pagé (ed.), *Profil économique de la France au seuil des années 80* (Paris, 1981).

Thompson, V. and Adloff, R., 'French Economic Policy in Tropical Africa', in L.H. Gann and P. Duignan (eds), *Colonialism in Africa 1870–1960. Volume 4. The Economics of Colonialism* (Cambridge, 1975).

Toutain, J.-C., *Histoire quantitative de l'économie française* (Paris, 1961).

United Nations, *Economic Survey of Europe in 1950* (Geneva, 1951), p. 147.

UN Food and Agriculture Organization, *Commodity Policy Studies*, no. 2, April 1953.

Vincent, L.A., 'Population active, production et productivité dans 21 branches de l'économie française 1896–1962', *Etudes et Conjoncture*, no. 7, July 1963.

Volle, M., *Pour Une Histoire de la statistique* (Paris, 1977).

Wall, I.M., *The United States and the Making of Postwar France 1945–1954* (Cambridge, 1991).

Wexler, I., *The Marshall Plan Revisited. The European Recovery Program in Economic Perspective* (Westport, 1983}.

Williams, P., *Politics in Postwar France* (London, 1955).

Williams, P., *French Politicians and Elections 1951–1969* (London, 1970).

Wilson, J.C.S., *French Banking Structure and Credit Policy* (London, 1957).

Wright, G., *Rural Revolution in France* (Stanford, 1964).

Wright, G., *France in Modern Times* (New York, 1987).

Wurm, C. (ed.), *Western Europe and Germany. The Beginnings of European Integration, 1945–1960* (Oxford and Washington, DC, 1995).

INDEX